SHIFTING PARADIGMS

SHIFTING PARADIGMS

Growth, Finance, Jobs, and Inequality in the Digital Economy

EDITED BY
ZIA QURESHI
CHEONSIK WOO

BROOKINGS INSTITUTION PRESS
Washington, D.C.

The Brookings Institution is a private nonprofit organization devoted to research, education, and publication on important issues of domestic and foreign policy. Its principal purpose is to bring the highest quality independent research and analysis to bear on current and emerging policy problems. Interpretations or conclusions in Brookings publications should be understood to be solely those of the authors.

Library of Congress Control Number: 2021950374

ISBN 9780815739005 (pbk)
ISBN 9780815739012 (ebook)

9 8 7 6 5 4 3 2 1

Typeset in Janson Text

Composition by Westchester Publishing Services

Contents

Preface

Ours is an era of exciting technological innovations. Digital technologies are driving transformative change. Economic paradigms are shifting. The new technologies are reshaping product and factor markets and profoundly altering business and work—and society at large. The latest advances in artificial intelligence and related innovations are expanding the frontiers of the digital revolution. Digital transformation is accelerating in the wake of the COVID-19 pandemic. The future is arriving faster than expected.

The new technologies hold great promise. They create new avenues and opportunities for a more prosperous future. But they also pose new challenges. While digital technologies have dazzled with their potential, they have so far not delivered the expected dividend in productivity growth. Indeed, aggregate productivity growth has slowed in the past couple of decades in many economies. Consequently, economic growth has trended lower. At the same time, income inequality and social disparities have been rising.

One important reason for these outcomes is that policies and institutions have been slow to adjust to the unfolding transformations. To realize the promise of today's smart machines, policies need to be smarter too. They must be more responsive to change.

As technology reshapes markets and alters growth and distributional dynamics, policies must ensure that markets remain inclusive and support wide access to the new opportunities for firms and workers. The digital economy must be broadened to disseminate new technologies and productive opportunities among smaller firms and wider segments of the labor force.

This book examines the challenges of digital transformation and suggests how responsive policies can make it more productive and inclusive. It is the second book produced under a joint research project of the Brookings Institution and the Korea Development Institute that explores how technological change is reshaping economies and public policy agendas. The first book, *Growth in a Time of Change*, was published by the Brookings Institution Press in 2020. The project analyzes the implications of technological change from both global and country perspectives, including a specific focus on the Korean economy.

Digital technologies offer large productivity payoffs but create new challenges for firms as production processes and market structures shift. Is rising industrial concentration, as reflected in the increasing market dominance of tech giants, inevitable with these technologies? Or can their benefits be more widely diffused across firms to lift aggregate productivity and foster more robust economic growth? Digital transformation is driving rapid change in financial markets. How can the promise of Fintech be captured while managing risks? The nature of work and skill needs are changing. Should workers fear the new automation? Income inequality has been rising in many countries, feeding social discontent and political conflict. Are technology-driven shifts in business and work causing economic disparities to widen? How should public policy respond?

This book addresses these questions. A theme running through the book is that policies matter. New thinking and adaptations are needed to realign policies and institutions with the digital economy. The book discusses an agenda for change spanning competition policy and regulation of data and digital platforms, the innovation ecosystem, digital infrastructure, regulation of Fintech, workforce development, social protection frameworks, and tax policies. It also calls attention to the need for new frameworks for international collaboration in areas such as regulation of cross-border data flows and taxation of cross-border digital business.

Enabling broader participation of firms in the innovation economy, widening the diffusion of new technologies, and building complementary capabilities in the workforce can deliver both stronger and more inclusive economic growth. Policy actions in these areas can reduce inequality and economic insecurity more effectively than fiscal redistribution alone. Inevitably, major economic reform is politically complex. But one thing reform should not be paralyzed by is continued trite debates about conflicts between growth and inclusion. In capturing the full promise of digital transformation, the growth and inclusion agendas are one and the same.

Zia Qureshi and Cheonsik Woo

Acknowledgments

This book is the second produced under a joint research project of the Brookings Institution and the Korea Development Institute (KDI) that explores the implications of today's technological change for economies and public policy. Zia Qureshi (Brookings) and Cheonsik Woo (KDI) coedited the book. The editors would like to thank Jeong Pyo Choi (former president of KDI), Jang Pyo Hong (current president of KDI), and Brahima Coulibaly (vice president of the Global Economy and Development Program at Brookings) for the support from the two institutions.

The book consists of chapters contributed by a team of experts from Brookings, KDI, and other institutions. The team included, in addition to the editors who contributed chapter 1 that provides an overview of the book, the following: Flavio Calvino and Chiara Criscuolo (OECD; chapter 2); Minho Kim (KDI; chapter 3); Thomas Philippon (New York University; chapter 4); Harry Holzer (Georgetown University and Brookings; chapter 5); Sunghoon Chung and Sangmin Aum (KDI and Myongji University; chapter 6); François Bourguignon (Paris School of Economics; chapter 7); and Jungsoo Park (Sogang University; chapter 8). The editors would like to thank their coauthors for their important scholarly contributions.

The chapters in the book were initially presented as papers at a joint Brookings-KDI research conference held on October 7 and 8, 2020, and were subsequently finalized in light of the comments received. Discussants of the papers included Martin Baily (Brookings), Simeon Djankov (Peterson Institute for International Economics), Romain Duval (IMF), Jason Furman (Harvard University), Charles Kenny (Center for Global Development), Aaron Klein (Brookings), Ratna Sahay (IMF), and Hoon Sahib Soh (World Bank). Their thoughtful comments and suggestions are gratefully acknowledged. Helpful comments were also received from session chairs, including Kaushik Basu (Cornell University), Dong Soo Kang (KDI), Alfonso Garcia Mora (International Finance Corporation), and Darrell West (Brookings). The editors would also like to thank other participants at the conference for sharing their valuable thoughts.

Janina Curtis Bröker, Helena Hlavaty, Sungjin Jung, and Hyemin Yoon very ably provided research support for the book as well as help with coordination. David Batcheck and Sebastian Strauss assisted in the organization of the research conference. For assistance with administrative and budgetary matters, thanks are due to Drew Badolato, Antwan Brown, Justine Hufford, Jacqueline Sharkey, Molly Sugrue, and Yvonne Thurman-Dogruer.

The publication of the book was managed by the Brookings Institution Press. The editors would like to thank William Finan, Elliott Beard, Cecilia González, and Kristen Harrison at the Brookings Institution Press for their advice and support in the book's production, and Angela Piliouras, Kelley Blewster and the team at Westchester Publishing Services for editorial services.

SHIFTING PARADIGMS

ONE

Overview

Digital Metamorphosis and Economic Change

ZIA QURESHI AND CHEONSIK WOO

Economic paradigms are shifting. Digital technologies are driving trans-formative change. Economies are experiencing an unfolding digital metamorphosis. Latest advances in artificial intelligence (AI) and related innovations are expanding the frontiers of the digital revolution. Digital transformation is accelerating as a consequence of the COVID-19 pandemic. The future is arriving faster than expected.

The new technologies hold immense promise. But they also pose new challenges. While digital technologies have dazzled with the brilliance and prowess of their applications, they have not so far delivered the expected dividend in higher aggregate productivity growth. And inequality has been rising. As these technologies transform markets, policies must rise to the challenges of change. The digital economy must be broadened to disseminate new technologies and productive opportunities among smaller firms and wider segments of the labor force. Policies must play their part to better harness the potential of innovation in our digital era and turn it into a driver of stronger and more inclusive growth in economic prosperity.

This book is the second of a two-book research project that examines how today's technological change is transforming growth and distributional dynamics and reshaping public policy agendas. The project is a collaboration between the Brookings Institution and the Korea Development Institute.[1] It analyzes the implications of technological change from both global and country perspectives, including a specific focus on the Korean economy. The country perspective enriches the analysis by providing both affirmation of and contrast with trends observed at the global level.

World Going Digital

We are living in an era of exciting new technologies. It is often referred to in epochal terms—as a time of technological renaissance powered by brilliant new technologies, a second machine age, and a new industrial revolution.[2] Some scenarios see the world approaching a technological singularity of accelerating technological change—and a consequent economic singularity of a takeoff in productivity and economic growth.[3] While some characterizations of the ongoing technological change may be overly grand and visionary, the pace and scope of the advances being made are surely impressive.

Technology has been booming in recent decades, led by an expanding array of digital innovations. Ranging from increasingly sophisticated computer systems, software, and mobile telephony to digital platforms and robotics, these innovations have been reshaping markets and the worlds of business and work. New advances in AI, machine learning, cyber-physical systems, and the internet of things are driving digital transformation farther. This latest wave of innovations can take the digital revolution to a whole new level.[4]

The automation and digitalization of economic activity is intensifying in the wake of the COVID-19 pandemic.[5] The pandemic may be remembered as the Great Digital Accelerator, marking an inflection point in the advance of digital transformation. It has reinforced firm incentives to automate production processes. Trade, commerce, and finance are going digital at a faster clip. Digital platforms are expanding their economic sway. Teleworking has increased sharply. Education and training have rapidly shifted online. The use of automated and online processes is speeding up across most sectors of the economy.

This trajectory of further technological change was expected, but the pandemic is making it happen sooner. Even as economies recover from the pandemic, some of its effects will be long lasting. This is certainly the case with the pandemic's impetus to digital transformation. Prior to the pandemic, a paradigm shift toward digitalization was already well underway. The pandemic has accelerated the shift.

But Productivity Slowing and Inequality Rising

Technology is a key determinant of productivity and long-term economic growth. Paradoxically, as digital technologies have boomed, productivity growth has slowed rather than accelerated.[6] Economic growth has trended lower. Productivity growth has slowed significantly in advanced economies since the 1980s. The slowdown extends across Organization for Economic Cooperation and Development (OECD) economies. It is broad based, affecting more than two-thirds of the sectors.[7] For the past decade or so, productivity growth has slowed in many emerging economies as well. Over the five-year period 2013–2017, productivity growth was lower than the long-term average in about 65 percent of all countries.[8]

Meanwhile, income inequality within countries has been rising. Inequality has risen in all major advanced economies since the 1980s, and quite appreciably in several of them. There has been a particularly sharp increase in income concentration at the top end of the distribution. Trends in income distribution are more mixed across emerging economies, but many of them have also experienced rising inequality over the same period.

Inequality between countries has been falling, thanks to the rise of faster-growing emerging economies that are narrowing the income gap with advanced economies. But technological change poses new challenges for this economic convergence. Manufacturing-led growth in emerging economies has been propelled by their comparative advantage in labor-intensive manufacturing based on large pools of low-skilled, low-wage workers. This source of comparative advantage increasingly will matter less as automation of low-skilled work expands, disrupting traditional pathways to development.[9] The COVID-19 pandemic could add to the challenges emerging economies face in recalibrating their growth models by disrupting

FIGURE 1-1. **Slowing Productivity Growth and Rising Inequality:**
United States, 1985–2019

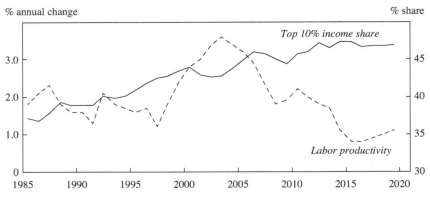

Source: Qureshi (2020).

global supply chains and prompting stronger moves to reshore production in advanced economies.

The trends of slowing productivity growth and rising within-country inequality are vividly illustrated by the US economy. The United States has been the global leader in the digital revolution. Yet productivity growth has slowed considerably since the early 2000s (figure 1-1).[10] Over the last ten years, labor productivity growth has averaged less than half the growth rate of the decade prior to the slowdown. Total factor productivity growth shows a similar trend. Productivity growth picked up in the latter half of the 1990s, partly spurred by increased initial investment in the adoption of digital technologies. But this surge proved short-lived. Even as these technologies continued their advance in the subsequent two decades, and automation of production deepened and became more sophisticated, productivity growth slowed, settling into a longer-term trend of persistent weakness.

Concurrently, income inequality has been rising in the United States— and more sharply than in other major advanced economies (figure 1-1). Since the early 1980s, the share of the top 10 percent in national income has risen from 35 percent to 47 percent.[11] The income share of the top 1 percent has roughly doubled, from 11 percent to 21 percent. The share of the top 1 percent in wealth has risen from 23 percent to around 40 percent. Those with middle-class incomes have been squeezed. For the median worker, real wages have been largely stagnant over long periods. Real median wage growth has been weighed down not only by slower productivity

growth but also by wages lagging productivity growth and rising wage inequality. Job insecurity has increased, with mounting fears of a "robocalypse": large job/wage losses from automation.[12] As income inequality has
risen, intergenerational economic mobility has declined.[13]

Rising inequality and related disparities and anxieties are stoking social discontent. They are a major driver of the increased popular disaffec-
tion and political polarization—and the rise of nationalist populism—that
are so evident today.

The trends noted above reveal a striking contrast between the promise of
brilliant new technologies and the actual economic and social outcomes. The
national economic pie has been growing more slowly and more unequally.
The benefits of technological transformation have been shared highly
unevenly. This should not, however, lead to a Luddite backlash against
technology. Technology itself is not the problem. On the contrary, the new
technologies hold immense potential to boost productivity and economic
growth, create new and better jobs to replace old ones, and raise human welfare. The challenge for policymakers is to better harness this potential.

Shifting Market Dynamics but Policies Slow to Catch Up

By its very nature, technological change is disruptive. It entails difficult
transitions as it unleashes a process of—using Schumpeter's famous
characterization—creative destruction.[14] It inevitably creates winners and
losers. Policies have a crucial role to play to improve the enabling environment for firms and workers—to broaden access to the new opportunities
that come from technological change and to enhance capabilities to adjust
to the new challenges. Unfortunately, policies and institutions have been
slow to rise to the challenges of technological change as it shifts dynamics
across product and labor markets. The outcomes of slowing productivity
growth and rising inequality are interconnected, and are closely linked to
the way new technologies have interacted with the prevailing policy and
institutional environment.[15]

Shifts in Product Markets

Business models and market structures are being reshaped by digital advances. How technology diffuses within the economy matters greatly for
both productivity growth and income distribution. But the benefits of

digital innovations have so far not been diffusing widely across firms. They have been captured predominantly by a relatively small number of large firms. There is a pronounced gap between the digital "haves" and the "have-mores." Even the economy at the digital frontier—the United States—may be reaching only about a fifth of its digital potential.[16]

The slowdown in productivity fundamentally reflects a growing inequality in productivity performance between firms. For firms at the technological frontier, productivity growth has remained relatively robust. But it has slowed considerably in the vast majority of other firms, depressing aggregate productivity growth. Over a fifteen-year period since 2000, labor productivity among frontier firms in OECD economies rose by around 45 percent; among nonfrontier firms, the increase was well below 10 percent.[17] Productivity divergence between firms is wider in more digital-intensive industries.[18]

Weakening competition is one important cause of this trend. Barriers to competition and related market frictions have prevented a broader diffusion of new technologies, contributing to a persistent rise in productivity and profitability gaps between firms. Evidence for OECD economies shows that in industries with diminished competitive intensity, technological innovation and diffusion have been weaker, interfirm productivity divergence has been wider, and aggregate productivity growth has been slower.[19]

The decline of competition in markets is reflected in a range of indicators: rise in market concentration in industries, higher markups showing increased market power of dominant firms, these firms' supernormal profits (rents) that account for a rising share of total corporate profits, low churning among high-return firms, and decline in new firm formation and business dynamism.[20] The rise in market concentration and the decline in business dynamism are greater in industries that are more intensive users of digital technologies.

While these trends are observable broadly across advanced economies, they have been particularly pronounced in the United States. The share of the top four US companies in total sales has risen since the 1980s in all major sectors of the economy—and more sharply in digital-intensive sectors.[21] Markups over marginal cost for US publicly traded firms are estimated to have nearly tripled between 1980 and 2016, with the increase concentrated in high-markup firms gaining market share, indicating a strong rise in their market power.[22] Over roughly the same period, rents (profits in excess of those under competitive market conditions) are estimated to have risen from a negligible share of national income to about one-fifth.[23] The distribution of returns on capital has become more unequal, with a relatively small number of firms reaping supernormal profits.[24] The share of young firms (five years old or less) in the total number of US firms has declined from about one-half to one-third.[25] American markets, a model of competition for the world, have been shifting toward more monopolistic structures.[26]

Digital technologies have led to increased market concentration because they promote a winner-takes-all form of competition. They offer first-mover advantages, strong economies of scale and network effects, and the leverage of big data that encourage the rise of "superstar firms."[27] The rise of the "intangible economy"—where assets such as data, software, knowledge embodied in patents, and other intellectual property matter more for economic success—has been associated with a stronger tendency toward the emergence of dominant firms.[28] The winner-takes-all dynamics are most marked in the high-tech sectors, as reflected in the rise of tech giants such as Apple, Facebook, and Google. But they are increasingly affecting economies more broadly as digitalization penetrates business processes in other sectors, such as transportation, communications, finance, and commerce. In retail trade, for example, the big box stores, which previously had replaced mom-and-pop outlets, are now losing market share to online megastores such as Amazon.

These technology-driven forces producing higher market concentration have been reinforced by failures in competition policy. Competition policy has failed to adapt to the shift in market structures and the new challenges to keep markets competitive, notably those related to data and the digital economy. Antitrust enforcement has been weak in the face of rising monopoly power and takeover activity. Facebook alone, for example, has acquired more than seventy companies over roughly fifteen years, including potential competitors such as Instagram and WhatsApp.[29] Increased overlapping ownership, by large institutional investors, of companies that compete also has affected competition. Regulatory policies have not consistently supported competition, sometimes overregulating and restricting competition and sometimes deregulating without safeguards to protect competition.

Moreover, flaws in patent systems have acted as barriers to new or follow-on innovation and wider diffusion of knowledge embodied in new technologies. These systems, typically designed many decades ago, have been slow to adapt to the knowledge dynamics of the digital era. In the United States, since the 1980s, the ownership of patents has become more concentrated in the hands of firms with the largest stock—mirroring broader patterns of market concentration—coupled with more strategic use of patents by market leaders to limit knowledge diffusion.[30]

Shifts in Labor Markets

In labor markets, an interplay between rapid technology-driven change and lagging policies that is similar to the interplay seen in product markets has been at work, limiting productivity gains from new technologies and exacerbating inequality. While product markets have seen rising inequality between firms, labor markets have seen rising inequality between workers.

Technology is transforming the nature and future of work. Automation and digital advances have shifted labor demand toward higher-level skills. In advanced economies, globalization has exerted pressure in the same direction. Demand has shifted, in particular, away from routine, middle-level skills that are more vulnerable to automation, as in jobs like clerical work and repetitive production. Job markets have seen an increasing polarization, with the employment share of middle-skill jobs falling and that of higher-skill jobs, such as technical professionals and managers, rising. The employment share of low-skill jobs has also increased, such as jobs in services like personal care that are hard to automate.

Over the two decades since the mid-1990s, the share of middle-skill jobs in total employment fell by about 9.5 percentage points in OECD economies on average, while the shares of high-skill and low-skill jobs rose by about 7.5 and 2 percentage points, respectively.[31] Part of the workforce displaced from middle-skill jobs is having to move to lower-skill, lower-productivity, lower-wage jobs, giving rise to an "inverse Lewis economy."[32]

Looking ahead, as AI advances, displacement risks will affect some higher-level skills as well, in contrast to previous waves of automation. However, the displacement risk at higher-level skills is likely to apply more at the task level than at the level of entire jobs or occupations as has been the case with low- to middle-level skills.[33] Higher-skilled workers typically also have greater ability to adjust by gaining new skills and new employment than less-skilled workers.

As demand for skills has shifted, adjustment on the supply side has been slow in equipping workers with skills that complement the new technologies and in supporting their transition to new tasks and jobs. Education and training have been losing the race with technology.[34] Even in an advanced economy such as the United States, almost two-thirds of workers do not have a college degree. Growth in the years of education completed slowed considerably in the United States around the 1980s. So just when demand for higher-level skills picked up as the digital revolution gathered steam, the attainment of those skills slowed. While precollege education gaps by family income level have narrowed, gaps in college and higher-level education have widened. The slowing of improvement in educational attainment around this period is observable more broadly across economies—both advanced and emerging.[35] Moreover, the capacity of systems for continuing education has been far exceeded by the fast-growing need for worker upskilling and reskilling. Access to retraining is typically more difficult for lower-skilled workers.

The lag in the supply of new and higher-level cognitive, technical, and managerial skills demanded by the digital economy has hampered technology diffusion across firms and broader productivity gains. Across industries, skills mismatches have increased: in OECD countries, on average around one-quarter of workers report a mismatch between their skills and those required by the job.[36] Workers with skills complementary to the new technologies have increasingly clustered in dominant firms at the technological frontier.

The changing balance between skills demand and supply has increased skill premia and wage differentials, contributing to higher labor income inequality and diminished job prospects for less-skilled workers. The skill premium has been rising since the 1980s and has more recently risen particularly sharply at the higher end of educational attainment—graduate and professional education. Skill-biased technological change is causing a "convexification" of returns to education and training.[37]

Wage inequality between firms has increased as well. Across OECD economies, increased interfirm inequality in firm productivity and profitability is mirrored by increased interfirm inequality in labor incomes.[38] As profitability gaps have widened between firms, so have wage gaps. Rent sharing also has contributed to wider wage differences between firms. Better-performing firms have reaped a higher share of total profits and have shared part of their supernormal profits with their workers. Between-firm wage inequality has risen more in industries that invest more intensively in digital technologies.

Although workers in firms at the technological frontier are earning more than those in other firms, gains from higher productivity at these firms have been shared unevenly, with wage growth lagging productivity growth. Wages have risen in the better-performing firms but by less than the rise in productivity. For most other firms, limited wage growth has reflected limited productivity growth, although even at these firms wage growth has tended to fall short of the meager gains in productivity. In the United States, between the mid-1970s and the mid-2010s, labor productivity rose by about 75 percent and average worker compensation in real terms rose by about 50 percent—with the productivity and compensation growth divergence increasing in the most recent decades. Over the same period, real compensation for the median worker rose by less than 15 percent, reflecting rising wage inequality.[39]

The decoupling of wages from productivity has contributed to a shift in income distribution from labor to capital. In the past couple of decades, most major economies have experienced both increasing inequality of labor earnings and declining shares of labor in total income.[40] In the United States, for example, the percentage share of labor in nonfarm business income fell from the mid-60s around 2000 to the mid-50s around 2015. Increased market concentration in product markets also has played a role in shifting income from labor to capital as it has reallocated labor within industries to dominant firms with supernormal profits and lower labor income shares.[41] Dominant firms are acquiring not only more monopoly power in product markets to increase markups and extract higher rents but also monopsony power to dictate wages in the labor market.[42] While employer market power has strengthened, worker bargaining power has weakened with a decline in unionization and erosion of minimum wage laws.

These developments in labor and product markets have reinforced the effect of the labor-substituting nature of many of the new technologies on the distribution of income between labor and capital. Production is shifting toward firms and processes using more capital (tangible and intangible) and less labor. The largest US firm in 2017 (Apple) had a market capitalization forty times as high as that of the largest US firm in 1962 (AT&T), but its total employment was only one-fifth that of the latter.[43] The shift of income from labor to capital has increased overall income inequality, as capital ownership is highly uneven.[44]

International trade and offshoring also have contributed to the shift in income toward capital in advanced economies by putting downward pressure on wages, especially of lower-skilled workers in tradable sectors. The expanding digital trade—the new phase of globalization—can add to these pressures. With a growing range of digitally deliverable services, workers farther up the skill spectrum also will face more competition from across borders.[45] Overall, globalization has played a significant role in the decline of the labor income share in advanced economies. However, its role has been much smaller than that of technology—about half or less.[46]

COVID-19 Reinforcing Technology-Driven Shifts in Market Dynamics

The COVID-19 pandemic is accelerating the digitalization of production, commerce, and work. As economies recover from the immediate crisis, the further advances in digital transformation can spur productivity and boost economic growth. But they can also reinforce the technology-driven shifts in product and labor markets that have in recent years inhibited productivity growth and increased economic inequality.

In product markets, the pandemic is intensifying the trend toward more monopolistic structures.[47] The big shift in demand toward online modes of business is adding to the pre-existing advantages of technologically advanced, well-positioned large firms. The pandemic is likely to disproportionately cull the ranks of smaller, less automation-intensive firms—also because smaller firms lack the liquidity and access to credit needed to survive in a crisis. While smaller firms struggle, tech giants are further increasing market shares. This is already evident in some industries, such as in retail trade, where an unfolding wave of bankruptcies is pushing more business toward big tech retail giants. Market dynamism and competition will face added challenges with more firm exits and fewer new entrants—and increased takeover opportunities. The reinforcement of the dominant positions of large firms associated with more demand shifting online will not be limited to the period of COVID-19 shutdowns but will extend into the future.

In labor markets, the pandemic is further tilting the balance against less-skilled, low-wage workers.[48] Firms are automating even more, especially in industries with business models more reliant on human contact and a less-skilled workforce. The further consolidation of economic activity in large firms in product markets will reinforce recent trends toward higher wage inequality and lower labor income share. Moreover, the pandemic has caused an overnight revolution in telework. The beneficiaries of telework are primarily higher-educated workers. Low-skilled workers have fewer options to telework, and they also face job losses as telework reduces demand for a range of personal and business services that employ them in large numbers, such as office space maintenance, transportation, and hospitality. Even after the pandemic has passed, the number of people teleworking could be three to four times higher than before, with remote work potentially accounting for more than 30 percent of working time in advanced economies. Up to 25 percent more workers than previously estimated may need to switch occupations as a result of increased telework, e-commerce, and automation triggered by the pandemic.[49]

Rebooting Policies for the Digital Era

Digital technologies are reshaping markets, and the COVID-19 pandemic will accelerate this transformation. But technological change is not delivering its full potential to boost productivity and economic growth. And it is pushing income inequality higher, with the distribution of both capital and labor income becoming more unequal and income shifting from labor to capital. These outcomes are not inevitable, however. With more responsive policies, better outcomes are possible.

Digital technologies can be the source of as much as two-thirds—or perhaps even more—of potential productivity growth over the next decade.[50] How to realize the potential of these technologies to deliver stronger and more inclusive economic growth lies at the core of the forward policy agenda. Today's innovation economy must be broadened from its narrow confines to enable wider segments of firms and workers to contribute to and share in its promise. Innovation must be "democratized."[51]

Policies to reduce inequality are often considered narrowly in terms of redistribution—tax and transfer policies. This is of course an important element, especially given the erosion of the state's redistributive role in recent decades as tax progressivity has declined and social programs have felt the pressure of tighter fiscal constraints. In particular, systems for taxing income and wealth should be bolstered in light of the new distributional dynamics. But there is a much broader policy agenda of "predistribution" to make the growth process itself more inclusive.[52] Much of the reform agenda to achieve more inclusive outcomes from technological change is also an agenda to achieve stronger growth outcomes, given the linked dynamics between the recent rise in inequality and the slowdown in productivity.

Specific policy needs and priorities evidently differ across groups of economies, especially between advanced and emerging economies.

Broadly, there are five areas that need more focused attention from national policymakers.

First, as technology transforms the world of business, policies and institutions governing markets must keep pace. Competition policy should be revamped for the digital age to ensure that markets continue to provide an open and level playing field for firms, keep competition strong, and check the growth of monopolistic structures.

Antitrust enforcement should be strengthened. Laws and guidelines on mergers and acquisitions (M&As)—covering not only horizontal M&As but also nonhorizontal ones—and prevention of anti-competitive practices need to be reviewed and updated in light of the new dynamics of the digital economy. Recent congressional activity (antitrust hearings and legislative proposals) and filings of antitrust lawsuits against tech giants (Amazon, Apple, Facebook, and Google) in the United States, together with related actions in the European Union (EU), suggest that momentum may be building for reform of the antitrust legal framework and stronger enforcement.

The digital economy poses a range of new regulatory challenges that must be addressed. These include regulatory responses to proprietary agglomeration of data, competition issues relating to digital platforms that have emerged as gatekeepers in the digital world, and market concentration resulting from tech giants that resemble natural or quasi-natural monopolies. An overarching issue is the regulation of data, the lifeblood of the digital economy. Issues relating to how data are handled—use, access, portability, openness while protecting privacy and security—matter for consumer protection but also for competition. To date, there has been more action on these issues in Europe than in the United States. The EU enacted the General Data Protection Regulation in 2018 and has proposed important new legislation—the Digital Services Act and the Digital Markets Act—as part of its Shaping Europe's Digital Future initiative.[53]

To strengthen institutional capabilities to address the competition policy challenges of the digital economy, some countries—such as Australia, France, Germany, and the United Kingdom—are now establishing or contemplating new regulatory bodies focused on digital markets.[54] These bodies would be tasked to develop procompetition standards, rules, and codes of conduct for digital markets (including approaches to addressing new competition issues that may arise as AI and machine learning algorithms advance), and could also serve as focal points for international coordination on regulation of digital markets. There are also emerging proposals for similar reform in the United States.[55] As a related step, in July 2021, the Biden administration announced the establishment of a White House Competition Council to coordinate and advance government efforts to address overconcentration, monopolization, and unfair competition.

Second, the innovation ecosystem should be improved so that it spurs new knowledge and technological advances but also promotes their wide diffusion. In a knowledge-driven economy, its role is increasingly vital in continuing to push the technological frontier while at the same time fostering broader economic impacts from the new advances.

"The copyright and patent laws we have today look more like intellectual monopoly than intellectual property."[56] Patent systems should be reformed to better balance incumbent interests and the wider promotion and dissemination of innovation. This involves changing excessively broad or stringent protections, addressing the problems of patent thickets and patent trolling, aligning the rules with today's realities, and giving freer rein to competition that, ultimately, is the primary driver of technological innovation and diffusion. One possible reform is to replace the one-size-fits-all approach of current systems with a differentiated approach.[57] While a relatively long patent term may continue to be appropriate for some innovations, notably in pharmaceuticals that involve protracted and expensive testing, the case is less clear for digital technologies that have much shorter gestation periods and typically build on previous innovations in an incremental fashion.[58]

A rebalancing is needed also in investment in research and development (R&D). Public R&D investment has been falling in many countries: in the United States, for example, it has fallen from 1.2 percent of GDP in the early 1980s to half that level in recent years, with its share in total R&D investment declining from 45 percent to less than a quarter.[59] It should be revitalized, as it supplies the public good of basic research that produces broad knowledge spillovers and complements the focus of private R&D on narrower, applied research. Also, a robust public R&D program can influence the direction of technological change toward innovation that serves broader economic and social goals rather than the interests of narrow groups of investors. It can, for example, address the concern that the current private technological paradigm is geared toward "excessive automation," producing technologies that displace labor without much gain in productivity.[60] Correcting biases in the tax system that favor capital relative to labor would also help.[61]

Access to innovation financing should be broadened. Well-designed small business research and technology transfer programs can provide vital support to small and young firms that typically face greater hurdles in accessing innovation financing. In the United States, venture capital plays a major role in financing startups, but the industry is highly concentrated, with the top 5 percent of investors accounting for 50 percent of the capital raised.[62] Digital innovations in finance—Fintech—are now creating promising new financing possibilities for innovative entrepreneurs that public policy should foster.

Incentives provided to private R&D through tax relief should ensure that small and young firms are not at a disadvantage in accessing them. Best practices include payroll tax relief for researchers and refundable R&D tax credits. Support encouraging R&D collaboration between universities and firms can facilitate technological diffusion by providing smaller firms with access to sources of knowledge. Innovations are concentrated in high-income groups. Support for internship programs at firms to increase exposure to innovation among disadvantaged groups can boost overall innovation by helping the many "lost Einsteins" in these groups.[63]

Many breakthrough innovations developed commercially by private firms originate from government-supported research. Examples include Google's basic search algorithm, key features of Apple smartphones, and even the internet itself.[64] Governments should explore ways of better recouping some of their investments in research—not least to replenish their research budgets—producing a better balance in sharing risks and rewards of public research investment compared to the current paradigm, where risks are socialized but rewards are privatized. Ensuring that companies do not take advantage of loopholes in the tax system and pay adequate taxes on their profits is the obvious way. Other possibilities include requiring companies to repay research grants if their products succeed financially, or acquiring equity stakes in the commercialization of successful technologies directly supported by public research funds.[65]

Third, the foundation of digital infrastructure must be strengthened to broaden access to new opportunities in the digital economy. This calls for increased public investment and frameworks to encourage more private investment to improve digital access for underserved groups and areas. Broadband is becoming as much of a necessity in this century as electricity was in the twentieth century. But the digital divide remains wide within economies, a fact brought into starker relief by the COVID-19 crisis. Even in the United States, the economy at the digital frontier, most sectors are less than 15 percent as digitalized as the leading sectors, and there are large gaps in access between major urban/industrial centers and other areas.[66]

In developing economies, the digital divide is still wider. Stronger digital infrastructure will be crucial for these economies as technology forces a shift toward growth models less reliant on low-skill, low-wage manufacturing. A robust digital infrastructure is essential to capturing the new growth opportunities that technology offers, such as the expanding trade in digitally deliverable services. Success in many countries in using mobile telephony to connect large populations to the formal economy, including to financial markets through expanding Fintech applications, illustrates the leapfrogging possibilities in development offered by the new technologies, given a supportive enabling environment.

Fourth, investment in skills must be boosted, with education and training programs revamped to emphasize skills that complement the new technologies. This will require innovation in the content, delivery, and financing of these programs, including new models of public-private partnerships. Persistent inequalities in access to education and (re)training must be addressed. While gaps in basic capabilities across income groups have narrowed, those in higher-level capabilities that will drive success in the twenty-first century are widening.[67]

With the fast-changing demand for skills and the growing need for upskilling, reskilling, and lifelong learning, the availability and quality of continuing education should be greatly scaled up.[68] This effort should span both the general education system and the institutions for vocational education. It should include expanded partnerships with employers, including exploring a larger role for apprenticeship arrangements—which have been used successfully in some European countries, notably Germany. To improve workers' access to retraining, one approach is through Lifelong Learning Accounts, allowing workers to accumulate rights to training that are portable across jobs.[69] Such accounts have recently been introduced at the national level in some countries, such as France and Singapore. More flexibility can be built into government student aid programs (grants, loans, tax incentives) so that they benefit not just first-time college entrants but also returning older adults.

Technology is changing not only which skills are in demand but also how skills are acquired. The potential of technology-enabled solutions must be harnessed. The COVID-19 pandemic has dramatically demonstrated the scope for scaling up the use of online learning tools. Broader access to these tools will require a stronger foundation of digital infrastructure and digital literacy.

Fifth, labor market policies and social protection systems should be reformed to realign them with the changing economy and the nature of work. This means shifting the focus from backward-looking policies, such as stringent job protection laws that seek to keep workers in existing jobs (even as they are being rendered obsolete by technological change), to forward-looking policies that improve workers' ability to move to new and better jobs. Unemployment insurance schemes should better support workers in adjusting to change, retraining, and transitioning to new jobs. They should be designed to provide adequate coverage and encourage re-employment, complemented by enhanced placement services.

Other barriers to worker mobility and competition in labor markets, such as the ever-increasing professional licensing requirements and non-compete covenants in worker contracts, should also be addressed.[70] Well-functioning labor market institutions—collective bargaining, minimum wage laws, labor standards—are important to ensure that workers get a fair share of economic returns, especially at a time of rising market power of dominant firms.

Worker benefits systems, covering benefits such as pensions and health care, which traditionally have been based on formal long-term employer-employee relationships, will need to adjust to a job market with more frequent job transitions and more diverse work arrangements. This means greater portability and adaptability to address the needs of more people working independently. The gig economy is expanding.[71] The increased use of teleworking stemming from the pandemic will spur it further.

Finally, international cooperation needs to play its part. While the dominant part of the policy agenda to make technology work better for all lies at the national level, especially in the five areas discussed above, there is a complementary agenda at the international level. The rise of nationalist populism has increased protectionist sentiment. The pandemic can further stoke the backlash against globalization. Concerns about the security of critical supplies can spur more reshoring of supply chains. International cooperation will need to ensure that past gains in establishing an open, rules-based global trading system are shielded from these headwinds.

At the same time, new rules and cooperative arrangements must be devised to underpin the next phase of globalization led by digital flows to ensure open access and fair competition.[72] This includes adequate disciplines for digital trade, cross-border data flows, and the fast-growing digitally deliverable services. The rise of multinational tech giants that can affect competition across national markets calls for increased international cooperation in competition policy. In a more knowledge-intensive globalization, well-balanced frameworks governing intellectual property—that reward innovation but prevent intellectual monopolies—take on added significance. International cooperation on tax matters becomes even more important in view of the new tax challenges of the digital economy.

The chapters that follow flesh out some key elements of the agenda summarized above, discussing in more detail the potential and the unfolding impacts of digital transformation, the opportunities and challenges it presents, and how responsive and creative policies can make it more productive and inclusive. The chapters approach these issues from both a global perspective and the perspective of a major individual economy: Korea.

Promoting Technology Diffusion

In chapter 2, Flavio Calvino and Chiara Criscuolo focus on technology diffusion dynamics in the digital era, reviewing a large body of research, including their own at the OECD. They document the uneven diffusion of digital technologies and widening productivity gaps across firms. Aggregate productivity growth has slowed not because innovation has slowed at the technological frontier but because the spread of innovation across firms has slowed. The shift to a digital and knowledge-based economy has created new challenges for firms, including the increasing importance of intangible assets, the need for complementary investments in human and organizational capital, and the winner-takes-all dynamics associated with the new technologies. To promote technology diffusion, the authors emphasize policies to boost competition in markets and address the new regulatory issues of the digital economy (especially those relating to data), improve knowledge production and sharing (including through sensible patent policies), upskill and reskill workers, and strengthen digital infrastructure.

A similar mix of policies will be important to harness the potential of AI, the new wave of technologies that mark the next phase of the digital revolution. Data and analyses on the diffusion and impact of AI are still relatively scant. The productivity effects of AI will not fully materialize until a range of complementary innovations are developed and deployed. The new technologies may strengthen the importance of intangible capital and investments in higher-level skills and organizational changes, which may produce a J-curve effect on productivity and wider productivity dispersion between leading and lagging firms, and accentuate market dynamics toward more concentrated structures.[73]

In chapter 3, Minho Kim investigates the relationship between digital technologies, intangible capital, and productivity, using a large database of Korean firms in manufacturing and service industries. He finds that the adoption of digital technologies and investment in intangible capital boost productivity but require complementary innovations and investments in management practices (organizational capital) to deliver their full potential. Even though Korea is home to several leading high-tech companies, the diffusion of new technologies among smaller firms has been weak, limiting gains from digital transformation—which echoes the theme of chapter 2. Reviewing some policy initiatives in Korea to promote technology diffusion, the author calls upon policymakers to pay attention to the diversity of needs across firms, avoiding one-size-fits-all solutions.

Harnessing Digital Transformation in Finance

Digital transformation is also driving rapid change in financial markets. Innovations range from the use of smartphones and digital platforms for a variety of banking and investing services to blockchain and digital currencies. In chapter 4, Thomas Philippon examines the question of how to realize the potential of Fintech while managing associated risks. Digital innovations in finance are improving financial inclusion, lowering the cost of financial intermediation while offering new products and services, and introducing more competition into financial markets. They have the potential to significantly broaden access to finance and open new gateways to entrepreneurship.[74]

But the digital transformation of finance also creates new risks to cybersecurity, financial integrity, consumer protection, and financial stability. It poses new regulatory challenges, ranging from putting in place clear and consistent rules on data ownership and access, to tackling regulatory arbitrage, to developing capacities and tools to regulate the new world of financial platforms and algorithms. Policymakers will need to adopt regulatory approaches that strike the right balance between enabling financial innovation and managing risks. Some countries—Australia, Canada, Japan, Korea, Singapore, and the United Kingdom, for example—are using a "sandbox" approach that encourages innovation and generates learning to inform the development of appropriate regulatory policies.

As in product markets, policymakers need to ensure that financial markets remain sufficiently competitive as digital finance expands. The finance industry now has three sets of players: traditional financial intermediaries such as banks, which are expanding investment in digitalizing their business; young Fintech firms that are trying to grow beyond their niche markets; and big tech firms that are becoming more involved in finance. The economies of scale and network effects associated with the technologies driving digital finance can potentially lead to increased concentration in financial markets, especially given the pre-existing advantages of big tech firms with large customer networks established through e-commerce platforms or information and communication services, vast collection of proprietary data, and use of advanced technologies such as AI and machine learning. Regulators will need to avoid excessive concentration and market dominance by a few financial services providers and their overlapping control over finance and other sectors of the economy.

Revamping Workforce Development

In labor markets, technology will continue to shift demand for skills. In chapter 5, Harry Holzer argues that labor market effects of digitalization and automation in coming years will be similar to what we have seen in recent decades—with both job displacements and rising inequality—only more so. The pace of these developments could well accelerate as automation intensifies in the aftermath of the COVID-19 pandemic. Also, advances in AI could increasingly displace workers higher up in the skill distribution than those previously affected. Against these challenges, workforce development policies will need to be rethought, with significant reform and adaptation to support workers and equip them with skills complementary with the new technologies.

The author discusses a range of policy reforms in the education and training system, including placing greater emphasis on "twenty-first-century skills" in K–12 education systems, making the acquisition of technical and higher-level skills at institutions of vocational and higher education more accessible, expanding opportunities for continuing education and lifelong learning, designing incentives to encourage employers to retrain rather than displace workers, and complementing improvements in training/retraining with enhanced workforce support services such as labor market information, career guidance, and placement assistance. The chapter also examines the role of other policies, such as provision of incentives for "good job" creation, wage subsidies or earned income tax credits for low-income workers to "make work pay," wage insurance, more "voice" for workers in the workplace and corporate governance, and changes in retirement and immigration policies that can all help address some of the effects of automation as well as the changing demographics and labor market institutions that complicate these effects. The author emphasizes policies that help workers adjust to automation and encourage (re)employment, drawing a contrast with policies—such as a universal basic income advocated by some—that may have the effect of paying workers to withdraw from the labor force, besides entailing high fiscal costs.[75]

The need for stepped-up worker retraining and lifelong learning is underscored by Sunghoon Chung and Sangmin Aum in chapter 6. Analyzing firm-level data for Korea, they find strong complementarity between firms' investment in the continuous learning of their workforce and successful digital transformation. As the digital revolution advances from information technology applications of recent years to major new innovations based on AI and other new technologies, the role of the firm in adapting and updating the skills of their workers will take on added importance, as will the use of technology-based delivery of learning content. The new technologies will demand complementary technical skills but also more soft skills such as critical thinking and problem solving, creativity, adaptiveness, communication, and teamwork. The role of institutions of formal education will remain important in the digital era, but the role of the firm as a teacher and supporter of learning will grow. Greater cooperation between these two suppliers of learning will be needed to better match skill supply and demand and support lifelong learning. Public policy should promote such cooperation.

Addressing Rising Inequality

Technology's implications for income distribution are an important concern. In chapter 7, François Bourguignon analyzes in detail the increase in income inequality in recent decades, particularly in advanced economies. The role of digitalization-led technological change in pushing inequality higher is examined through three channels: rise in earnings inequality as the new technologies favor higher-level skills and polarize labor markets; shift in income from labor to capital with rising automation; and shift toward more concentrated market structures and the associated rise in corporate rents. Absent countervailing policies, a "tsunami" of AI and other new innovations could exacerbate inequality. Even as new technologies increase productivity and produce greater economic affluence, and new jobs and tasks emerge to replace those displaced to prevent large technological unemployment, inequality could reach much higher levels.[76] Continuing and large increases in inequality may not be a sustainable path given associated social and political risks.

While calling for adaptations in education and training systems to upskill and reskill workers for the digital era, as stressed by Holzer and by Chung and Aum, the author also argues for a key role for tax policy reforms. Tax policy can be deployed to prevent an excessive increase in disposable income inequality, help finance stronger safety nets for occupational transitions in the labor market, and influence the direction of technological change. The author proposes higher taxation of capital and more progressive taxation of household income. Some have suggested directly taxing robots and using fiscal incentives to favor specific types of innovations relative to others. The author cautions against such actions, which may be difficult to implement, create unintended distortions, and risk hurting an economy's innovation capacity. Re-establishing a better balance between the taxation of capital and labor against a history of tax changes that have favored capital would be a more efficient way to address biases in the current tax system that encourage excessive automation, incentivize more employment-friendly innovation, and help facilitate economic and social adjustments to new technology. Some international coordination would be essential if meaningful reform of capital taxation is to be implemented, given the high mobility of capital.

In chapter 8, Jungsoo Park analyzes technology and inequality dynamics in Korea, using both macroeconomic data and data at the level of firms, workers, and households. Contrary to some other studies that show a declining labor income share in Korea in recent decades, he finds that the long-run labor share appears relatively stable if the large self-employed sector in Korea is correctly taken into account in calculating factor income shares. Skill-biased technological change seems to have been having offsetting effects on the incomes of higher- and lower-skilled workers, leaving the aggregate long-run labor income share relatively unchanged. Meanwhile, wage disparity has been rising. In particular, wage gaps have been widening between large firms well-positioned to take advantage of the new technologies and boost productivity and small firms that are lagging behind. The rising wage disparity has been pushing overall household income inequality higher. Another interesting finding is that rising female participation in the labor force also has been pushing inequality higher, by widening income gaps between multiple-income and single-income households.

The author stresses the need for improvements in the business environment to foster broader opportunities for firms and their workers to benefit from technological transformation. He calls on Korean policymakers to redirect policies regarding smaller firms away from overprotecting existing businesses (which leaves them uncompetitive) to promoting their productivity, competitiveness, and growth in the innovation economy and revitalizing firm dynamics. The social safety net should be strengthened to support necessary firm turnover and worker transitions. Also, redistribution policies should take into account ongoing shifts in labor market participation and demographic transition.

Conclusion

Digital technologies are a defining feature of our time as they drive transformative change. They are reshaping product and factor markets and profoundly altering business and work—and society at large. And we may be on the cusp of a significant deepening and acceleration of this transformation as AI spawns a new wave of innovations and the COVID-19 pandemic gives added impetus to automation and online processes.

Our era of an ever-expanding array of smart machines holds considerable promise. It creates new avenues and opportunities for a more prosperous future. But it also demands smarter policies to realize that promise.

Policies will need to be more responsive to change to capture potential gains in productivity and economic growth and to address rising inequality.

New thinking and adaptations are needed to realign institutions and policies with the digital economy. As technology reshapes markets and alters growth and distributional dynamics, policies must ensure that markets remain inclusive and support broad access to the new opportunities for firms and workers. Areas for policy attention include competition policy and regulation of data and digital platforms, the innovation ecosystem, digital infrastructure, regulation of Fintech, workforce development, social protection frameworks, and tax policies. The digital economy also calls for new frameworks for international collaboration in areas such as regulation of cross-border data flows and taxation of cross-border digital business.

An agenda to enable broader participation of firms in the innovation economy, widen the diffusion of new technologies, and build complementary capabilities in the workforce can deliver both stronger and more inclusive economic growth. These reforms can reduce inequality and economic insecurity more effectively than fiscal redistribution alone. In capturing the full promise of digital transformation, the growth and inclusion agendas are one and the same. Inevitably, major economic reform is politically complex, even more so in today's climate of increased political divisiveness. But one thing reform should not be paralyzed by is continued trite debates about conflicts between growth and inclusion. Research increasingly shows this to be a false dichotomy.

NOTES

1. The first book, *Growth in a Time of Change: Global and Country Perspectives on a New Agenda*, Brookings Institution Press, was published in 2020.

2. See, for example, Brynjolfsson and McAfee (2014) and Schwab (2016).

3. Nordhaus (2015).

4. West and Allen (2020).

5. Chernoff and Warman (2020).

6. It should be noted that current statistical methods may not fully capture the new value created in the digital space. The rising importance of intangibles in business and production processes adds to the measurement challenges (Brynjolfsson, Rock, and Syverson 2021). Overall, research shows that, even allowing for these measurement issues, the productivity slowdown is real, not illusory. See Derviş and Qureshi (2016). See also Qureshi (2016) for the debate among "techno-pessimists" and "techno-optimists" on the productivity growth potential of digital technologies.

7. McKinsey Global Institute (2018).

8. World Bank (2018). See also World Bank (2020).

9. Coulibaly and Foda (2020).

10. The productivity series in figure 1-1 shows five-year moving averages to smooth year-to-year fluctuations.

11. The income shares in figure 1-1 are based on pretax national income.

12. Autor and Salomons (2017).

13. Chetty and others (2017). The negative relationship between income inequality and intergenerational mobility has been famously captured in a curve termed the Great Gatsby Curve by Alan Krueger (2012).

14. Schumpeter (1950).

15. On the nexus connecting technology, policies, and the productivity and distributional outcomes, see Brookings Institution and Chumir Foundation (2019) and Furman and Orszag (2018b).

16. McKinsey Global Institute (2015).

17. Andrews, Criscuolo, and Gal (2016) and Orbis Database (Bureau Van Dijk n.d.). Frontier firms in this estimate are defined as the top 5 percent of firms with the highest labor productivity within each two-digit industry. Nonfrontier firms cover all other firms.

18. Berlingieri and others (2020).

19. See, for example, Andrews, Criscuolo, and Gal (2016), Cette, Lopez, and Mairesse (2016), and Égert (2016). These studies use panel data for a broad range of OECD economies and industries. For a recent review of research on the productivity slowdown, see Goldin and others (2020).

20. Qureshi (2019). See also Akcigit and others (2021).

21. Autor and others (2020).

22. De Loecker, Eeckhout, and Unger (2020).

23. Eggertsson, Robbins, and Wold (2018). Mordechai Kurz (2018) estimates that, between 1985 and 2015, as monopoly profits boosted the market value of corporate stocks and produced outsize capital gains, the share of total US stock market value reflecting monopoly power (what he terms monopoly wealth) rose from negligible levels to around 80 percent.

24. Furman and Orszag (2018a).

25. Decker and others (2017).

26. Philippon (2019) and Tepper (2019).

27. Autor and others (2020).

28. See Haskel and Westlake (2017) and Crouzet and Eberly (2019).

29. Reich (2020). In an influential article, Khan (2017) makes the case that the current US antitrust legal framework is ill-equipped to address the competition policy challenges of the digital economy, such as those posed by business models based on online platforms like that of Amazon.

30. Akcigit and Ates (2019).

31. OECD Employment Database (OECD n.d.). See also World Bank (2019).

32. See Taylor and Ömer (2020) and Temin (2017).

33. Autor, Mindell, and Reynolds (2019) and Webb (2020).

34. Autor, Goldin, and Katz (2020) and Goldin and Katz (2008).

35. Barro and Lee (2013) and Morrisson and Murtin (2013).

36. Adalet McGowan and Andrews (2017).

37. Autor, Goldin, and Katz (2020).

38. Criscuolo and others (2020), Song and others (2019), and Berlingieri, Blanchenay, and Criscuolo (2017).

39. Stansbury and Summers (2018).

40. OECD (2018) and Schwellnus and others (2018). See also Gutiérrez and Piton (2020) for measurement issues relating to the labor income share and how they affect the estimated trend in some countries.

41. Autor and others (2020).

42. Council of Economic Advisers (2016) and Azar, Marinescu, and Steinbaum (2017).

43. West (2018).

44. The roles of uneven capital ownership and returns on capital as sources of inequality have been particularly emphasized by Thomas Piketty in his 2014 bestseller (Piketty 2014).

45. Baldwin (2019).

46. International Monetary Fund (2017). The study finds that, in advanced economies, technology accounts for about half of the decline in the labor income share, global integration accounts for about a quarter, and policies and institutions and other factors such as measurement issues account for the remainder.

47. Rose (2020).

48. Autor and Reynolds (2020).

49. McKinsey Global Institute (2021).

50. McKinsey Global Institute (2018).

51. Qureshi (2020) and Rodrik (2020).

52. Hacker (2011).

53. The 2018 regulation has become a model for several national laws outside the EU, for example, in Japan and Korea. For the proposed new legislation, see European Union (2020).

54. For the United Kingdom, for example, see Digital Competition Expert Panel (2019).

55. See Wheeler, Verveer, and Kimmelman (2020) and Stigler Committee on Digital Platforms (2019).

56. Lindsey and Teles (2017).

57. In advanced economies, patents typically carry terms of twenty years. Copyright protections typically run for seventy-plus years.

58. Roin (2014) and Qureshi (2018). See also Galasso and Schankerman (2015) on differentiating patent policy by firm size. In tailoring patents to different types of innovation and innovators, care must be taken not to complicate the patent regime excessively. More research on possible approaches is needed.

59. Shambaugh, Nunn, and Portman (2017).

60. Acemoglu and Restrepo (2019). The authors refer to these technologies as so-so technologies.

61. Acemoglu, Manera, and Restrepo (2020). The authors find that, in the United States, labor is taxed much more heavily than capital and that this difference has increased in recent years. They estimate that the US effective tax rate in the 2010s was 25.5–33.5 percent for labor and 5–10 percent for capital. See also Saez and Zucman (2019).

62. Lerner and Nanda (2020).

63. Bell and others (2019).

64. Mazzucato (2015).

65. Mazzucato (2015) and Rodrik (2015). Ideas such as government acquiring equity stakes are not without controversy. Government stakes could be "passive" and temporary, with the research investments focused in priority areas that entail high risks that private investors would not take on their own, and managed by independent entities shielded from day-to-day political pressures.

66. McKinsey Global Institute (2015).

67. United Nations (2019).

68. The need to scale up continuing education is reinforced by the aging of the workforce in many countries.

69. Fitzpayne and Pollack (2018).

70. In the United States, almost one in three workers requires a government occupational license (Council of Economic Advisers 2016). Noncompete restrictions cover about a quarter of all workers, with the ratio rising for higher-level technical and professional occupations (Shambaugh and Nunn 2018).

71. Brynjolfsson and McAfee (2017) and Sundarajan (2016).

72. Schwab (2019) and World Economic Forum (2019).

73. See also Brynjolfsson, Rock, and Syverson (2017).

74. See also Sahay and others (2020).

75. See also Holzer (2021) for detailed specific proposals focused on the United States.

76. Spence (2021) sketches a similar scenario, arguing that we should worry less about technological unemployment and more about inequality.

REFERENCES

Acemoglu, Daron, Andrea Manera, and Pascual Restrepo. 2020. "Does the U.S. Tax Code Favor Automation?" *Brookings Papers on Economic Activity* (Spring).

Acemoglu, Daron, and Pascual Restrepo. 2019. "The Wrong Kind of AI? Artificial Intelligence and the Future of Labor Demand." NBER Working Paper 25682 (Cambridge, MA: National Bureau of Economic Research).

Adalet McGowan, Muge, and Dan Andrews. 2017. "Labor Market Mismatch and Labor Productivity: Evidence from PIAAC Data." *Research in Labor Economics* 45, pp. 199–241.

Akcigit, Ufuk, and Sina Ates. 2019. "What Happened to U.S. Business Dynamism?" NBER Working Paper 25756 (Cambridge, MA: National Bureau of Economic Research).

Akcigit, Ufuk, Wenjie Chen, Federico Díez, Romain Duval, Philipp Engler, Jiayue Fan, Chiara Maggi, Marina Tavares, Daniel Schwarz, Ippei Shibata, and Carolina Villegas-Sánchez. 2021. "Rising Corporate Market Power: Emerging Policy Issues." IMF Staff Discussion Note SDN/21/01 (Washington, DC: International Monetary Fund).

Andrews, Dan, Chiara Criscuolo, and Peter Gal. 2016. "The Best versus the Rest: The Global Productivity Slowdown, Divergence across Firms and the Role of Public Policy." OECD Productivity Working Paper 5 (Paris: OECD Publishing).

Autor, David, David Dorn, Lawrence Katz, Christina Patterson, and John Van Reenen. 2020. "The Fall of the Labor Share and the Rise of Superstar Firms." *Quarterly Journal of Economics* 135, no. 2, pp. 645–709.

Autor, David, Claudia Goldin, and Lawrence Katz. 2020. "Extending the Race between Education and Technology." NBER Working Paper 26705 (Cambridge, MA: National Bureau of Economic Research).

Autor, David, David Mindell, and Elisabeth Reynolds. 2019. *The Work of the Future: Shaping Technology and Institutions.* MIT Task Force on the Work of the Future (Massachusetts Institute of Technology).

Autor, David, and Elisabeth Reynolds. 2020. *The Nature of Work after the COVID Crisis: Too Few Low-Wage Jobs.* Hamilton Project (Brookings Institution).

Autor, David, and Anna Salomons. 2017. "Robocalypse Now: Does Productivity Growth Threaten Employment?" in *Proceedings of the ECB Forum on Central Banking: Investment and Growth in Advanced Economies* (Sintra: European Central Bank).

Azar, José, Ioana Marinescu, and Marshall Steinbaum. 2017. "Labor Market Concentration." NBER Working Paper 24147 (Cambridge, MA: National Bureau of Economic Research).

Baldwin, Richard. 2019. *The Globotics Upheaval: Globalization, Robotics, and the Future of Work* (Oxford University Press).

Barro, Robert, and Jong-Wha Lee. 2013. "A New Data Set of Educational Attainment in the World, 1950–2010." *Journal of Development Economics* 104 (September), pp. 184–98.

Bell, Alex, Raj Chetty, Xavier Jaravel, Neviana Petkova, and John Van Reenen. 2019. "Who Becomes an Inventor in America? The Importance of Exposure to Innovation." *Quarterly Journal of Economics* 134, no. 2, pp. 647–713.

Berlingieri, Giuseppe, Patrick Blanchenay, and Chiara Criscuolo. 2017. "The Great Divergences." OECD Science, Technology and Industry Policy Papers 39 (Paris: OECD Publishing).

Berlingieri, Giuseppe, Sara Calligaris, Chiara Criscuolo, and Rudy Verlhac. 2020. "Laggard Firms, Technology Diffusion, and Its Structural and Policy Determinants." OECD Science, Technology and Industry Policy Papers 86 (Paris: OECD Publishing).

Brookings Institution and Chumir Foundation. 2019. *Productive Equity: The Twin Challenges of Reviving Productivity and Reducing Inequality*. Report. Washington, DC.

Brynjolfsson, Erik, and Andrew McAfee. 2014. *The Second Machine Age: Work, Progress, and Prosperity in a Time of Brilliant Technologies* (New York: Norton).

Brynjolfsson, Erik, and Andrew McAfee. 2017. *Machine, Platform, Crowd: Harnessing Our Digital Future* (New York: Norton).

Brynjolfsson, Erik, Daniel Rock, and Chad Syverson. 2017. "Artificial Intelligence and the Modern Productivity Paradox: A Clash of Expectations and Statistics." NBER Working Paper 24001 (Cambridge, MA: National Bureau of Economic Research).

Brynjolfsson, Erik, Daniel Rock, and Chad Syverson. 2021. "The Productivity J-Curve: How Intangibles Complement General Purpose Technologies." *American Economic Journal: Macroeconomics* 13, no. 1, pp. 333–72.

Bureau Van Dijk. n.d. Orbis Database. https://www.bvdinfo.com/en-us/our -products/data/international/orbis.

Cette, Gilbert, Jimmy Lopez, and Jacques Mairesse. 2016. "Market Regulations, Prices, and Productivity." *American Economic Review* 106, no. 5, pp. 104–8.

Chernoff, Alex, and Casey Warman. 2020. "COVID-19 and Implications for Automation." NBER Working Paper 27249 (Cambridge, MA: National Bureau of Economic Research).

Chetty, Raj, David Grusky, Maximilian Hell, Nathaniel Hendren, Robert Manduca, and Jimmy Narang. 2017. "The Fading American Dream: Trends in Absolute Income Mobility since 1940." *Science* 356, no. 6336, pp. 398–406.

Coulibaly, Brahima, and Karim Foda. 2020. "The Future of Global Manufacturing," in *Growth in a Time of Change: Global and Country Perspectives on a New Agenda*, edited by Hyeon-Wook Kim and Zia Qureshi (Brookings Institution Press).

Council of Economic Advisers. 2016. *Labor Market Monopsony: Trends, Consequences, and Policy Responses* (Washington, DC: The White House).

Criscuolo, Chiara, Alexander Hijzen, and others. 2020. "Workforce Composition, Productivity, and Pay: The Role of Firms in Wage Inequality." OECD Social, Employment and Migration Working Papers 241 (Paris: OECD Publishing).

Crouzet, Nicolas, and Janice Eberly. 2019. "Understanding Weak Capital Investment: The Role of Market Concentration and Intangibles." NBER Working Paper 25869 (Cambridge, MA: National Bureau of Economic Research).

Decker, Ryan, John Haltiwanger, Ron Jarmin, and Javier Miranda. 2017. "Declining Business Dynamism, Allocative Efficiency, and the Productivity Slowdown." *American Economic Review* 107, no. 5, pp. 322–26.

De Loecker, Jan, Jan Eeckhout, and Gabriel Unger. 2020. "The Rise of Market Power and the Macroeconomic Implications." *Quarterly Journal of Economics* 135, no. 2, pp. 561–644.

Derviş, Kemal, and Zia Qureshi. 2016. "The Productivity Slump—Fact or Fiction: The Measurement Debate." Research Brief (Brookings Institution).

Digital Competition Expert Panel. 2019. *Unlocking Digital Competition: Report of the Digital Competition Expert Panel* (London).

Égert, Balázs. 2016. "Regulation, Institutions and Productivity: New Macroeconomic Evidence from OECD Countries." *American Economic Review* 106, no. 5, pp. 109–13.

Eggertsson, Gauti, Jacob Robbins, and Ella Getz Wold. 2018. "Kaldor and Piketty's Facts: The Rise of Monopoly Power in the United States." NBER Working 24287 (Cambridge, MA: National Bureau of Economic Research).

European Union. 2020. *Shaping Europe's Digital Future* (Luxembourg: European Commission).

Fitzpayne, Alastair, and Ethan Pollack. 2018. *Lifelong Learning and Training Accounts: Helping Workers Adapt and Succeed in a Changing Economy* (Washington, DC: Aspen Institute).

Furman, Jason, and Peter Orszag. 2018a. "A Firm-Level Perspective on the Role of Rents in the Rise in Inequality," in *Toward a Just Society: Joseph Stiglitz and Twenty-First Century Economics*, edited by M. Guzman (Columbia University Press).

Furman, Jason, and Peter Orszag. 2018b. "Slower Productivity and Higher Inequality: Are They Related?" Working Paper 18-4 (Washington, DC: Peterson Institute for International Economics).

Galasso, Alberto, and Mark Schankerman. 2015. "Patent Rights and Innovation by Small and Large Firms." NBER Working Paper 21769 (Cambridge, MA: National Bureau of Economic Research).

Goldin, Claudia, and Lawrence Katz. 2008. *The Race between Education and Technology* (Harvard University Press).

Goldin, Ian, Pantelis Koutroumpis, François Lafond, and Julian Winkler. 2020. "Why Is Productivity Slowing Down?" OMPTEC Working Paper 2020-1 (Oxford, UK: Oxford Martin School).

Gutiérrez, Germán, and Sophie Piton. 2020. "Revisiting the Global Decline of the (Non-Housing) Labor Share." *American Economic Review: Insights* 2, no. 3, pp. 321–38.

Hacker, Jacob. 2011. "The Institutional Foundations of Middle Class Democracy." *Policy Network* (May 6).

Haskel, Jonathan, and Stian Westlake. 2017. *Capitalism without Capital: The Rise of the Intangible Economy* (Princeton University Press).

Holzer, Harry. 2021. *After COVID-19: Building a More Coherent and Effective Workforce Development System in the United States.* Hamilton Project (Brookings Institution).

International Monetary Fund. 2017. "Understanding the Downward Trend in Labor Income Shares," in *World Economic Outlook* (Washington, DC).

Khan, Lina. 2017. "Amazon's Antitrust Paradox." *Yale Law Journal* 126, no. 3, pp. 710–805.

Krueger, Alan. 2012. "The Rise and Consequences of Inequality in the United States." Paper presented at the Center for American Progress, Washington, DC, January 12.

Kurz, Mordecai. 2018. "On the Formation of Capital and Wealth: IT, Monopoly Power and Rising Inequality." Institute of Economic Policy Research, Working Paper 17-016, Stanford University, Stanford, CA.

Lerner, Josh, and Ramana Nanda. 2020. "Venture Capital's Role in Financing Innovation: What We Know and How Much We Still Need to Learn." *Journal of Economic Perspectives* 34, no. 3 (Summer), pp. 237–61.

Lindsey, Brink, and Steven Teles. 2017. *The Captured Economy: How the Powerful Enrich Themselves, Slow Down Growth, and Increase Inequality* (Oxford University Press).

Mazzucato, Mariana. 2015. *The Entrepreneurial State: Debunking Public vs Private Sector Myths* (London: Anthem Press).

McKinsey Global Institute. 2015. *Digital America: A Tale of the Haves and Have-Mores* (McKinsey & Company).

McKinsey Global Institute. 2018. *Solving the Productivity Puzzle: The Role of Demand and the Promise of Digitization* (McKinsey & Company).

McKinsey Global Institute. 2021. *The Future of Work after COVID-19* (McKinsey & Company).

Morrisson, Christian, and Fabrice Murtin. 2013. "The Kuznets Curve of Human Capital Inequality: 1870–2010." *Journal of Economic Inequality* 11, no. 3, pp. 283–301.

Nordhaus, William. 2015. "Are We Approaching an Economic Singularity? Information Technology and the Future of Economic Growth." NBER Working Paper 21547 (Cambridge, MA: National Bureau of Economic Research).

OECD. n.d. Employment Database. https://www.oecd.org/employment/emp/onlineoecdemploymentdatabase.htm.

OECD. 2018. "Decoupling of Wages from Productivity: What Implications for Public Policies?" in *OECD Economic Outlook* no. 2 (Paris: OECD Publishing).

Philippon, Thomas. 2019. *The Great Reversal: How America Gave Up on Free Markets* (Harvard University Press).

Piketty, Thomas. 2014. *Capital in the Twenty-First Century* (Harvard University Press).

Qureshi, Zia. 2016. "The Productivity Outlook: Pessimists versus Optimists." Research Brief (Brookings Institution).

Qureshi, Zia. 2018. "Intellectual Property, Not Intellectual Monopoly." *Project Syndicate*, July 11. https://www.project-syndicate.org/commentary/intellectual-property-regime-tends-toward-monopoly-by-zia-qureshi-2018-07?barrier=accesspaylog.

Qureshi, Zia. 2019. "The Rise of Corporate Market Power." *Up Front* (blog), Brookings Institution, May 21. https://www.brookings.edu/blog/up-front/2019/05/21/the-rise-of-corporate-market-power/.

Qureshi, Zia. 2020. *Democratizing Innovation: Putting Technology to Work for Inclusive Growth*. Report (Brookings Institution).

Reich, Robert. 2020. "Resurrect Antitrust." *Project Syndicate*, June 23. https://www.project-syndicate.org/onpoint/break-up-big-tech-companies-by-robert-b-reich-2020-04?barrier=accesspaylog.

Rodrik, Dani. 2015. "From Welfare State to Innovation State." *Project Syndicate*, January 14. https://www.project-syndicate.org/commentary/labor-saving-technology-by-dani-rodrik-2015-01?barrier=accesspaylog.

Rodrik, Dani. 2020. "Democratizing Innovation." *Project Syndicate*, August 11. https://www.project-syndicate.org/commentary/policymakers-should-influence-course-of-technological-innovation-by-dani-rodrik-2020-08?barrier=accesspaylog.

Roin, Benjamin. 2014. "The Case for Tailoring Patents Based on Time-to-Market." *UCLA Law Review* 61, pp. 672–759.

Rose, Nancy. 2020. *Will Competition Be Another COVID-19 Casualty?* Hamilton Project (Brookings Institution).

Saez, Emmanuel, and Gabriel Zucman. 2019. *The Triumph of Injustice: How the Rich Dodge Taxes and How to Make Them Pay* (New York: Norton).

Sahay, Ratna, Ulric Eriksson von Allmen, Amina Lahreche, Purva Khera, Sumiko Ogawa, Majid Bazarbash, and Kim Beaton. 2020. *The Promise of Fintech: Financial Inclusion in the Post COVID-19 Era* (Washington, DC: International Monetary Fund).

Schumpeter, Joseph. 1950. *Capitalism, Socialism, and Democracy*, 3rd ed. (New York: Harper & Row).

Schwab, Klaus. 2016. *The Fourth Industrial Revolution* (Geneva: World Economic Forum).

Schwab, Klaus. 2019. "Globalization 4.0: A New Architecture for the Fourth Industrial Revolution." *Foreign Affairs*, January 2019.

Schwellnus, Cyrille, Mathilde Pak, Pierre-Alain Pionnier, and Elena Crivellaro. 2018. "Labor Share Developments over the Past Two Decades: The Role of Technological Progress, Globalization and 'Winner-Takes-Most' Dynamics." Economics Department Working Paper 1503 (Paris: OECD Publishing).

Shambaugh, Jay, and Ryan Nunn, eds. 2018. *Revitalizing Wage Growth: Policies to Get American Workers a Raise*. Hamilton Project (Brookings Institution).

Shambaugh, Jay, Ryan Nunn, and Becca Portman. 2017. *Eleven Facts about Innovation and Patents*. Hamilton Project (Brookings Institution).

Song, Jae, David Price, Faith Guvenen, Nicholas Bloom, and Till von Wachter. 2019. "Firming Up Inequality." *Quarterly Journal of Economics* 134, no. 1, pp. 1–50.

Spence, Michael. 2021. "Winners and Losers in the Digital Transformation of Work." *Project Syndicate*, February 25. https://www.project-syndicate.org /commentary/distributional-effects-of-automation-artificial-intelligence -by-michael-spence-2021-02?barrier=accesspaylog.

Stansbury, Anna, and Lawrence Summers. 2018. "Productivity and Pay: Is the Link Broken?" Working Paper 18–5 (Washington, DC: Peterson Institute for International Economics).

Stigler Committee on Digital Platforms. 2019. *Final Report* (University of Chicago Booth School of Business).

Sundarajan, Arun. 2016. *The Sharing Economy: The End of Employment and the Rise of Crowd-Based Capitalism* (MIT Press).

Taylor, Lance, with Özlem Ömer. 2020. *Macroeconomic Inequality from Reagan to Trump: Market Power, Wage Repression, Asset Price Inflation, and Industrial Decline* (Cambridge University Press).

Temin, Peter. 2017. *The Vanishing Middle Class: Prejudice and Power in a Dual Economy* (MIT Press).

Tepper, Jonathan. 2019. *The Myth of Capitalism: Monopolies and the Death of Competition* (Hoboken, NJ: Wiley & Sons).

United Nations. 2019. *Human Development Report 2019: Beyond Income, Beyond Averages, Beyond Today—Inequalities in Human Development in the 21st Century* (New York).

Webb, Michael. 2020. "The Impact of Artificial Intelligence on the Labor Market." Economics Department Paper (Stanford University).

West, Darrell. 2018. *The Future of Work: Robots, AI, and Automation* (Brookings Institution Press).

West, Darrell, and John Allen. 2020. *Turning Point: Policymaking in the Era of Artificial Intelligence* (Brookings Institution Press).

Wheeler, Tom, Phil Verveer, and Gene Kimmelman. 2020. *New Digital Realities; New Oversight Solutions in the U.S.—The Case for a Digital Platform Agency and a New Approach to Regulatory Oversight* (Harvard Kennedy School).

World Bank. 2018. *Global Economic Prospects: Broad-Based Upturn, but for How Long?* (Washington, DC).

World Bank. 2019. *The Changing Nature of Work: World Development Report 2019* (Washington, DC).

World Bank. 2020. *Global Productivity: Trends, Drivers, and Policies*, edited by Alistair Dieppe (Washington, DC).

World Economic Forum. 2019. "Globalization 4.0: Shaping a New Global Architecture in the Age of the Fourth Industrial Revolution." White paper (Geneva).

TWO

Gone Digital

Technology Diffusion in the Digital Era

FLAVIO CALVINO AND CHIARA CRISCUOLO

Productivity is a key driver of economic growth and explains a signifi-cant portion of cross-country differences in income per capita. How-ever, productivity growth has been slowing in recent decades, depressing economic growth, and this is a cause for major concern in many Organ-ization for Economic Cooperation and Development (OECD) countries.[1]

However, not all firms have fared equally during the slowdown in pro-ductivity growth. While firms at the global frontier of productivity have continued to increase their productivity steadily, the rest of the business population has not kept pace (figure 2-1). The productivity gap between frontier firms and the rest has increased significantly in recent years, espe-cially in digital-intensive sectors, raising challenges for the inclusiveness of growth.[2]

Analyzing the dynamics of technology diffusion, together with the changes brought by digital transformation, is key to explaining these trends. Such analysis is central to understanding the paradox of slowing aggregate

FIGURE 2-1. **A Widening Labor Productivity Gap between Frontier Firms and Other Firms**

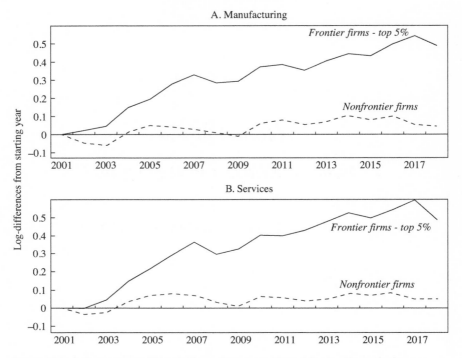

A. Manufacturing

B. Services

Source: Calculations using the Orbis database of Bureau van Dijk, following the methodology described in Andrews, Criscuolo, and Gal (2016).

Note: The "frontier" is measured by the average of log labor productivity, based on value added over employment, for the top 5 percent of firms with the highest productivity levels in each two-digit industry. "Nonfrontier" corresponds to the average of the log-productivity distribution of all other firms. Data shown are unweighted averages across two-digit industries over the period 2001–2018 across twenty-one OECD countries. The series are normalized to zero in the starting year (2001 = 0). The vertical axes show log differences from the starting year. The coverage of firms in the last year, 2018, is more limited than in previous years, hence the figures for that year might be less accurate. Services refer to nonfinancial business services.

productivity growth in the midst of a boom in new technologies. This chapter focuses on the process of technology diffusion in the digital era, critically discussing and interpreting stylized facts and evidence based on academic and policy literature.[3] Research suggests that technology diffusion has weakened in the last few decades. The chapter analyzes possible factors behind weak technology diffusion—with particular attention to the shifts to a digital and knowledge economy. It discusses the implications of the diffusion slowdown for economic outcomes. Finally, it looks at the role of public policy in improving technology diffusion.

The chapter devotes considerable attention to the increasing role of intangibles and digital transformation, which are key to understanding the slowdown of technology diffusion. It focuses on recent trends, but also attempts to look ahead, including to the possible role of the latest advances in digital technologies, notably in artificial intelligence (AI), which may not yet have delivered their full potential.

Intangible assets—such as research and development (R&D), software and data, and other intellectual property—are increasingly important in the knowledge economy and may have contributed to allowing a few superstar firms to thrive and gain considerable market shares, especially when these assets are proprietary.[4] These dynamics may, however, involve important trade-offs for technology diffusion, especially when accompanied by excessive accumulation of market power, anticompetitive patenting behavior, or policies favoring established firms.[5]

Weakening technology diffusion is not only related to increasing productivity divergence, but it also affects other important economic outcomes. It plays a role in explaining the recent declines in business dynamism and the rise in concentration and markups in many industries in the United States and a number of other countries, and possibly also trends in labor income shares and wage inequality.[6]

Digital transformation and the concomitant shift to a knowledge economy are linked to the observed slowdown in technology diffusion and play a key role in explaining important recent changes in market economies. Digital technologies may lower entry costs and ease market penetration and the sharing of ideas, but at the same time they require complementary investments in intangible assets that take time and are costly to implement. Furthermore, digital technologies, once installed, are scalable at low cost. Economies of scale and network externalities associated with these technologies can give rise to winner-takes-most dynamics, contributing to increasing barriers to technology diffusion for firms left behind, reducing incentives for experimentation, and consolidating the advantage of market leaders.

Governments can play an important role in fostering technology diffusion, even more crucially now as the COVID-19 pandemic may amplify some of the trends noted above. They can help remove barriers to diffusion and increase firms' absorptive capacity by addressing skill and financial constraints to technology adoption, implementing effective competition and research and innovation policies, and regulating data access and ownership.[7]

No single policy can foster technology diffusion alone. A broad policy mix affecting firms' incentives and capabilities is needed, one that includes both demand-side and supply-side measures. Demand-side measures would raise awareness about new technologies, develop absorptive capacity, and reduce risks. Supply-side measures would foster competition and the provision of new credit tools, address the new regulatory issues of the digital economy, improve knowledge production and sharing (including through sensible patent policies), strengthen the foundation of digital infrastructure and skills, and enable experimentation.[8]

Supporting wider technology diffusion, in particular for small and young firms, together with business dynamism and fair labor markets would allow the achievement of economic growth that is stronger as well as more inclusive and sustainable.[9]

Section 1 of the chapter conceptualizes technology diffusion, discussing different elements of the diffusion process and its measurement. Section 2 presents some key findings and stylized facts, especially focusing on technology diffusion in the digital era. Section 3 analyzes factors that may have contributed to the slowdown in diffusion, with particular attention to the role of digital transformation, and examines the implications of the slowdown for key economic outcomes. Section 4 focuses on the role of public policy to boost diffusion. The final section concludes with some implications for the future.

Defining and Measuring Technology Diffusion

Following Comin and Mestieri (2014), technology diffusion can be seen as the dynamic consequence of adopting a new technology. In this sense, the concept of technology diffusion appears somewhat different from the more general phenomenon of knowledge diffusion, which is more related to the exchange and spread of knowledge and ideas that may lead to invention, innovation, and new applications, or imitation.

Technology diffusion may be analyzed at different levels of aggregation and across different users, including individuals and households (consumers), or businesses (producers). Consumers or producers may be located in different cities, regions, or countries, and businesses operate in different sectors of economic activity. Here we will focus mainly on technology adoption by firms and diffusion in and across businesses.[10] This is not always an easy task given that a considerable part of the literature focuses on country-specific patterns in technology diffusion, where both consumers and producers play an important role.

Conceptualizing Technology Diffusion: Four Key Steps

The steps that characterize the technology diffusion process across businesses are (1) existence of a technology, (2) knowledge about its existence and potential, (3) adoption decision, and (4) capability to effectively use the technology adopted.[11]

Evidently, the first step to allow a technology to be adopted by businesses is the existence of the technology itself. Technology diffusion may be thought of as coming after invention (the development of a new would-be product or process) and innovation (its introduction and economic exploitation by businesses).[12] Although invention, innovation, and diffusion are conceptually different phenomena, they are interlinked. Indeed, diffusion may be seen as intrinsic to the broader process of technological change, with learning and feedback effects that may enhance or change the original new technology, which evolves over the course of its diffusion.

A second step prior to adoption is the awareness of the existence of a technology by the firm. This has importantly to do with understanding which technology is best suited to produce desired goods or services, or to improve efficiency in production processes. Awareness of the existence of a technology or understanding its potential benefits for the firm may depend on several factors. Some of these are technology specific and are related to intellectual property strategies (i.e., whether information about the technology is available or is kept secret),[13] the stage of the technology life cycle, and the nature of the technology itself. The benefits of adoption may increase over time, while awareness of technologies that have a general purpose may be different from that of technologies that have a narrower scope or less significant network externalities.

Knowledge flows are important drivers influencing the awareness of the existence of a technology and its potential gains. Geographic and social proximity play a role in knowledge diffusion, as do trade flows, relationships with suppliers or customers, interactions with institutional knowledge sources such as universities and research institutions, and government policies and incentives.[14] Knowledge diffusion may also be facilitated by worker mobility and migration.[15]

Firms' considerations about adoption benefits or returns, which can be expressed in terms of expected revenue streams or other economic outcomes, are not solely driven by rational behaviors, but also by heuristics or imitation of competitors. Observation of realized gains from technology adoption by competitors may inform firms about the potential benefits of adoption, and these may be more evident as the stock of adopters increases.

A third step in the diffusion of technology across firms is their adoption decision, which, like many other choices made by businesses, is made under uncertainty, with limited available information, and is path dependent. Adoption decisions may also be constrained by financial and nonfinancial barriers, which hit different groups of firms in different ways. Financial costs associated with the investments needed to adopt new technology include not only direct costs, such as purchasing a new machine, but also indirect costs, such as adapting the production process and organization or training workers.[16] Some firms (typically the smallest and the youngest) may be willing to adopt a technology but are financially constrained and unable to do so. Adoption decisions may also be constrained by nonfinancial barriers. One such barrier relates to intellectual property. Akcigit and Ates (2019b) find that strategic use of intellectual property by incumbent firms may hinder technology diffusion.

The nature of the social system, the environment in which firms operate, institutions, and public policy may facilitate or constrain adoption decisions by providing incentives to adopt new technologies or by imposing extra costs and creating institutional obstacles that, for instance, hinder access to finance or raise the risks of experimentation.[17]

Finally, once the adoption decision is taken, businesses need to be able to use the technology effectively in relation to their products or production processes and leverage the investment. Effectively using a technology requires absorptive capacity, that is, the ability of firms to assimilate new knowledge and exploit it commercially,[18] which depends importantly on the degree of tacitness of the knowledge and expertise required, the stock of knowledge already available relating to previous technology vintages, and the applicability of such stock to the use of new technology.

Different forms of learning may boost firms' ability to effectively use the technology adopted and translate adoption into efficiency gains. These include learning by doing, learning by using, and learning from interaction or from interindustry spillovers, which can also lead to improvements of the technology adopted.[19] Absorptive capacity is also linked to the extent to which firms carry out R&D activities, as these not only are related to new discoveries but also increase firms' ability to assimilate and process existing information.[20]

Market size is an important factor that affects the extent to which firms can leverage investments in new technologies,[21] ultimately influencing their effective use. It allows spreading fixed costs and increases the expected returns of technology adoption. This is closely linked with the role of digital technologies in boosting business process replication.[22]

Management, skills, and organizational capital are key to successful technology adoption. On the one hand, significant complementarities exist between the effective use of technology—in particular, information and communication technologies (ICTs)—and these factors. Bloom, Sadun, and Van Reenen (2012) show how high-quality managers are crucial to fully benefiting from digital technologies, based on their study of subsidiaries of US multinationals in Europe. Also, organizational redesign may be needed to fully reap the benefits of digital technologies, with different technologies being more effective with different organizational structures.[23] On the other hand, the human capital of the workforce affects the way in which technology is used. Higher ICT and technical skills enhance the capabilities to fully profit from newly introduced digital technologies.[24]

Spillovers across firms also play a significant role in technology diffusion, notably with respect to knowledge about the existence and potential benefits of a technology and the acquisition of capabilities to effectively use it, given that technology is not fully codifiable.[25] This includes spillovers via the mobility of workers across firms.[26]

As is probably already clear, institutions and public policy play an important role for all the four steps in technology diffusion outlined above, and especially for boosting firms' absorptive capacities. We will draw the implications for policy more fully in section 4.

Measuring Technology Diffusion: Direct and Indirect Indicators

Measuring technology diffusion, especially across businesses, is not easy. There are different direct and indirect measures of technology diffusion, which are available for different sets of firms and over different time periods and countries.

Among direct measures, it is important to distinguish between measures of the extensive and the intensive margin of technology adoption, that is, between whether the technology is used or not, and how intensively it is used.[27] At the firm level, this corresponds to distinguishing between inter-firm and intrafirm technology diffusion.[28] Interfirm measures are relatively more common and focus on whether a certain technology has been adopted or not by a firm (for the first time), and on how many potential adopters use such technology. Intrafirm measures focus on the intensity and perva-siveness with which the technology is used within a firm.[29]

Direct measures of technology diffusion at the firm level are generally based on surveys, which encompass information on certain specific tech-nologies adopted by firms.[30] These are not widely available and tend to focus on samples of firms, with challenges in many cases in analyzing diffusion dynamics over time due to rotation in sampling. An example of such sur-veys in Europe, focusing on digital technologies, is the Eurostat ICT usage and e-commerce survey, which contains information on a range of digital technologies, from broadband to computers, e-commerce, and cloud computing.[31]

Regarding indirect measures, an emerging literature has interpreted changes in productivity differentials between the most productive and other firms, and changes in the pace of productivity convergence, as indicators of changes in technology diffusion.[32] These types of measures are more widely available via commercial and administrative data, which can reach whole populations of firms and can be more easily compared over time. However, these measures do not focus directly on technology adoption, but rather consider its effects on productivity for different groups of firms, assuming a close link between technology adoption and productivity performance.

An important difference to keep in mind between direct and indirect measures, in light of the conceptual framework for technology diffusion presented above, is that while direct measures capture the first three steps (until the adoption decision), indirect measures such as those based on pro-ductivity differentials capture also the extent to which the technology is effectively used (the fourth step).

Direct and indirect measures of technology diffusion can be aggregated at different levels, to analyze differences in the patterns of diffusion across industries and geographical areas. Different sectors are indeed character-ized by different adoption rates and intensities in using a given technology due to the specific nature of activities carried out. But even within the same sector of activity, there can be significant heterogeneity in the adoption of technologies by firms in different regions or countries, linked to differences in skill endowments, openness, institutions, and policies.[33]

Stylized Facts about Technology Diffusion in the Digital Era

This section presents some key findings and stylized facts on technology diffusion from recent academic and policy literature, especially focusing on diffusion in the digital era. In particular, it highlights that (1) technology diffusion is a slow and gradual process, which tends to be characterized by S-shaped diffusion curves of successful technologies and by important technology-specific and country-specific differences in its pace; (2) the diffusion of technologies, particularly digital technologies, is uneven across countries, regions, sectors, and firms, and even within narrowly defined sectors in the same country; and (3) an increasing productivity gap between the most productive firms and the rest could be the reflection of a slowdown in technology diffusion, and this is particularly evident in the most digital-intensive sectors.

Fact 1: Technology Diffusion Takes Time, with Significant Differences across Countries and Technologies

One important stylized fact about technology diffusion—highlighted by classic contributions, including Mansfield (1961 and 1963), Mansfield and others (1971), Griliches (1957), Romeo (1975), and Davies (1979), and discussed in more extensive recent surveys, such as Stoneman and Battisti (2010) and Comin and Mestieri (2014)—is that diffusion is a time-consuming process, and its pace is technology specific and depends importantly on the country or geographical area in which it occurs.

Several contributions using measures of technology diffusion based on the extensive margin highlight that diffusion curves of successful new technologies tend to be S-shaped, and this is observed at different levels of aggregation.[34] This means that technology diffusion is slow in its initial stages, speeding up subsequently. This has been tested in the literature for different technologies, including major manufacturing innovations such as in the tool-and-die, bituminous coal, iron and steel, brewing, and railroad industries, and general-purpose technologies, with differences in the exact shape of the diffusion curve between major and minor innovations.[35]

Countries differ substantially in the speed with which new technologies are adopted for the first time and in the extent to which they diffuse after adoption, with cross-country differences that appear to be persistent.[36] Furthermore, different technologies have diffused at different speeds. Newer technologies—including some digital technologies—have been adopted faster across countries on average.[37] However, their penetration within countries after adoption has become more divergent across countries.[38]

Research on the intensive margin of technology adoption provides additional insights. Battisti and Stoneman (2005) show that at the beginning of the diffusion process, interfirm diffusion contributes importantly to the intensity of technology use, while at later stages intrafirm diffusion plays a more important role. Taking a broader country-level perspective, Comin, Hobijn, and Rovito (2006) show that once the intensive margin is taken into account, the shape of the diffusion curve does not typically resemble an S-shaped function but is rather concave.

Research reviewed above does not focus on technology adoption at the firm level exclusively, since it is challenging to collect such data consistently over time, and does not focus only on (process) technologies but also on products. The next subsection focuses more closely on the diffusion of digital technologies.

Fact 2: Diffusion of Digital Technologies Is Uneven across Countries, Sectors, and Firms

Digital transformation, driven by the spread of ICTs, has characterized the last few decades, reshaping markets and the production of goods and services, and societies more broadly. Different from other new technologies, ICTs are general-purpose technologies.[39] They are characterized by pervasiveness of applications in different domains of the economy and aspects of business, and also by continuing improvement over time as applications induce more innovation among users.[40] Digital technologies have, therefore, deeper and broader consequences for firms than the adoption of a single specific innovation.

An important characteristic of technologies, and in particular ICTs, is the significant heterogeneity in their uptake and use across countries, sectors, and businesses.[41] Focusing on the extensive margin, OECD (2019b) finds that there was substantial uptake of ICTs between 2010 and 2018, but the share of adopters varied greatly between different types of these technologies and between countries.[42] For instance, while on average about 90 percent of businesses employing ten or more persons in the OECD countries covered by the study had access to broadband in 2018, only about 30 percent used enterprise resource planning (ERP) software or cloud computing systems (in 2017). Across countries, the share of businesses using cloud computing ranged from a high of about 60 percent to a low of 10 percent (figure 2-2, panel A).

The diffusion of digital technologies affects all sectors of the economy, but it does so with varying speeds and to different extents, which depend on the particular facets of the digital transformation considered. A recent OECD study has proposed a taxonomy of digital-intensive sectors, focusing on different dimensions of digital transformation, including investments, intermediate inputs, labor, automation, and markets.[43] This work shows significant heterogeneity in the extent to which different sectors have gone digital. Some sectors, such as information technology (IT) services and telecommunications, are positioned consistently at the top of the digital intensity distribution across all indicators. Some others, such as agriculture, mining, and real estate, score low on most indicators. Sectors in the middle of the distribution are engaged in digital transformation at different rates depending on the dimension considered. The analysis finds that sectors at the top are those that experienced the fastest increases in digital intensity over time. It also reconfirms the presence of considerable cross-country heterogeneity in the sectoral uptake of digital technologies.

Focusing more directly on differences across firms, OECD (2019b) shows that the diffusion of digital technologies is uneven for different groups of businesses. Focusing on their size, a key firm characteristic, figure 2-2, panel B, shows that large firms tend to exhibit higher adoption rates, with, for instance, 56 percent of large firms but only 27 percent of small firms adopting cloud computing services. This heterogeneity is also evident (although with different magnitudes) across other types of digital technologies.[44]

Fact 3: Increasing Productivity Gaps between the Best and the Rest Mirror a Slowdown in Diffusion

While the previous subsection reviewed evidence based on direct measures of technology diffusion, some recent studies have focused on broader indirect measures, notably productivity patterns across firms. Analyzing productivity trends over time for different groups of firms, and the extent to

FIGURE 2-2. **Significant Heterogeneity in the Diffusion of Digital Technologies across Countries and Firms**

Panel A - Cross-Country Heterogeneity in the Diffusion of Selected ICT Tools in Enterprises

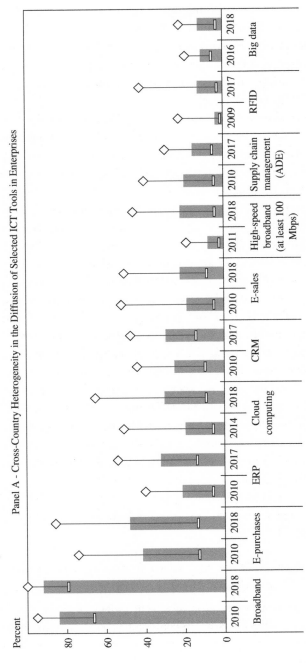

■ Average   ◇ Highest country   = Lowest country

Panel B - Heterogeneity in the Diffusion of Selected ICT Tools in Large vs. Small Enterprises

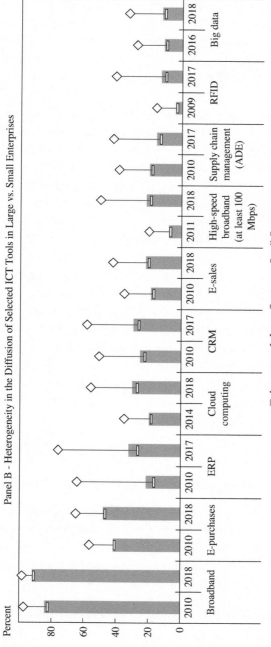

Source: OECD (2019b).

Note: The figures show the diffusion of selected ICT tools in enterprises in OECD countries, in terms of percentages of enterprises (with ten or more persons employed) using these tools, based on data available in the OECD ICT Access and Use by Business Database. ERP stands for enterprise resource planning; CRM for customer relationship management; ADE for automated data exchange; and RFID for radio-frequency identification.

which productivity convergence or divergence occurs between the most efficient businesses and the laggards, provides valuable additional information on patterns in technology diffusion. As an all-encompassing measure of technology, productivity reflects not only technology adoption, but also management quality and firms' capabilities to effectively use technology, as well as market or institutional conditions in which they operate.

Andrews, Criscuolo, and Gal (2015 and 2016) have analyzed the performance of frontier and laggard firms across more than twenty OECD countries since the early 2000s. Their analysis suggests the presence of steady productivity divergence, contrary to the predictions of neo-Schumpeterian growth theory, with rising productivity growth at the global frontier combined with rising gaps between the best performers and the rest. These patterns are also confirmed, using highly representative data collected in the framework of the OECD MultiProd project, to occur within detailed country-sector pairs.[45]

Interestingly, Andrews, Criscuolo, and Gal (2016) find that gaps between the most productive firms and the laggards have increased more in the more digital-intensive sectors, pointing to the role of digital transformation in generating winner-takes-most dynamics (figure 2-3). Furthermore, the rising gaps between the best and the rest mainly reflect divergence in (revenue-based) multifactor productivity rather than capital deepening, and they do not simply reflect the ability of most efficient firms to charge higher markups. The analysis points to rising obstacles to technology diffusion for laggard firms that have slowed catch-up rates.

Drivers and Implications of the Slowdown in Diffusion

Digital technologies have accelerated the innovation machine, but as suggested by the evidence reviewed above, the diffusion machine has slowed. What does research say about the factors behind the slowdown in technology diffusion? What are the implications of the slowdown for key economic outcomes? We now turn to these questions.

Drivers of the Slowdown in Technology Diffusion

Shifts to a digital and knowledge economy play a key role in shaping the recent productivity dynamics and are important in understanding the

FIGURE 2-3. Increasing Productivity Gaps between the Best and the Rest, Especially in ICT-Intensive Sectors

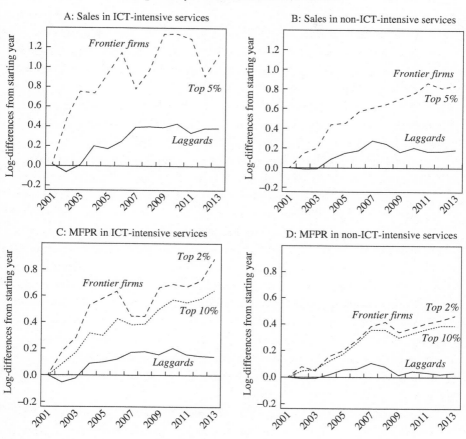

Source: Andrews, Criscuolo, and Gal (2016).

Note: In panels A and B, the global frontier is defined by the top 5 percent of firms with the highest revenue-based multifactor productivity (MFPR) levels within each two-digit industry, while in panels C and D it is defined by the top 2 percent and 10 percent of the MFPR distribution. Laggards are all other firms. Data shown are unweighted averages across two-digit industries over the period 2001–2013 across twenty-four OECD countries. *Services* refers to nonfinancial business services. *ICT-intensive services* refers to information and communication and postal and courier activities.

observed slowdown in technology diffusion. These shifts are related to the rising importance of intangible assets, such as R&D or software development, an increasing role of tacit knowledge, and rising technological complexity that has increased the sophistication of complementary investments.[46]

The need for complementary investments in intangible assets, which are costly and complex, the nonrivalry and low-cost scalability of digital technologies, and the associated economies of scale as well as network externalities create and reinforce winner-takes-most dynamics, especially in digital-intensive sectors. These factors can allow a few superstar firms to succeed and gain considerable market shares while acting as barriers for other firms to benefit from the new technologies.[47]

Berlingieri and others (2020) analyze patterns in catch-up using harmonized productivity data across thirteen OECD countries over the 1994–2014 period and find that the transition to a digital and knowledge economy has contributed significantly to increased barriers to technology diffusion. They show, using different sectoral proxies of digital technologies, that laggard firms face higher obstacles and catch up at a lower speed in the more digital-intensive and knowledge-intensive industries (figure 2-4). Importantly, they find that digital and knowledge intensity is related to higher productivity dispersion, which suggests that the potential benefits of digital transformation are not spread equally across firms.

Gal and others (2019) confirm these findings using a different framework that combines industry-level data on digital technology adoption and firm-level productivity data. Focusing on four key digital technologies (high-speed broadband, enterprise resource planning, customer relationship management, and cloud computing), they show that higher digitalization is associated with faster productivity growth, but that gains are significantly larger for frontier firms.

Indeed, gains from digital transformation and the knowledge-based economy depend importantly on intangible assets, absorptive capacity, worker skills, complementary investments, organizational capital, and management abilities, which may be scarcer in laggard firms. The above evidence is consistent with the potential of digital transformation to increase dispersion in business outcomes as noted by Brynjolfsson and McAfee (2011) and with the analysis of Comin and Mestieri (2018), which shows slower penetration rates of newer technologies within countries notwithstanding their faster initial adoption.[48]

Shifts to a digital economy increasingly based on intangibles may have also affected financing constraints, which are an important barrier to adoption, given stronger information asymmetries associated with intangible assets and the challenges to pledge them as collateral.[49] This is particularly relevant given that financing constraints may be particularly binding for

FIGURE 2-4. Laggard Firms Catch Up at a Lower Rate in Digital- and Knowledge-Intensive Industries

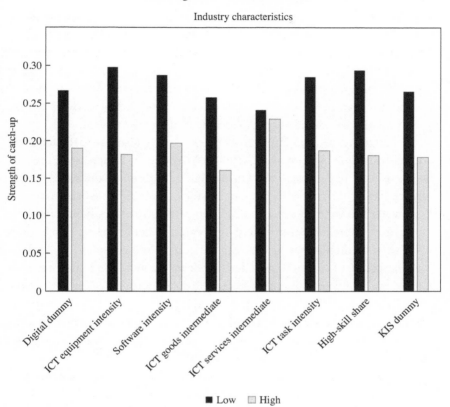

Industry characteristics

■ Low ☐ High

Source: Berlingieri and others (2020).

Note: The vertical axis shows the difference in labor productivity (LP) growth, due to the catch-up effect, between firms at the average level of LP gap in the percentile (0–10) group and firms at the average LP gap in the percentile (10–40) group, in industries with low versus high values of the indicators of digital- and knowledge-intensity shown on the horizontal axis. The LP gap is computed as the difference between log productivity at the frontier (top 10 percent most productive firms in the same country, industry, and year) and firms in the percentile (0–10) and percentile (10–40) groups. Black and gray bars show industries with low and high values, respectively, of the indicators shown. For dummy variables, the low and high values are simply 0 and 1. For other indicators, the low and high values correspond to the 10th and 90th percentiles. High-skill share is the share of hours worked by high-skilled workers, and KIS denotes knowledge-intensive services.

laggard firms. Ongoing OECD work is further exploring this channel using firm-level data.

Besides digital transformation and the shift to a knowledge economy, other concomitant factors may help explain the slowdown in technology diffusion. Liu, Mian, and Sufi (2019) argue that low interest rates may have favored market concentration, increasing leaders' incentives to gain strategic advantages, and suggest that the fall in interest rates may provide part of the explanation for why gaps between the most productive firms and the rest have increased and aggregate productivity growth has slowed.

Changes relating to intellectual property may also have affected technology diffusion. Akcigit and Ates (2019b) document an increase in the concentration of patenting in the United States, with more and more patents in the hands of firms with the largest stock. They find that the nature of patenting has been changing since 2000, with innovators increasing strategic use of intellectual property by creating patent thickets that protect their market dominance by erecting barriers to knowledge diffusion.[50]

Increasing uncertainty may deter or delay the adoption of new technologies, making firms—possibly lagging firms in particular—more cautious about investing.[51] Baker, Bloom, and Davis (2016), using a new measure of economic policy uncertainty based on newspaper coverage frequency, document increasing uncertainty trends in recent decades in the United States and several other major economies.

Migration, and in particular high-skilled immigration, can contribute importantly to innovation and the spread of new ideas.[52] Declines in or higher barriers to skilled international migration may, therefore, also have dampened knowledge diffusion, considering that immigrants benefit from networks with diasporas, and are known to be more likely to start new ventures, which are often also more innovative.[53] Economic history documents how big waves of immigration resulted in great spurts of innovation and how restrictive quotas damaged innovation and research productivity.[54]

Trade flows and openness are major drivers of knowledge spillovers[55] and ultimately technology diffusion. However, recent years have experienced a slowdown in the relative growth of world trade,[56] which likely contributed to the slowing of technology diffusion—and productivity.

Finally, although it is hard to disentangle causal effects given the close interrelation between trends in technology diffusion and business dynamics, including declines in business dynamism and competition, or in worker reallocation and mobility, research finds these factors as important in understanding the diffusion slowdown. In particular, lower competition and declining worker reallocation can weaken technology diffusion by increasing barriers to adoption and reducing interactions that promote the spread of knowledge.

Implications for Economic Outcomes

A slowdown in technology diffusion may be associated with changes in key economic and social outcomes. It affects aggregate productivity growth (and in turn economic growth), business dynamism, wages, and the inclusiveness of economic growth.

A recent strand of the literature pioneered by OECD contributions has suggested that slower technology diffusion may be one of the key drivers of the slowdown in productivity growth that many advanced countries have experienced over the last few decades.[57] Sluggish productivity growth at aggregate levels hides a significant divergence between the best performers and the rest. Aggregate productivity performance has been weaker in sectors with more pronounced productivity divergence, indicating that such divergence was driven not only by the best performers pushing the technology frontier and by more efficient reallocation of resources, but also by increasing obstacles to technology diffusion faced by laggard firms that have depressed their productivity and have slowed aggregate productivity growth.

This helps explain the paradox of fast technological improvements but slower productivity growth. Sluggish productivity growth may not have been caused by unavailability of advanced technologies at the frontier or their slower pace of improvement,[58] but rather by limited successful adoption of these technologies by a large number of firms. It is not technological progress at the frontier that appears to have slowed but the catch-up process for lagging firms, especially in the digital- and knowledge-intensive sectors.

Increased productivity divergence associated with weaker technology diffusion has implications for inclusiveness and other social outcomes.[59] In particular, Berlingieri, Blanchenay, and Criscuolo (2017), using data for sixteen OECD countries, find that divergences in productivity are closely linked with divergences in wages. They find that these trends are driven more by differences between firms within sectors than by differences across sectors. These findings are confirmed by the analysis of Criscuolo and others (2020) showing that a large proportion of changes in between-firm wage inequality is accounted for by productivity-related premia, and that this explains about half of overall wage inequality on average across countries.

Recent research finds that a slowdown in technology diffusion has contributed to changes in a number of business dynamism indicators, such as declining business entry and job reallocation rates, increases in market concentration and markups, and declines in the labor income share. Digital transformation and shifts toward a knowledge economy, linked with increasing barriers to diffusion and strong advantages enjoyed by leading firms at the technological frontier, are likely to have influenced these patterns.

Akcigit and Ates (2019a and 2019b) focus on alternative factors affecting ten trends related to declining business dynamism in the United States. Calibrating on US data a theoretical model featuring endogenous market power and strategic competition between new firms and incumbents, they argue that a slowdown in knowledge diffusion is the most powerful force driving the decline in business dynamism.

Relatedly, Calvino, Criscuolo, and Verlhac (2020) document a steady decline over the last two decades in job reallocation rates and business entry rates within country-sector pairs, using harmonized data for eighteen (mostly OECD) countries across twenty-two industries. They find weakening knowledge diffusion to have been an important structural driver of these trends. Country-sector pairs with larger productivity gaps between the most productive firms and the rest experienced stronger declines in business dynamism.

Declines in business dynamism have occurred not only across many countries, but also at the top of industries, with falling turnover among industry-leading firms.[60] Interestingly, a study also finds that start-up formation has declined for firms operated by US Ph.D. recipients in science and engineering—the kind of start-ups that may be considered a key source of new technological and business opportunities.[61] Declining dynamism, as measured by business entry rates, has been stronger in digital-intensive sectors (figure 2-5), suggesting links between the patterns of diffusion of digital technologies and firm demographics.[62]

The polarization between leading and lagging firms is likely to be amplified by the COVID-19 pandemic. For instance, while teleworking has been crucial to sustaining production during the crisis, not all firms are able to organize their activities remotely, and the pandemic may add to the ad-

FIGURE 2-5. Stronger Decline in Business Entry Rates in Digital-Intensive Sectors

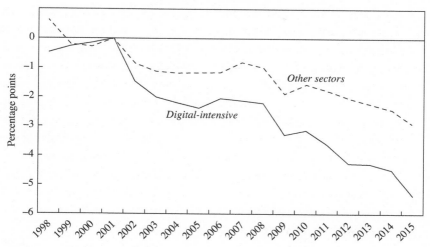

Source: Calvino and Criscuolo (2019).

Note: The figure shows average within-country-industry trends, based on the year coefficients of regressions within country-sector, with and without interaction with a digital-intensity dummy. Each point represents average cumulative change in percentage points since 2001. The figure covers fifteen mostly OECD countries.

vantages of digitally advanced firms.[63] Similarly, not all firms face the same financial vulnerabilities or have the same access to finance, and many viable but financially vulnerable nonleading firms may be forced to exit the market.[64] These effects, together with shocks to business registrations, may amplify declines in business dynamism, increase industry concentration, and weaken competition.[65] The effects of the pandemic reinforce the need for policies to boost digital technology diffusion and foster conditions for broad-based growth of firms in a changing economy, as discussed next.

The Role of Public Policy in Boosting Technology Diffusion in the Digital Era

Public policy can play an important role in fostering technology diffusion in the digital era, with actions that remove barriers to diffusion and help boost firms' absorptive capacity. Recent research, including several OECD studies, provides useful guidance for policymakers.[66] Key policies to boost technology diffusion relate to competition, worker skills and mobility, trade openness, access to finance, human and organizational capital, and R&D.

Competitive pressures are a major driver of technology adoption and of organizational and managerial improvements by firms that boost returns to adoption. Andrews, Criscuolo, and Gal (2016) focus on the role of product market regulation for the catch-up of laggard firms. Using a rich database of product market regulations combined with firm-level data across more than twenty OECD countries, and focusing in particular on service sectors where productivity divergence has been stronger, they find that several sectors could benefit from procompetition product market regulatory reforms, especially retail and professional services—sectors where the pace of such reform has been slower than in network industries over the 2000s.[67] Their analysis shows that productivity divergence is greater in sectors where product market reforms have been less extensive.

In a more and more digital world, data portability and interoperability and, more broadly, regulations related to data flows are increasingly important for competition and technology diffusion. As new technologies unleash the "next production revolution," improving access to and sharing of data, while protecting privacy and security, will be a key focus of regulatory policies governing competition in markets.[68] Antitrust policies also will need to be more responsive to the competition challenges posed by the dominance of digital markets by a few big firms.

Another channel that links competition and diffusion is related to the mobility of workers, which can bolster knowledge spillovers and help build firm organizational capabilities more broadly.[69] Excessive occupational licensing and noncompete clauses limit mobility and in turn innovation and diffusion.[70] Policy should seek to reduce barriers to job mobility and support transitions into new jobs.[71]

Trade openness intensifies competitive pressures on incumbents. It also promotes knowledge spillovers that arise among trading partners, and increases market size and the expected profits from technology adoption.[72] Reducing barriers to trade, therefore, fosters technology diffusion.

Focusing more directly on laggard firms, Perla and Tonetti (2014) highlight their potential for fueling productivity growth and spurring technology diffusion by imitation and risk taking. Supportive policies can facilitate this process. In this context, Berlingieri, Blanchenay, and Criscuolo (2020) carry out a comprehensive analysis of the role of public policy in promoting catch-up by less productive firms, with a particular focus on digital- and skill-intensive industries where barriers to diffusion are stronger. Policies relating to the skills of workers, financial conditions, and R&D are found to be key to lowering barriers to diffusion and boosting absorptive capacity. Lower skills mismatches and lower shares of underqualified workers are associated with higher speeds of catch-up, indicating the importance of worker upskilling, reskilling, and lifelong learning. More favorable financing conditions for small and medium enterprises can help laggard firms to catch up faster, reducing their financing constraints for technology adoption. Greater government support for business R&D can expand opportunities for laggard firms to innovate and adapt new technologies for their purposes.

In a similar vein, Andrews, Nicoletti, and Timiliotis (2018) highlight the role of factors boosting capabilities and incentives for the adoption of two core sets of digital technologies: cloud computing and back- and front-office integration. Using cross-country data, their results show that building organizational capital, enhancing ICT competencies and training, and better matching worker skills with jobs (capabilities), together with strong competitive pressures and availability of risk capital (incentives), promote digital technology adoption—with significant complementarities between enhancement of capabilities and incentives.

What is clear from this discussion is that no single policy would be able to foster technology diffusion alone. Policymakers should keep in mind all the four steps in the technology diffusion process described at the beginning of this chapter. This means: boosting innovation, increasing information on the availability and potential of new technologies, removing barriers to adoption, and increasing the ability of firms to effectively use new technologies.

A broad policy mix affecting incentives and capabilities is required, one that would also capture synergies across different policy areas. Although one size does not fit all, and country-specific characteristics and institutional features may call for stronger focus on specific dimensions, an optimal policy mix would include both demand-side and supply-side measures. Demand-side measures would raise awareness about new technologies, develop absorptive capacity, and reduce uncertainty and risks. Supply-side measures would foster competition, provide credit tools that are able to overcome the challenges of financing intangibles, address the new regulatory issues of the digital economy, improve knowledge production and sharing (including through sensible intellectual property policies), and strengthen the foundation of digital infrastructure and skills. Careful policy design needs to be complemented by evaluation, especially in areas where the new challenges of the digital economy demand innovation and adaptation in policies.

Such policy reforms can bring a double dividend in our digital era: they can not only boost technology diffusion and productivity and strengthen economic growth, but they can also promote more inclusive economic and social outcomes. The COVID-19 pandemic reinforces the case for some of these reforms as it amplifies unevenness in access to opportunities offered by the digital economy.

Conclusion

This chapter has focused on technology diffusion in the digital era. The diffusion of digital technologies has been quite uneven across firms. This is reflected in increasing productivity gaps between firms at the technological frontier and other firms. Aggregate productivity growth has slowed, but this appears to be the result not of a slowdown in innovation at the technological frontier but rather of a slowdown in the spread of innovation across most firms.

While several factors affect technology diffusion, the analysis suggests a key role played by factors associated with the shift to a digital and knowledge-based economy. These include the increasing importance of intangible assets, the challenges posed by required complementary investments in human and organizational capital, and winner-takes-most dynamics linked to rising market concentration and declining business dynamism.

Governments can promote technology diffusion through a mix of policies that enhance firm incentives and capabilities and improve the market setting for a wider adoption of new technologies. Key areas for policy attention include fostering competition and addressing the new regulatory issues of the digital economy (importantly those relating to data), improving knowledge production and sharing (including through sensible patent policies), upskilling and reskilling workers as digital transformation shifts the demand for skills, and strengthening the foundation of digital infrastructure.

Looking ahead, attention is now focusing more and more on the next phase of the digital revolution, led by AI, and how it may impact productivity. There is much discussion about the potential of AI to be the next major general-purpose technology, spawning complementary innovations in a range of applications across sectors.[73] These could be related to specific software or hardware, big data analytics, machine learning, cyber-physical systems, or applications embodied in robots or other artifacts, with different technologies having different characteristics and skill requirements.

There has been a dramatic acceleration in the number of AI-related publications—the knowledge base of AI—in recent years, combined with a marked increase in the share of AI-related inventions as a part of total inventions since 2015.[74] This suggests an increasing spread of AI across economies, although data and analyses about diffusion across firms and sectors are still very scant.[75] The diffusion and impact of AI is an important area for future research—and is the focus of a significant ongoing research effort at the OECD.[76]

Although there are signs of an increasing spread of AI, it will take time to see its potential more fully reflected in indirect measures of technology diffusion, such as those related to productivity dispersion. Indeed, Brynjolfsson, Rock, and Syverson (2017) note that, as in the case of other general-purpose technologies, the productivity effects of AI will not fully materialize until waves of complementary innovations are developed and deployed. These technologies may strengthen the importance of intangible capital and complementary investments in higher-level skills and related organizational changes, which may produce a J-curve effect on productivity and wider productivity dispersion between leading and lagging firms.

The continuing advances in digital transformation reinforce the case for policies to ensure that gains from frontier technologies are spread broadly across the economy. Supporting wider technology diffusion, particularly among small and young firms, can deliver both stronger and more inclusive growth.

NOTES

The views expressed here are those of the authors and cannot be attributed to the OECD or its member countries. The authors would like to thank Martin Baily and Zia Qureshi for useful comments and suggestions, and Natia Mosiashvili for updating figure 2-1.
    1. OECD (2015).
    2. Andrews, Criscuolo, and Gal (2016), Berlingieri, Blanchenay, and Criscuolo (2017), and OECD (2018c).

3. See, among others, the work of Aghion and Howitt (1992), Comin and Mestieri (2014), and Akcigit and Ates (2019b).

4. Haskel and Westlake (2018), Crouzet and Eberly (2019), Autor and others (2020), Bajgar, Criscuolo, and Timmis (2021), and Bessen (2017).

5. Calvino, Criscuolo, and Menon (2016), Van Reenen (2018), and Akcigit and Ates (2019b).

6. See, for example, Gutiérrez and Philippon (2017), Calligaris, Criscuolo, and Marcolin (2018), Decker and others (2018), Akcigit and Ates (2019b), Covarrubias, Gutiérrez, and Philippon (2019), Autor and others (2020), Bajgar, Criscuolo, and Timmis (2021), and Calvino, Criscuolo, and Verlhac (2020). Note also that, due to measurement challenges, most studies follow trends in industry concentration rather than "market" concentration. Throughout the chapter, we will use the term *concentration* in this sense. A notable exception is the work by Affeldt and others (2021) that focuses on antitrust markets in Europe.

7. Philippon (2019), Berlingieri and others (2020), and Jones and Tonetti (2020).

8. Additional policy discussions can be found in OECD (2015), Andrews, Criscuolo, and Gal (2015 and 2016), Andrews, Nicoletti, and Timiliotis (2018), Calvino and Criscuolo (2019), and Berlingieri and others (2020).

9. OECD (2018b), and Sorbe and others (2019).

10. This is different from focusing on the diffusion patterns of new products in the sense of Gort and Klepper (1982), i.e., the number of businesses that engage in their production, which is the subject of a related but different strand of the literature. For additional discussion of individual- , household- , or overall country-level patterns in technology diffusion, see Keller (2004) or Comin and Mestieri (2014). See also Bass (1969) and related literature on the diffusion of given products across consumers.

11. For further insights on some of these issues, including theoretical discussions on different approaches to model technology diffusion, see Rosenberg (1972), Baptista (1999), Geroski (2000), Hall (2006), Stoneman and Battisti (2010), Dosi and Nelson (2010), Comin and Mestieri (2014), and Perla and Tonetti (2014).

12. Dosi and Nelson (2010).

13. See Hall and others (2014).

14. On geographic and social proximity, see Jaffe, Trajtenberg, and Henderson (1993) and Breschi and Lissoni (2009). On trade flows, see Crespi, Criscuolo, and Haskel (2008), Criscuolo, Haskel, and Slaughter (2010), Perla, Tonetti, and Waugh (2015), and Bloom, Draca, and Van Reenen (2016). On interactions with institutional knowledge sources, see Belenzon and Schankerman (2013).

15. Kerr (2018) and Lissoni (2018).

16. Brynjolfsson and Hitt (2000).

17. Andrews, Nicoletti, and Timiliotis (2018).

18. Cohen and Levinthal (1990).

19. Malerba (1992) and Hall (2006).

20. Cohen and Levinthal (1989) and Griffith, Redding, and Van Reenen (2004).

21. Acemoglu and Linn (2004).

22. Brynjolfsson and others (2007).

23. Bloom and others (2014).

24. Gal and others (2019). Using German data, Bender and others (2018) find significant complementarities between the skills of managers and those of the workforce.

25. Keller (2004).

26. Stoyanov and Zubanov (2012), Braunerhjelm, Ding, and Thulin (2020), and Cassiman and Veugelers (2002).

27. Comin and Mestieri (2014).

28. Stoneman and Battisti (2010).

29. Battisti and Stoneman (2005).

30. Canepa and Stoneman (2004).

31. Examples in the United States include the Annual Survey of Manufacturers (see, for instance, Jin and McElheran, 2017), and the recent digital technology module of the Annual Business Survey (see Zolas and others, 2021). Additional sources of information include surveys of management practices; see, for instance, Bloom and Van Reenen (2007).

32. Andrews, Criscuolo, and Gal (2015 and 2016) and Berlingieri and others (2020).

33. Measuring patterns of technology diffusion for firms across different countries may be challenging for a number of reasons, including data availability constraints.

34. Jovanovic and Rousseau (2005) and Stoneman and Battisti (2010). It is worth highlighting the focus on *successful* innovations since, as pointed out by Dosi and Nelson (2010), many technologies introduced by some initial adopters never diffuse further and fail.

35. Mansfield (1961 and 1963), Romeo (1975), Jovanovic and Rousseau (2005), and Davies (1979).

36. Comin, Hobijn, and Rovito (2006) and Comin, Easterly, and Gong (2010).

37. Comin and Hobijn (2010).

38. Comin and Mestieri (2018).

39. Prior examples of general-purpose technologies include, for example, the internal combustion engine and electricity.

40. Jovanovic and Rousseau (2005) and Bresnahan (2010).

41. The OECD has led significant efforts to improve the measurement and understanding of digital transformation across countries, in the framework of its ongoing project Going Digital.

42. See also Andrews, Nicoletti, and Timiliotis (2018).

43. Calvino and others (2018).

44. See also Galindo-Rueda, Verger, and Ouellet (2020) for patterns of advanced technology use by firms in Canada.

45. Berlingieri, Blanchenay, and Criscuolo (2017). The MultiProd project studies productivity patterns and investigates the extent to which different policy frameworks can shape firm- and industry-level productivity, on the basis of comparable data collected across countries. See OECD (n.d.).

46. Haskel and Westlake (2018) and Andrews, Criscuolo, and Gal (2016).

47. Andrews, Criscuolo, and Gal (2016), Crouzet and Eberly (2019), Autor and others (2020), and Bajgar, Criscuolo, and Timmis (2021).

48. Another possible mechanism related to the shifts to a digital and knowledge economy is that, with more rapid technological change, new technologies become obsolete faster, which may induce wait-and-see strategies limiting technology adoption among noninnovators (Hoppe, 2002).

49. Demmou, Stefanescu, and Arquie (2019).

50. These findings can be related to other recent research that suggests that ideas may have become harder to find (Bloom and others, 2020).

51. Bloom, Bond, and Van Reenen (2007).

52. Khanna and Lee (2018), Hunt and Gauthier-Loiselle (2010), Kerr (2013), Bahar and Rapoport (2018).

53. Frey (2009), Kerr (2018), Kerr and Kerr (2019), Bratti, De Benedictis, and Santoni (2020), and Brown and others (2019).

54. Moser, Voena, and Waldinger (2014) and Moser and San (2020).

55. Keller (2010).

56. Ollivaud and Schwellnus (2015) and Constantinescu, Mattoo, and Ruta (2020).

57. OECD (2015) and Andrews, Criscuolo, and Gal (2015 and 2016).

58. Gordon (2012).

59. OECD (2018c).

60. Bessen and others (2020).

61. Astebro, Braguinsky, and Ding (2020).

62. Calvino and Criscuolo (2019). This may be consistent with the work on industry life cycles pioneered by Klepper (1996). When new technologies are introduced and their diffusion starts, they may find various and competing applications, and may be embodied in different new products produced by a number of new firms. Over time, industries employing the new technology are likely to consolidate, with a few remaining dominant applications and increasing attention devoted to process innovation, until the introduc-

tion and diffusion of another new technology that initiates new life-cycle dynamics.

63. OECD (2020b).

64. OECD (2020a).

65. OECD (2020c).

66. For earlier work on public policy and technology diffusion, see, for example, Stoneman and David (1986), Stoneman and Diederen (1994), and Stoneman and Battisti (2010).

67. See also Gal and Hijzen (2016).

68. OECD (2019a) and OECD (2018a).

69. Stoyanov and Zubanov (2012), Braunerhjelm, Ding, and Thulin (2020), and Cassiman and Veugelers (2002).

70. Marx, Strumsky, and Fleming (2009), Marx and Fleming (2012), and Hermansen (2019).

71. Policies should factor in the fact that the COVID-19 crisis, by reducing worker mobility, and by more generally limiting interactions among workers and firms (including through disruption of global value chains), may have additional negative implications for knowledge spillovers and technology diffusion (OECD, 2020b).

72. See Acemoglu and Linn (2004) for a theoretical model and an empirical application to the pharmaceutical industry.

73. Agrawal, Gans, and Goldfarb (2018), Trajtenberg (2018), and West and Allen (2018).

74. Baruffaldi and others (2020).

75. Seamans and Raj (2018).

76. Ongoing OECD work is investigating the characteristics of AI adopters across countries, with a particular focus on their productivity and on understanding whether the advent of AI could amplify existing gaps between leading and lagging firms. Related work is focusing on the role of AI in the productivity of science.

REFERENCES

Acemoglu, D., and J. Linn. 2004. "Market Size in Innovation: Theory and Evidence from the Pharmaceutical Industry." *Quarterly Journal of Economics* 119, no. 3, pp. 1049–90.

Affeldt, P., T. Duso, K. Gugler, and J. Piechucka. 2021. "Market Concentration in Europe: Evidence from Antitrust Markets." CESifo Working Paper 8866 (Munich: Munich Society for the Promotion of Economic Research).

Aghion, P., and P. Howitt. 1992. "A Model of Growth through Creative Destruction." *Econometrica* 60, no. 2, pp. 325–51.

Agrawal, A., J. Gans, and A. Goldfarb. 2018. *The Economics of Artificial Intelligence* (University of Chicago Press).

Akcigit, U., and S. T. Ates. 2019a. "Ten Facts on Declining Business Dynamism and Lessons from Endogenous Growth Theory." NBER Working Paper 25755 (Cambridge, MA: National Bureau of Economic Research).

Akcigit, U., and S. T. Ates. 2019b. "What Happened to US Business Dynamism?" NBER Working Paper 25756 (Cambridge, MA: National Bureau of Economic Research).

Andrews, D., C. Criscuolo, and P. Gal. 2015. "Frontier Firms, Technology Diffusion and Public Policy: Micro Evidence from OECD Countries." OECD Productivity Working Paper 2 (Paris: OECD Publishing).

Andrews, D, C. Criscuolo, and P. N. Gal. 2016. "The Best versus the Rest: The Global Productivity Slowdown, Divergence across Firms and the Role of Public Policy." OECD Productivity Working Paper 2016-05 (Paris: OECD Publishing).

Andrews, D., G. Nicoletti, and C. Timiliotis. 2018. "Digital Technology Diffusion: A Matter of Capabilities, Incentives or Both?" OECD Economics Department Working Paper 1476 (Paris: OECD Publishing).

Astebro, T. B., S. Braguinsky, and Y. Ding. 2020. "Declining Business Dynamism among Our Best Opportunities: The Role of the Burden of Knowledge." NBER Working Paper 27787 (Cambridge, MA: National Bureau of Economic Research).

Autor, D., D. Dorn, L. F. Katz, C. Patterson, and J. Van Reenen. 2020. "The Fall of the Labor Share and the Rise of Superstar Firms." *Quarterly Journal of Economics* 135, no. 2, pp. 645–709.

Bahar, D., and H. Rapoport. 2018. "Migration, Knowledge Diffusion and the Comparative Advantage of Nations." *Economic Journal* 128, no. 612, pp. 273–305.

Bajgar, M., C. Criscuolo, and J. Timmis. Forthcoming 2021. "Supersize Me: Intangibles and Industry Concentration." OECD Productivity Working Paper.

Baker, S. R., N. Bloom, and S. J. Davis. 2016. "Measuring Economic Policy Uncertainty." *Quarterly Journal of Economics* 131, no. 4, pp. 1593–1636.

Baptista, R. 1999. "The Diffusion of Process Innovations: A Selective Review." *International Journal of the Economics of Business* 6, no. 1, pp. 107–29.

Baruffaldi, S., B. van Beuzekom, H. Dernis, D. Harhoff, N. Rao, D. Rosenfeld, and M. Squicciarini. 2020. "Identifying and Measuring Developments in Artificial Intelligence: Making the Impossible Possible." OECD Science, Technology and Industry Working Paper 2020/05 (Paris: OECD Publishing).

Bass, F. M. 1969. "A New Product Growth for Model Consumer Durables." *Management Science* 15, no. 5, pp. 215–27.

Battisti, G., and P. Stoneman. 2005. "The Intra-Firm Diffusion of New Process Technologies." *International Journal of Industrial Organization* 23, pp. 1–22.

Belenzon, S., and M. Schankerman. 2013. "Spreading the Word: Geography, Policy, and Knowledge Spillovers." *Review of Economics and Statistics* 95, no. 3, pp. 884–903.

Bender, S., N. Bloom, D. Card, J. Van Reenen, and S. Wolter. 2018. "Management Practices, Workforce Selection, and Productivity." *Journal of Labor Economics* 36, S1, pp. S371–S409.

Berlingieri, G., P. Blanchenay, and C. Criscuolo. 2017. "The Great Divergence(s)." OECD Science, Technology and Industry Policy Paper 39 (Paris: OECD Publishing).

Berlingieri, G., S. Calligaris, C. Criscuolo, and R. Verlhac. 2020. "Last but Not Least: Laggard Firms, Technology Diffusion and Its Structural and Policy Determinants." OECD Science, Technology and Industry Policy Paper 86 (Paris: OECD Publishing).

Bessen, J. 2017. "Information Technology and Industry Concentration." Boston University School of Law, Law and Economics Paper Series 17–41 (Boston University).

Bessen, J. E., E. Denk, J. Kim, and C. Righi. 2020. "Declining Industrial Disruption." Boston University School of Law, Law and Economics Research Paper 20–28 (Boston University).

Bloom, N., S. Bond, and J. Van Reenen. 2007. "Uncertainty and Investment Dynamics." *Review of Economic Studies* 74, no. 2, pp. 391–415.

Bloom, N., M. Draca, and J. Van Reenen. 2016. "Trade Induced Technical Change? The Impact of Chinese Imports on Innovation, IT and Productivity." *Review of Economic Studies* 83, no. 1, pp. 87–117.

Bloom, N., L. Garicano, R. Sadun, and J. Van Reenen. 2014. "The Distinct Effects of Information Technology and Communication Technology on Firm Organization." *Management Science* 60, no. 12, pp. 2859–85.

Bloom, N., C. I. Jones, J. Van Reenen, and M. Webb. 2020. "Are Ideas Getting Harder to Find?" *American Economic Review* 110, no. 4, pp. 1104–44.

Bloom, N., R. Sadun, and J. Van Reenen. 2012. "Americans Do IT Better: US Multinationals and the Productivity Miracle." *American Economic Review* 102, no. 1, pp. 167–201.

Bloom, N., and J. Van Reenen. 2007. "Measuring and Explaining Management Practices across Firms and Countries." *Quarterly Journal of Economics* 122, no. 4, pp. 1351–1408.

Bratti, M., L. De Benedictis, and G. Santoni. 2020. "Immigrant Entrepreneurs, Diasporas, and Exports." *Journal of Regional Science* 60, no. 2, pp. 249–72.

Braunerhjelm, P., D. Ding, and P. Thulin. 2020. "Labour Market Mobility, Knowledge Diffusion and Innovation." *European Economic Review* 123, 103386.

Breschi, S., and F. Lissoni. 2009. "Mobility of Skilled Workers and Co-Invention Networks: An Anatomy of Localized Knowledge Flows." *Journal of Economic Geography* 9, no. 4, pp. 439–68.

Bresnahan, T. 2010. "General Purpose Technologies," in *Handbook of the Economics of Innovation*, vol. 2, edited by B. H. Hall and N. Rosenberg (Amsterdam: North-Holland).

Brown, J. D., J. S. Earle, M. J. Kim, and K. M. Lee. 2019. "Immigrant Entrepreneurs and Innovation in the US High-Tech Sector." NBER Working Paper 25565 (Cambridge, MA: National Bureau of Economic Research).

Brynjolfsson, E., and L. M. Hitt. 2000. "Beyond Computation: Information Technology, Organizational Transformation and Business Performance." *Journal of Economic Perspectives* 14, no. 4, pp. 23–48.

Brynjolfsson, E., and A. McAfee. 2011. *Race against the Machine: How the Digital Revolution Is Accelerating Innovation, Driving Productivity, and Irreversibly Transforming Employment and the Economy* (Lexington, MA: Digital Frontier Press).

Brynjolfsson, E., A. McAfee, M. Sorell, and F. Zhu. 2007. "Scale without Mass: Business Process Replication and Industry Dynamics." Harvard Business School Working Paper 07-016 (Harvard Business School).

Brynjolfsson, E., D. Rock, and C. Syverson. 2017. "Artificial Intelligence and the Modern Productivity Paradox: A Clash of Expectations and Statistics." NBER Working Paper 24001 (Cambridge, MA: National Bureau of Economic Research).

Calligaris, S., C. Criscuolo, and L. Marcolin. 2018. "Mark-Ups in the Digital Era." OECD Science, Technology and Industry Working Paper 2018/10 (Paris: OECD Publishing).

Calvino, F., and C. Criscuolo. 2019. "Business Dynamics and Digitalisation." OECD Science, Technology and Industry Policy Paper 62 (Paris: OECD Publishing).

Calvino, F., C. Criscuolo, L. Marcolin, and M. Squicciarini. 2018. "A Taxonomy of Digital Intensive Sectors." OECD Science, Technology and Industry Working Paper 2018/14 (Paris: OECD Publishing).

Calvino, F., C. Criscuolo, and C. Menon. 2016. "No Country for Young Firms?: Start-Up Dynamics and National Policies." OECD Science, Technology and Industry Policy Paper 29 (Paris: OECD Publishing).

Calvino, F., C. Criscuolo, and R. Verlhac. 2020. "Declining Business Dynamism: Evidence and Causes." OECD Science, Technology and Industry Policy Paper 94 (Paris: OECD Publishing).

Canepa, A., and P. Stoneman. 2004. "Comparative International Diffusion: Patterns, Determinants and Policies." *Economics of Innovation and New Technology* 13, no. 3, pp. 279–98.

Cassiman, B., and R. Veugelers. 2002. "R&D Cooperation and Spillovers: Some Empirical Evidence from Belgium." *American Economic Review* 92, no. 4, pp. 1169–84.

Cohen, W. M., and D. A. Levinthal. 1989. "Innovation and Learning: The Two Faces of R&D." *Economic Journal* 99, no. 397, pp. 569–96.

Cohen, W. M., and D. A. Levinthal. 1990. "Absorptive Capacity: A New Perspective on Learning and Innovation." *Administrative Science Quarterly* 35, no. 1, pp. 128–52.

Comin, D., W. Easterly, and E. Gong. 2010. "Was the Wealth of Nations Determined in 1000 B.C.?" *American Economic Journal: Macroeconomics* 2, no. 3, pp. 65–97.

Comin, D., and B. Hobijn. 2010. "An Exploration of Technology Diffusion." *American Economic Review* 100, no. 5, pp. 2031–59.

Comin, D., B. Hobijn, and E. Rovito. 2006. "Five Facts You Need to Know about Technology Diffusion." NBER Working Paper 11928 (Cambridge, MA: National Bureau of Economic Research).

Comin, D., and M. Mestieri. 2014. "Technology Diffusion: Measurement, Causes, and Consequences," in *Handbook of Economic Growth*, vol. 2B (Amsterdam: Elsevier).

Comin, D., and M. Mestieri. 2018. "If Technology Has Arrived Everywhere, Why Has Income Diverged?" *American Economic Journal: Macroeconomics* 10, no. 3, pp. 137–78.

Constantinescu, C., A. Mattoo, and M. Ruta. 2020. "The Global Trade Slowdown: Cyclical or Structural?" *World Bank Economic Review* 34, no. 1, pp. 121–42.

Covarrubias, M., G. Gutiérrez, and T. Philippon. 2019. "From Good to Bad Concentration? U.S. Industries over the Past 30 Years." NBER Working Paper 25983 (Cambridge, MA: National Bureau of Economic Research).

Crespi, G., C. Criscuolo, and J. Haskel. 2008. "Productivity, Exporting, and the Learning-By-Exporting Hypothesis: Direct Evidence from UK Firms." *Canadian Journal of Economics/Revue canadienne d'économique* 41, no. 2, pp. 619–38.

Criscuolo, C., J. Haskel, and M. Slaughter. 2010. "Global Engagement and the Innovation Activities of Firms." *International Journal of Industrial Organization* 28, no. 2, pp. 191–202.

Criscuolo, C., A. Hijzen, C. Schwellnus, E. Barth, W.-H. Chen, R. Fabling, P. Fialho, K. Grabska, R. Kambayashi, T. Leidecker, O. Nordström Skans, C. Riom, D. Roth, B. Stadler, R. Upward, and W. Zwysen. 2020. "Workforce Composition, Productivity and Pay: The Role of Firms in Wage Inequality." OECD Social, Employment and Migration Working Paper 241 (Paris: OECD Publishing).

Crouzet, N., and J. C. Eberly. 2019. "Understanding Weak Capital Investment: The Role of Market Concentration and Intangibles." NBER Working Paper 25869 (Cambridge, MA: National Bureau of Economic Research).

Davies, S. 1979. *The Diffusion of Process Innovations* (Cambridge University Press).

Decker, R. A., J. Haltiwanger, R. Jarmin, and J. Miranda. 2018. "Changing Business Dynamism and Productivity: Shocks vs. Responsiveness." NBER Working Paper 24236 (Cambridge, MA: National Bureau of Economic Research).

Demmou, L., I. Stefanescu, and A. Arquie. 2019. "Productivity Growth and Finance: The Role of Intangible Assets—A Sector Level Analysis." OECD Economics Department Working Paper 1547 (Paris: OECD Publishing).

Dosi, G., and R. R. Nelson. 2010. "Technical Change and Industrial Dynamics as Evolutionary Processes," in *Handbook of the Economics of Innovation*, vol. 1 (Amsterdam: North-Holland).

Frey, W. 2009. *The Great American Migration Slowdown*. Metropolitan Policy Program (Brookings Institution).

Gal, P., and A. Hijzen. 2016. "The Short-Term Impact of Product Market Reforms: A Cross-Country Firm-Level Analysis." OECD Economics Department Working Paper 1311 (Paris: OECD Publishing).

Gal, P., G. Nicoletti, T. Renault, S. Sorbe, and C. Timiliotis. 2019. "Digitalisation and Productivity: In Search of the Holy Grail—Firm-Level Empirical Evidence from EU Countries." OECD Economics Department Working Paper 1533 (Paris: OECD Publishing).

Galindo-Rueda, F., F. Verger, and S. Ouellet. 2020. "Patterns of Innovation, Advanced Technology Use and Business Practices in Canadian Firms." OECD Science, Technology and Industry Working Paper 2020/02 (Paris: OECD Publishing).

Geroski, P. A. 2000. "Models of Technology Diffusion." *Research Policy* 29, no. 4–5, pp. 603–25.

Gordon, R. 2012. "Is U.S. Economic Growth Over? Faltering Innovation Confronts the Six Headwinds." NBER Working Paper 18315 (Cambridge, MA: National Bureau of Economic Research).

Gort, M., and S. Klepper. 1982. "Time Paths in the Diffusion of Product Innovations." *Economic Journal* 92, no. 367, pp. 630–53.

Griffith, R., S. Redding, and J. Van Reenen. 2004. "Mapping the Two Faces of R&D: Productivity Growth in a Panel of OECD Industries." *Review of Economics and Statistics* 86, no. 4, pp. 883–95.

Griliches, Z. 1957. "Hybrid Corn: An Exploration in the Economics of Technological Change." *Econometrica, Journal of the Econometric Society* 25, no. 4, pp. 501–22.

Gutiérrez, G., and T. Philippon. 2017. "Declining Competition and Investment in the US." NBER Working Paper 23583 (Cambridge, MA: National Bureau of Economic Research).

Hall, B. 2006. "Innovation and Diffusion," in *The Oxford Handbook of Innovation*, edited by J. Fagerberg and D. C. Mowery (Oxford University Press).

Hall, B., C. Helmers, M. Rogers, and V. Sena. 2014. "The Choice between Formal and Informal Intellectual Property: A Review." *Journal of Economic Literature* 52, no. 2, pp. 375–423.

Haskel, J., and S. Westlake. 2018. *Capitalism without Capital: The Rise of the Intangible Economy* (Princeton University Press).

Hermansen, M. 2019. "Occupational Licensing and Job Mobility in the United States." OECD Economics Department Working Paper 1585 (Paris: OECD Publishing).

Hoppe, H. C. 2002. "The Timing of New Technology Adoption: Theoretical Models and Empirical Evidence." *Manchester School* 70, no. 1, pp. 56–76.

Hunt, J., and M. Gauthier-Loiselle. 2010. "How Much Does Immigration Boost Innovation?" *American Economic Journal: Macroeconomics* 2, no. 2, pp. 31–56.

Jaffe, A. B., M. Trajtenberg, and R. Henderson. 1993. "Geographic Localization of Knowledge Spillovers as Evidenced by Patent Citations." *Quarterly Journal of Economics* 108, no. 3, pp. 577–98.

Jin, W., and K. McElheran. 2017. "Economies before Scale: Survival and Performance of Young Plants in the Age of Cloud Computing." Rotman School of Management Working Paper 3112901 (Rotman School of Management, University of Toronto).

Jones, C. I., and C. Tonetti. 2020. "Nonrivalry and the Economics of Data." *American Economic Review* 110, no. 9, pp. 2819–58.

Jovanovic, B., and P. L. Rousseau. 2005. "General Purpose Technologies," in *Handbook of Economic Growth*, vol. 1, edited by P. Aghion and S. N. Durlauf (Amsterdam: Elsevier).

Keller, W. 2004. "International Technology Diffusion." *Journal of Economic Literature* 42, no. 3, pp. 752–82.

Keller, W. 2010. "International Trade, Foreign Direct Investment, and Technology Spillovers," in *Handbook of the Economics of Innovation*, vol. 2 (Amsterdam: North-Holland).

Kerr, W. R. 2013. "US High-Skilled Immigration, Innovation, and Entrepreneurship: Empirical Approaches and Evidence." NBER Working Paper 19377 (Cambridge, MA: National Bureau of Economic Research).

Kerr, W. R. 2018. *The Gift of Global Talent: How Migration Shapes Business, Economy and Society* (Stanford University Press).

Kerr, S. P., and W. R. Kerr. 2019. "Immigrant Networking and Collaboration: Survey Evidence from CIC." NBER Working Paper 25509 (Cambridge, MA: National Bureau of Economic Research).

Khanna, G., and M. Lee. 2018. "High-Skill Immigration, Innovation, and Creative Destruction." NBER Working Paper 24824 (Cambridge, MA: National Bureau of Economic Research).

Klepper, S. 1996. "Entry, Exit, Growth, and Innovation over the Product Life Cycle." *American Economic Review* 86, no. 3, pp. 562–83.

Lissoni, F. 2018. "International Migration and Innovation Diffusion: An Eclectic Survey." *Regional Studies* 52, no. 5, pp. 702–14.

Liu, E., A. Mian, and A. Sufi. 2019. "Low Interest Rates, Market Power, and Productivity Growth." NBER Working Paper 25505 (Cambridge, MA: National Bureau of Economic Research).

Malerba, F. 1992. "Learning by Firms and Incremental Technical Change." *Economic Journal* 102, no. 413, pp. 845–59.

Mansfield, E. 1961. "Technical Change and the Rate of Imitation." *Econometrica: Journal of the Econometric Society* 29, no. 4, pp. 741–66.

Mansfield, E. 1963. "The Speed of Response of Firms to New Techniques." *Quarterly Journal of Economics* 77, no. 2, pp. 290–311.

Mansfield, E., J. Rapoport, J. Schnee, S. Wagner, and M. Hamburger. 1971. "The Diffusion of a Major Manufacturing Innovation," in *Research and Innovation in the Modern Corporation* (London: Palgrave Macmillan).

Marx, M., and L. Fleming. 2012. "Non-compete Agreements: Barriers to Entry . . . and Exit?" *Innovation Policy and the Economy* 12, no. 1, pp. 39–64.

Marx, M., D. Strumsky, and L. Fleming. 2009. "Mobility, Skills, and the Michigan Non-compete Experiment." *Management Science* 55, no. 6, pp. 875–89.

Moser, P., and S. San. 2020. "Immigration, Science, and Invention: Lessons from the Quota Acts." SSRN, April 15. https://papers.ssrn.com/sol3/papers.cfm?abstract_id=3558718.

Moser, P., A. Voena, and F. Waldinger. 2014. "German Jewish Émigrés and US Invention." *American Economic Review* 104, no. 10, pp. 3222–55.

OECD. n.d. The MultiProd Project. www.oecd.org/sti/ind/multiprod.htm.

OECD. 2015. *The Future of Productivity* (Paris).

OECD. 2018a. "Artificial Intelligence and the Technologies of the Next Production Revolution," in *OECD Science, Technology and Innovation Outlook 2018: Adapting to Technological and Societal Disruption* (Paris).

OECD. 2018b. *Opportunities for All: A Framework for Policy Action on Inclusive Growth* (Paris).

OECD. 2018c. *The Productivity-Inclusiveness Nexus* (Paris).

OECD. 2019a. *Enhancing Access to and Sharing of Data: Reconciling Risks and Benefits for Data Re-use across Societies* (Paris). https://doi.org/10.1787/276aaca8-en.

OECD. 2019b. *Measuring the Digital Transformation: A Roadmap for the Future* (Paris).

OECD. 2020a. "Corporate Sector Vulnerabilities during the Covid-19 Outbreak: Assessment and Policy Responses." OECD Policy Responses to Coronavirus (COVID-19). May 5. www.oecd.org/coronavirus/policy-responses/corporate-sector-vulnerabilities-during-the-covid-19-outbreak-assessment-and-policy-responses-a6e670ea/.

OECD. 2020b. "Productivity Gains from Teleworking in the Post COVID-19 Era: How Can Public Policies Make It Happen?" OECD Policy Responses to Coronavirus (COVID-19). Updated September 7. www.oecd.org/coronavirus/policy-responses/productivity-gains-from-teleworking-in-the-post-covid-19-era-a5d52e99/.

OECD. 2020c. "Start-Ups in the Time of COVID-19: Facing the Challenges, Seizing the Opportunities." OECD Policy Responses to Coronavirus (COVID-19). May 13. www.oecd.org/coronavirus/policy-responses/start-ups-in-the-time-of-covid-19-facing-the-challenges-seizing-the-opportunities-87219267/.

Ollivaud, P., and C. Schwellnus. 2015. "Does the Post-crisis Weakness of Global Trade Solely Reflect Weak Demand?" *OECD Journal: Economic Studies* no. 1, pp. 269–97.

Perla, J., and C. Tonetti. 2014. "Equilibrium Imitation and Growth." *Journal of Political Economy* 122, no. 1, pp. 52–76.

Perla, J., C. Tonetti, and M. E. Waugh. 2015. "Equilibrium Technology Diffusion, Trade, and Growth." NBER Working Paper 20881 (Cambridge, MA: National Bureau of Economic Research).

Philippon, T. 2019. *The Great Reversal: How America Gave Up on Free Markets* (Harvard University Press).

Romeo, A. A. 1975. "Interindustry and Interfirm Differences in the Rate of Diffusion of an Innovation." *Review of Economics and Statistics* 57, no. 3, pp. 311–19.

Rosenberg, N. 1972. "Factors Affecting the Diffusion of Technology." *Explorations in Economic History* 10, no. 1, pp. 3–33.

Seamans, R., and M. Raj. 2018. "AI, Labor, Productivity and the Need for Firm-Level Data." NBER Working Paper 24239 (Cambridge, MA: National Bureau of Economic Research).

Sorbe, S., P. Gal, G. Nicoletti, and C. Timiliotis. 2019. "Digital Dividend: Policies to Harness the Productivity Potential of Digital Technologies." OECD Economic Policy Paper 26 (Paris: OECD Publishing).

Stoneman, P., and G. Battisti. 2010. "The Diffusion of New Technology." *Handbook of the Economics of Innovation*, vol. 2 (Amsterdam: North-Holland).

Stoneman, P. L., and P. A. David. 1986. "Adoption Subsidies vs Information Provision as Instruments of Technology Policy." *Economic Journal* 96, pp. 142–50.

Stoneman, P., and P. Diederen. 1994. "Technology Diffusion and Public Policy." *Economic Journal* 104, no. 425, pp. 918–30.

Stoyanov, A., and N. Zubanov. 2012. "Productivity Spillovers across Firms through Worker Mobility." *American Economic Journal: Applied Economics* 4, no. 2, pp. 168–98.

Trajtenberg, M. 2018. "AI as the Next GPT: A Political-Economy Perspective." NBER Working Paper 24245 (Cambridge, MA: National Bureau of Economic Research).

Van Reenen, J. 2018. "Increasing Differences between Firms: Market Power and the Macro-Economy." CEP Discussion Paper 1576 (London: Centre for Economic Performance).

West, D. M., and J. R. Allen. 2018. *How Artificial Intelligence Is Transforming the World.* Report. April 24 (Brookings Institution).

Zolas, N., Z. Kroff, E. Brynjolfsson, K. McElheran, D. N. Beede, C. Buffington, N. Goldschlag, L. S. Foster, and E. Dinlersoz. 2021. "Advanced Technologies Adoption and Use by U.S. Firms: Evidence from the Annual Business Survey." NBER Working Paper 28290 (Cambridge, MA: National Bureau of Economic Research).

THREE

Digital Technologies, Intangibles, and Firm Productivity

MINHO KIM

Many empirical studies have documented large differences in productivity performance between firms even within narrowly defined industries. Economists have tried to identify the sources of these differences. Syverson (2011) lists several potential factors driving productivity dispersion, such as managerial talent and practices, quality of labor or capital inputs, use of information technology (IT), investment in research and development (R&D), business environment, and others. Many developed economies have already moved toward knowledge-based economies and are now undergoing another transformation toward digital economies. Firms' investment in digital technologies and intangible assets, such as knowledge and organizational capital, is now considered to be a more important source of comparative advantage than investment in tangible capital assets. This chapter empirically investigates the role of digital technologies and intangibles as drivers of firm productivity in Korea.

Digital transformation is now taking place across industries and is considered indispensable for firms' competencies. Rapid innovations in digital technologies are transforming the production process, value chains, and business models. The ongoing COVID-19 pandemic is accelerating the speed of transformation. With the rising importance of digital transformation, demand for related data has surged among policymakers and analysts. International institutions and countries are devising tools to measure digital transformation, including technology development and utilization across industries and firms. The Organization for Economic Cooperation and Development's (OECD's) Going Digital Project provides indicators of digital transformation in various dimensions.[1] In Korea, from the year 2017, Statistics Korea has been collecting data on the utilization status of nine specific technologies that are considered key elements of digital transformation and the fourth industrial revolution. These data are included in the Survey of Business Activities, which also provides information on various aspects of business practices and performance. This allows us to analyze the role of digital technologies and intangibles in firm productivity.

We employ relatively large-scale data for our analysis. The Survey of Business Activities from Statistics Korea covers more than 6,000 firms in the manufacturing industry and more than 5,000 firms in the service industry.[2] The survey allows us to measure firm-level intangible capital and utilization status of nine key digital technologies. Once we measure productivity as the unexplained component after accounting for traditional inputs of capital and labor, we analyze the relationship between productivity, intangible capital, and digital technologies.

We observe a low rate of technology adoption among the large sample of companies included in the survey. In 2018, only 11 percent of firms were using any of the nine digital technologies. We find that the adoption of digital technologies is strongly correlated with a firm's productivity. Intangible capital also plays a significant role in firm productivity performance. We also find that the effect of intangible capital on productivity is larger when it is combined with incentive management practices, such as performance bonus schemes covering managers and workers. This finding on the complementary role of organizational practices is important to understanding the contribution of investment in intangibles and digital technologies to productivity. It also provides useful implications for innovation policies supporting firms.

This chapter is related to a rich literature that investigates the effects of intangibles on productivity. One strand of the literature studies the IT-related intangibles' role in productivity, using firm-level data. Brynjolfsson and Hitt (2003) found that increases in computer spending contributed to long-term multifactor productivity growth. Bartel, Ichniowski, and Shaw (2007) showed that new IT-enhanced equipment improved the efficiency of production processes. Bloom, Sadun, and Van Reenen (2012) found that management practices related to people's incentives mattered most in the ability of US multinational firms to attain higher productivity from IT investment compared to non-US multinationals. Brynjolfsson and McElheran (2019) measured data-related managerial practices of manufacturing firms in the United States and found that structured data-driven decision-making practices were significantly associated with productivity growth. This literature emphasizes the role of complementary organizational factors, such as management practices and human capital, in influencing returns to IT investment.

The literature on the effects of IT-related intangibles is only part of the large literature that covers various types of intangible assets. Demmou, Franco, and Stefanescu (2020) introduce several studies providing evidence at the firm level on other intangibles, including Doraszelski and Jaumandreu (2013) on R&D, and Crass and Peters (2014) on R&D and human capital. At the aggregate industry-country level, Corrado, Hulten, and Sichel (2009) and Corrado and Hulten (2010) estimate that intangible investments account for most of the productivity growth. Several recent studies analyze the effects of newly developed technologies, such as intangible capital related to artificial intelligence (AI) and smart factories.[3]

The following section describes data and measurement of digital technologies and intangible capital. The subsequent section presents the empirical model and results on the relationship between digital technologies, intangibles, and firm productivity. The last section concludes the chapter and discusses some policy implications.

Data and Measurement

As an economy shifts toward a knowledge-based economy, intangible investments become increasingly important factors of economic growth. Accordingly, proper measurement of such investments takes on added significance.

Measuring Intangibles and Digital Technologies at the Firm Level

A body of empirical literature has emerged on the measurement of intangible investments—both at the industry level and at the firm level—and assessment of their role as inputs into the productive process.[4] Intangible investments include investments in assets such as R&D, IT, human capital, organizational capital, product design, and marketing. Corrado, Hulten, and Sichel (2005) and Haskel and Westlake (2018) place intangible investments into three broad categories: computerized information, innovative property, and economic competencies.

Computerized information refers to the digitization of information and its utilization in business activities. The development or adoption of software or computerized databases is included in this category. Recent work by the OECD (2019) lays out a roadmap specifically for measuring digital transformation. Innovative property includes items such as R&D, patents and licenses, and product design. Economic competencies include human capital, marketing and branding, and organizational capital.

In our analysis, we try to measure firm-level intangible capital broadly by including variables that cover all three categories of intangible investments. We include intangible assets, R&D expense, advertising expense, and certain management practices. Digital transformation is measured by firms' utilization of nine specific digital technologies.

Data Description

We use annual firm-level data from the Survey of Business Activities by Statistics Korea. The survey covers all industries and targets firms with at least fifty full-time employees and 300 million Korean won (KRW) or more in capital stock.[5] The survey contains information for over 11,000 firms for each year since 2006. Due to the size restrictions on the survey target, the survey includes relatively large firms. Although the firms covered constitute less than 3 percent of all registered firms in Korea in number, they accounted for 80 percent of sales in the manufacturing industry and 31 percent in the service industry in 2017 (based on the input-output information provided by the Bank of Korea).

The Survey of Business Activities provides information on various business activities, including financial information and management practices. For productivity estimation, it contains variables such as revenue, costs, employment, and tangible assets. For intangible variables that may affect productivity, we use intangible assets, R&D expense, advertising expense, as well as firm management practices. The Survey of Business Activities contains a section on firm management practices. The section covers practices such as the method of incentive pay, types of strategic partnership with other firms, and outsourcing areas of the business. Management policies to align employee incentives with innovation and to network with other firms can be important in capturing the productivity potential of today's technologies. For incentive management policies, we use the range of managers and workers targeted with performance bonuses as an indicator in our analysis. The range of managers and employees who are under performance bonus schemes is measured on a scale from one to four: one (none), two (executives and managers), three (some employees), and four (all employees). We also use an indicator of whether a firm formed a strategic partnership with any other firm.

Moreover, since 2017, the Survey of Business Activities has started to collect information on the firms' utilization status of nine digital technologies considered key to digital transformation and the fourth industrial revolution. The technologies include the internet of things (IoT), cloud computing, big data, 5G mobile, AI, blockchain, 3D printing, robotics, and augmented reality (AR) or virtual reality (VR). The survey data allow us to analyze the relationship between specific digital technologies and performance at the firm level. We restrict the empirical analysis to the 2017 and 2018 surveys to study the effects of digital technologies on firm productivity. The proportion of firms utilizing any of the nine technologies was 11 percent in 2018, up from 8 percent in 2017.

In this study, a few industries for which productivity measurement is difficult were excluded from the analysis. These industries, and their International Standard Industrial Classification Revision 4 codes, are financial services, insurance (64–66); real estate, rental (68, 69); public administration and defense (84); education (85); health (86); social work (88); and arts, entertainment, personal services (90–99). All variables except tangible assets were deflated using industry-specific producer price indexes issued by the Bank of Korea. The tangible assets variable was deflated by the price index for fixed capital published by the Bank of Korea. The value added of a firm is calculated using the following equation, with data drawn from the Survey of Business Activities:[6]

$$\text{Value Added} = \text{Sales Revenue} - \text{Cost of Sales} - \text{Selling}$$
$$\text{and Administrative Expenses} + \text{Cost of Labor} +$$
$$\text{Depreciation} + \text{Bad Debt Expense} + \text{Taxes and Dues}$$

Table 3-1 provides descriptive statistics for the main variables, which will be used in our empirical analysis, in manufacturing and service industries in 2018. The sample includes 6,134 firms in manufacturing and 5,264 firms in services. The average firm size is 312 employees (median 115) in manufacturing and 391 employees (median 129) in services. There is a large difference between the mean and median values not only in employment but also in other input variables and value added. This suggests that the firm-size distribution is positively skewed even though our survey contains relatively large firms.

The average manufacturing firm spends 7 million KRW per employee on R&D (which is equivalent to US$6,363 when converted at the 2018 yearly exchange rate). The average service firm spends 2.6 million KRW on R&D, less than half the amount spent by the average manufacturing firm. However, the average service firm invests much more in intangible assets than the average manufacturing firm, investing 18.8 million KRW compared to 8 million KRW. The average service firm also spends more on advertising than the average manufacturing firm, and the amount of spending on advertising exceeds its spending on R&D.

Besides firm intangible capital inputs, table 3-1 shows the diffusion of digital technologies among the sample firms. Only 9.9 percent of firms in manufacturing are utilizing any of the nine digital technologies. The proportion is slightly larger at 13.3 percent for firms in services. The proportion of firms using digital technologies in 2017 was 6.7 percent in manufacturing and 9.7 percent in services—implying an increase of between 3.2 and 3.6 percentage points between 2017 and 2018. The diffusion rate varies greatly across specific digital technologies, ranging from a low of 0.2 percent (blockchain technology in manufacturing) to a high of 6.4 percent (cloud computing in services). While digital technologies are considered to have considerable potential to augment worker capabilities and support more efficient business processes, the adoption rate of these technologies across firms in Korea is still in its infancy. For example, fewer than 3 percent of manufacturing firms are utilizing cloud computing and big data analytics. We will compare the adoption rate of these two digital technologies across OECD countries in the last section of this chapter.

Table 3-1. *Descriptive Statistics for Korean Firms, 2018*

	Manufacturing			Services		
	Mean	Median	Standard deviation	Mean	Median	Standard deviation
Labor productivity	11.35	11.33	0.67	11.10	11.09	0.87
TFP	9.39	9.22	1.88	11.16	11.05	1.41
Value added (million won)	52,900	9,430	938,000	34,100	9,240	172,000
Capital (tangible assets, million won)	97,500	16,100	1,180,000	47,700	2,920	451,000
Labor (employees)	312	115	1,989	391	129	1,222
R&D per employee (million won)	7	2.9	11.9	2.6	0.0	9.6
Intangible assets per employee (million won)	8	0.9	47.9	18.8	0.2	238
Advertising expenses per employee (million won)	2.3	0.1	13.2	6.1	0.1	26.4
Digital technology utilization status dummy (%)	9.9	0	29.8	13.3	0	33.9
(IoT)	3.5	0	18.4	4.3	0	20.4
(Cloud)	2.8	0	16.4	6.4	0	24.5
(Big Data)	2.6	0	16.0	6.0	0	23.7
(5G Mobile)	2.2	0	14.7	4.1	0	19.8
(AI)	1.7	0	12.9	3.7	0	18.8
(Blockchain)	0.2	0	4.9	1.9	0	13.7
(3D Printing)	2.2	0	14.6	0.8	0	8.9
(Robotics)	2.0	0	14.1	0.6	0	7.4
(AR, VR)	0.7	0	8.0	1.6	0	12.5
Strategic partnership dummy (%)	7.2	0	25.8	7.0	0	25.5
Incentive bonus range	2.83	4	1.35	2.64	3	1.36
Number of firms in sample	6,134			5,264		

Source: Author calculations based on Survey of Business Activities 2018 (Statistics Korea n.d.).

Note: Productivity is measured in logged value. TFP stands for total factor productivity. Variables with "(million won)" are expressed in nominal values in millions of KRW.

Table 3-1 also provides basic statistics on two variables relating to management practices. The proportion of firms that have a strategic partnership with any other firm is around 7 percent in both manufacturing and services. The average target range of managers and employees covered by performance bonuses scheme is between two (executives and managers) and three (some employees). Before we turn to econometric analysis in the next section, the descriptive statistics in table 3-1 help to indicate the relative use of different inputs by firms in each of the two industry groups.

Relationship between Digital Technologies, Intangibles, and Firm Productivity

To study the relationship between digital technologies, intangible capital, and productivity, we perform empirical estimation in two stages. In the first stage, we estimate firm-level productivity using traditional factors of production—labor and capital. In the second stage, we estimate regression models in which digital technologies and intangibles are used as explanatory variables for productivity. We adopt the two-step procedure used in Crass and Peters (2014), in which they study the impact of intangible assets on productivity. The other possible estimation method is to explicitly model the inputs of intangibles or digital technology in the production function, as in McGrattan (2020) or Bloom and others (2019). With several variables and their interactions to be taken into account in the analysis, we choose a simpler approach rather than incorporating all these variables in the production function.

Estimation of Firm Productivity

We first estimate total factor productivity (TFP) by positing a value-added production function. The TFP measure can be interpreted as the residual of value added after accounting for the traditionally measured inputs of capital and labor. This value-added productivity estimate has a direct implication for the economic welfare created by the firm. We use the following value-added specification of the Cobb-Douglas production function:

$$\ln VA_{it} = \ln A_{it} + \varepsilon_j^K \ln K_{it} + \varepsilon_j^L \ln L_{it} \qquad (3\text{-}1)$$

The production function is expressed in logs. VA_{it} denotes the real value-added of firm i in year t. A_{it} is the measure of TFP. K_{it} and L_{it} are the real capital and labor used as inputs by firm i. ε_j^K and ε_j^L are the elasticities of each production input (capital and labor), respectively. These elasticity parameters need to be estimated.

We estimate the elasticity parameters for each of forty-six two-digit industries using the estimation method in Wooldridge (2009). Correlation between unobserved productivity and the input level may cause simultaneity bias, since input decisions depend on the unobserved productivity. In that case, the estimates can be biased. Wooldridge (2009) tries to address the simultaneity problem by applying a generalized method of moments framework to the Levinsohn and Petrin (2003) method that uses intermediate inputs as proxy variables. Once we estimate the elasticity parameters, the estimate of firm-level TFP, $\ln \hat{A}_{it}$, is obtained from equation 3-1.

Empirical Model

Given the firm-level estimate of TFP, we use the following empirical specification to study the relationship between intangibles, digital technologies, and TFP at the firm level:

$$\ln \hat{A}_{it} = c + IC_{it}\beta + Tech_{it}\delta + X_{it}\gamma + f_j + f_t + \varepsilon_{it} \qquad (3\text{-}2)$$

The estimate of TFP is regressed on variables that represent intangible capital (IC_{it}), utilization status of digital technologies ($Tech_{it}$), and their interaction with certain firm management practices (X_{it}). Industry fixed effects (f_j) and a time dummy (f_t) are included in all analyses.

For the firm's input of intangible capital, we include not only intangible fixed assets but also R&D investment and advertising expense as proxies. Thus, the firm-level intangible capital (IC_{it}) is expressed as a vector of three variables, all scaled by size using the number of employees:

$$IC_{it}\beta = \beta_1 \ln(R\&D_{it}/L_{it}) + \beta_2 \ln(INT_{it}/L_{it}) + \beta_3 \ln(AD_{it}/L_{it}) \qquad (3\text{-}3)$$

R&D investment per employee, $R\&D_{it}/L_{it}$, represents the investment level of the firm in innovation activities and is calculated as the spending on R&D in a year divided by the number of employees. Intangible assets per employee, INT_{it}/L_{it}, cover the stock of intangibles the firm has invested up to year t. We use the survey item "asset value of intangible fixed assets," which is based on values from the firm's balance sheet. Intangible assets are nonphysical assets used over more than one year. They are listed in the firm's balance sheet when they are acquired and have an identifiable value. The intangible asset value consists of but is not limited to patents, trademarks, development costs, and goodwill. Some of the firm's past R&D investments can be included in intangible assets when they are recognized as assets generating future cash flow. It should be noted that the intangible asset value may differ from the true value of the firm's intangible assets since it is difficult to incorporate all intangible assets that are generated internally. We use advertising expense per employee, AD_{it} / L_{it}, as a proxy for a firm's investment in building its brand. We consider advertising as an intangible capital input that can affect a firm's productivity.

Besides a firm's investment in intangible capital, this study explicitly considers the firm's adoption of digital technology in the regression analysis. We utilize data collected from recent survey questions on firms' utilization status of the nine specific digital technologies. Previous studies relied on spending on information and communication technology (ICT) or physical capital such as computer assets to study the impact of technology on firm productivity. Recent rapid developments in digital technologies are broadening and deepening the digital transformation of production processes. Using firm-level data on the use of the nine key digital technologies, we study the association between the adoption of digital technology and firm productivity. Our baseline model incorporates the firm's digital technology adoption with a dummy variable, $Tech_{it}$ where it takes value 1 if a firm utilizes any of the nine digital technologies. In the other model, we include dummy variables for the adoption of each of the nine digital technologies separately to study which particular technologies were associated with the firm's productivity.

Thus far, our baseline model considers intangible capital and digital technology as explanatory variables. When we estimate the contribution of intangible capital or digital technology to productivity, it is important also to look for complementary inputs that affect productivity when combined with the investment in intangible capital or digital technologies. Among such inputs, we study complementarity with firms' management practices. Firm management practices can be considered a firm's organizational capital and can be included as a component of intangible capital. Bloom and others (2019) show that differences in management practices account for a significant fraction of variation in productivity across firms.

Even if we do not have a single measure such as a management practices score, we can look for evidence of complementarity with certain management practices. Here we use the range of managers and employees covered by performance bonus schemes and an indicator of whether a firm has formed strategic partnerships with other firms. In our analysis, we look at the interaction of the former with intangible assets per employee and of the latter with the adoption of digital technology. Detecting complementarity with management practices allows us to better understand the heterogeneous effects of investment in intangibles or adoption of digital technology on the productivity across firms.

We use panel data regression with random effects on two years of panel data, since only the 2017 and 2018 surveys contain information on the utilization status of digital technologies. The assumption is that any time constant unobserved characteristics of firms are not correlated with the explanatory variables.

Empirical Results

This section presents the estimation results of productivity regressed on intangibles and digital technologies based on equation 3-2. The estimation is conducted for two broad industry groups by splitting firm samples into manufacturing and services. Tables 3-2 and 3-3 report regression results for manufacturing and services, respectively. We discuss the results for manufacturing and then note the differences with the results for services.

Column 1 of tables 3-2 and 3-3 provides baseline results where we consider the inputs of three types of intangible capital and the adoption of digital technology. Among the three inputs of intangible capital, we find statistically significant coefficients for intangible assets and advertising expenses but not R&D expenses. In table 3-2, the coefficients for manufacturing suggest that a 100 percent increase in intangible assets per employee is associated with a 0.6 percent increase in TFP. A doubling of advertising expenses per employee is associated with a 1 percent increase in TFP. The coefficients are larger for services, as shown in table 3-3. In services, a doubling of intangible assets per employee and of advertising expenses per employee is associated with TFP increases of 1 percent and 1.5 percent, respectively.

The coefficient of R&D expenses per employee shows a negative sign but is not statistically significant for manufacturing. However, there is a statistically significant negative correlation between R&D expenses per

Table 3-2. *TFP, Digital Technologies, and Intangibles (Manufacturing)*

Independent variables	Dependent variable = TFP			
	(1)	(2)	(3)	(4)
R&D per employee	−0.001	−0.001	−0.002	−0.002*
Intangible assets per employee	0.006***	0.006***	0.002	0.002
Advertising expenses per employee	0.010***	0.010***	0.009***	0.009***
Digital technology utilization status dummy	0.058***	0.028	0.054***	0.026
Strategic partnership dummy		0.027		0.023
Digital technology X Strategic partnership		0.172***		0.161***
Incentive bonus range				
(executives and managers)			0.097**	0.097**
(some employees)			0.116***	0.115***
(all employees)			0.194***	0.194***
Intangible assets per employee X Incentive bonus range				
(executives and managers)			0.003	0.003
(some employees)			0.004	0.004
(all employees)			0.005**	0.005**
Year, Industry fixed effects, Constant	Yes	Yes	Yes	Yes
R^2	0.883	0.883	0.888	0.888
Observations	12,117	12,117	12,117	12,117

Source: Author calculations based on Survey of Business Activities 2017–2018 (Statistics Korea, n.d.).

Note: All coefficients are estimates from panel regression models with random effects. The significance levels of 1 percent, 5 percent, and 10 percent are indicated by asterisks ***, **, and *, respectively.

employee and TFP for service firms. The results appear at odds with the expectation of a positive correlation between R&D and productivity. One reason could be the way R&D was considered in the analysis. R&D expenditure values for the concurrent year are used with the measure of TFP in the analysis instead of R&D stock. We used current R&D expenditure as a proxy for a firm's investment in innovation. There can be time lags between R&D investment and discovery, application, and commercialization. There are a number of studies that investigate the effects of R&D on productivity. They point out the empirical difficulties in measuring R&D inputs. Without further analysis of the link between R&D in-

Table 3-3. *TFP, Digital Technologies, and Intangibles (Services)*

Independent variables	Dependent variable = TFP			
	(1)	(2)	(3)	(4)
R&D per employee	−0.006***	−0.006***	−0.007***	−0.007***
Intangible assets per employee	0.010***	0.010***	0.006**	0.006**
Advertising expenses per employee	0.015***	0.015***	0.014***	0.014***
Digital technology utilization status dummy	0.046**	0.038	0.037*	0.031
Strategic partnership dummy		0.031		0.023
Digital technology X Strategic partnership		0.078**		0.061*
Incentive bonus range				
(executives and managers)			0.130***	0.131***
(some employees)			0.090***	0.090***
(all employees)			0.191***	0.191***
Intangible assets per employee X Incentive bonus range				
(executives and managers)			0.008	0.008
(some employees)			0.003	0.003
(all employees)			0.006*	0.006*
Year, Industry fixed effects, Constant	Yes	Yes	Yes	Yes
R²	0.710	0.711	0.720	0.720
Observations	10,222	10,222	10,222	10,222

Source: Author calculations based on Survey of Business Activities 2017–2018 (Statistics Korea n.d.).

Note: All coefficients are estimates from panel regression models with random effects. The significance levels of 1 percent, 5 percent, and 10 percent are indicated by asterisks ***, **, and *, respectively.

puts and productivity, the estimated coefficient may suggest that R&D investment can have a negative effect on TFP in the same year.

The coefficient on the dummy variable for the utilization status of any of the nine digital technologies is statistically significant at 0.058 for manufacturing and 0.046 for services. This suggests that, in manufacturing, a firm utilizing digital technology is likely to have 5.8 percent higher TFP than a firm not equipped with such technology. The correlation between the adoption of digital technologies and TFP may arise due to omitted factors that affect both variables. Among possible factors that can affect the adoption of digital technology and the TFP measure, we considered an indicator of whether a firm formed a strategic partnership with any other firm. Digital technologies enable firms to utilize information to improve productivity by creating digital links not only within the organization but also with other businesses. New business models or values can be created through digital technologies. We examined whether the correlation between the productivity measure and digital technology was strong for firms that made strategic partnerships with other firms. In column 2 of tables 3-2 and 3-3, we included an interaction term between the digital technology and strategic partnership dummy variables. The magnitude of the coefficient for digital technology falls and loses its statistical significance while the coefficient of the interaction term shows a significant positive correlation. The magnitude of the interaction term coefficient suggests that, in manufacturing, a firm both utilizing any digital technology and forming a strategic partnership shows 17.2 percent higher TFP than a firm without any of the two. The magnitude is lower at 7.8 percent in services.

The results suggest that firm productivity can be affected by a complementary relationship between digital technology and management practices. We also looked at possible complementarity between intangible capital and management practices. Column 3 reports the results for the target range of performance bonus schemes and its interaction term with intangible assets per employee. The coefficient of the performance bonus range becomes larger as the target range widens, meaning that firms with broader performance bonus schemes are likely to have higher productivity. The coefficient of the interaction term is positive, but statistically significant only for performance bonus schemes that cover all employees. Column 4 presents results with full specification of equation 3-2. The results remain unchanged qualitatively.

Table 3-4 presents an extension of equation 3-2 by considering the nine specific digital technologies separately. This is to see which technologies were more strongly associated with firm productivity. We found that the effective digital technologies differed across industries. In manufacturing, big data technology showed a positive, statistically significant correlation with the TFP measure. In services, firms utilizing IoT and AR or VR had higher TFP than other firms. Other specific digital technologies did not show a correlation with TFP with strong statistical significance.

Table 3-4. *TFP, Digital Technologies, and Intangibles (Nine Individual Technologies)*

	Dependent variable = TFP			
	Manufacturing	Manufacturing	Services	Services
Independent variables	(1)	(2)	(3)	(4)
R&D per employee	−0.001	−0.002	−0.007***	−0.007***
Intangible assets per employee	0.006***	0.002	0.010***	0.006**
Advertising expenses per employee	0.010***	0.009***	0.015***	0.015***
Incentive bonus range				
(executives and managers)		0.096**		0.129***
(some employees)		0.116***		0.089***
(all employees)		0.194***		0.192***
Intangible assets per employee X Incentive bonus range				
(executives and managers)		0.002		0.008
(some employees)		0.004		0.003
(all employees)		0.005**		0.005*
Digital technology utilization status dummy				
(IoT)	−0.037	−0.043	0.070**	0.067**
(Cloud)	−0.011	−0.012	−0.021	−0.029
(Big Data)	0.097***	0.095***	−0.001	−0.005
(5G Mobile)	0.085*	0.084*	−0.009	−0.012
(AI)	0.019	0.016	0.03	0.03
(Blockchain)	−0.053	−0.037	0.074	0.072
(3D Printing)	0.028	0.024	−0.015	−0.008
(Robotics)	−0.061*	−0.060*	0.189	0.18
(AR, VR)	0.137	0.136	0.160***	0.164***
Year, Industry fixed effects, Constant	Yes	Yes	Yes	Yes
R^2	0.883	0.888	0.712	0.721
Observations	12,117	12,117	10,222	10,222

Source: Author calculations based on Survey of Business Activities 2017–2018 (Statistics Korea n.d.).

Note: All coefficients are estimates from panel regression models with random effects. The significance levels of 1 percent, 5 percent, and 10 percent are indicated by asterisks ***, **, and *, respectively.

Conclusion and Policy Implications

This study analyzes the relationship between digital technologies, intangible capital, and productivity using representative firm data for about 11,000 firms. We find that the adoption of digital technologies and intangible capital are strongly associated with a firm's productivity. We also find a complementary relationship between intangible assets and firms' incentive management practices. The positive impact of intangible assets on TFP was larger when the range of managers and workers covered by performance bonus schemes was wider. Moreover, the effects of digital technologies were larger for firms that made complementary strategic partnerships with other firms.

Even though Korea is considered one of the leading countries in ICT, the adoption rate of digital technologies among firms appears to be relatively low. While Korea has some leading ICT companies and high-quality digital infrastructure, the low rate of digital technology adoption among firms more widely tells a rather different story. What matters is not only the overall low rate of technology adoption but also the large differences in the rates of adoption across firms. Digital technologies are not being used at their potential.[7] The different rates of adoption across firms can arise naturally from different firm characteristics, but they can also result from barriers constraining firms' investment in digital technologies.

One firm characteristic influencing technology adoption is firm size. We can compare the usage rate of selected digital technologies by firm size across OECD countries using the OECD ICT Access and Usage by Business Database. Figures 3-1 and 3-2 present usage rates for big data analysis and cloud computing service, respectively. For both digital technologies, Korea's usage rate is low compared to that of other OECD countries. And the low rate is due mainly to the low rate of adoption among small and medium enterprises (SMEs). A wide gap exists between large enterprises and SMEs. Since our findings suggest that the adoption of digital technologies is positively associated with firm productivity, differences in technology adoption can amplify differences in firm productivity. Complementary organizational and other changes that must accompany new technology for successful adoption, which take time, can make a big difference in whether and when firms adopt the new technology. More research would be useful to better understand the determinants of and obstacles to technology adoption and investment in intangible capital, especially by SMEs.

FIGURE 3-1. Enterprises Performing Big Data Analysis, by Size, 2018

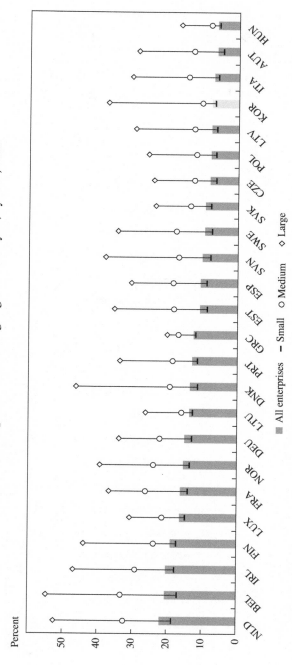

■ All enterprises   — Small   ○ Medium   ◇ Large

Source: OECD.Stat (n.d.), accessed September 2020.

Note: Firm size is defined by the number of employees: small (10–49), medium (50–249), and large (250 and more).

FIGURE 3-2. Enterprises Purchasing Cloud Computing Services, by Size, 2018

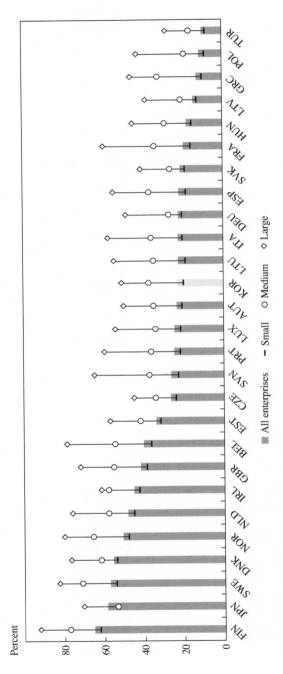

■ All enterprises   — Small   ○ Medium   ◇ Large

Source: OECD.Stat (n.d.), accessed September 2020.

Note: Firm size is defined by the number of employees: small (10–49), medium (50–249), and large (250 and more).

Many countries have introduced strategies to promote digital transformation to enhance the competitiveness of their industries, including manufacturing. The Korean government has pursued policies to encourage SMEs to adopt smart manufacturing, with an explicit goal of 30,000 smart factories by 2022. A total of 1 trillion KRW was earmarked for related projects in the 2019 budget alone. However, the particular approach being followed may have the same shortcomings as that of the SME IT Support Project of the early 2000s. That project also targeted 30,000 firms and encouraged SMEs to adopt either basic IT software or enterprise resource planning software. However, many firms reported that the software was either not used at all after installation or used only to a limited extent.[8] Government support can be inefficient when it focuses narrowly on the installation of a specific technology.

Chung and Kim (2021) make a distinction between installing smart factory technology and the smartness level of the factory. Using survey data on manufacturing factories in Korea, they show that an increase in the smartness level matters more for better performance than the mere adoption of a new smart technology. They find that structured incentive management practices are complementary with the adoption of new technologies in enhancing the level of smartness. Several previous studies also find complementarity between organizational capital and IT investment.[9] These findings suggest that complementary changes in organizational capital—including adaptation of management practices, alignment of worker incentives, and development of worker capabilities—are necessary to effectively capture the gains from investments in digital technologies. These considerations need to inform both firm decisions and government policy on new technologies.

We find that the effects of digital technologies on productivity differ across types of technology and across firms with different characteristics. This suggests that subsidizing the adoption of a particular technology may not be the best approach to technology promotion. There is no one-size-fits-all solution that serves diverse needs of firms. As part of a government's efforts to improve the access and capabilities of smaller firms to modernize their operations for the digital age, it can help disseminate practical information on the uses of digital technologies. Germany's online Industry 4.0 Map is a good example.[10] The map provides information on actual applications of smart factory technologies according to characteristics such as product type, development stage, and company size. It also provides information on related support services. Since the Korean government has already provided support for the adoption of digital technology to thousands of firms through recent initiatives, the lessons learned can provide valuable information for other firms, as well as for guiding future government policy in promoting digital transformation more widely across firms.

NOTES

1. For general information about the Going Digital Project, see OECD (n.d.). The project's publications include *Measuring the Digital Transformation: A Roadmap for the Future* (OECD, 2019), and the project provides related innovative policy examples.

2. Statistics Korea (n.d.).

3. Brynjolfsson, Rock, and Syverson (2021) and Chung and Kim (2021).

4. See Corrado and Hulten (2010) for references.

5. In the case of the "Wholesale and Retail Trade" industry, firms with full-time employees numbering five to forty-nine are included in the survey target when they have more than 1 billion KRW in capital stock.

6. Statistics Korea officially uses this equation for its published statistics on value added, based on the Survey of Business Activities.

7. OECD (2020).

8. Choi (2005).

9. Bresnahan, Brynjolfsson, and Hitt (2002) and Bloom, Sadun, and Van Reenen (2012), among others.

10. Industrie 4.0 Landkarte (n.d.).

REFERENCES

Bartel, Ann, Casey Ichniowski, and Kathryn Shaw. 2007. "How Does Information Technology Affect Productivity? Plant-Level Comparisons of Product Innovation, Process Improvement, and Worker Skills." *Quarterly Journal of Economics* 122, no. 4, pp. 1721–58.

Bloom, Nicholas, Erik Brynjolfsson, Lucia Foster, Ron Jarmin, Megha Patnaik, Itay Saporta-Eksten, and John Van Reenen. 2019. "What Drives Differences in Management Practices?" *American Economic Review* 109, no. 5, pp. 1648–83.

Bloom, Nicholas, Raffaella Sadun, and John Van Reenen. 2012. "Americans Do I.T. Better: U.S. Multinationals and the Productivity Miracle." *American Economic Review* 102, no. 1, pp. 167–201.

Bresnahan, Timothy F., Erik Brynjolfsson, and Lorin M. Hitt. 2002. "Information Technology, Workplace Organization, and the Demand for Skilled Labor: Firm-Level Evidence." *Quarterly Journal of Economics* 117, no. 1, pp. 339–76.

Brynjolfsson, Erik, and Lorin M. Hitt. 2003. "Computing Productivity: Firm-Level Evidence." *Review of Economics and Statistics* 85, no. 4, pp. 793–808.

Brynjolfsson, Erik, and Kristina McElheran. 2019. "Data in Action: Data-Driven Decision Making and Predictive Analytics in US Manufacturing." Rotman School of Management Working Paper No. 3422397. https://ssrn.com/abstract=3422397.

Brynjolfsson, Erik, Daniel Rock, and Chad Syverson. 2021. "The Productivity J-Curve: How Intangibles Complement General Purpose Technologies." *American Economic Journal: Macroeconomics* 13, no. 1, pp. 333–72.

Choi, Bo-keum. 2005. "An Analysis on the Status of ERP Adoption by SMEs." Master's dissertation. Kookmin University, Seoul.

Chung, Sunghoon, and Minho Kim. 2021. "How Smart Is 'Smart Factory'?: Causes and Consequences of Factory Smartization." Unpublished manuscript.

Corrado, Carol, and Charles Hulten. 2010. "How Do You Measure a Technological Revolution?" *American Economic Review* 100, no. 2, pp. 99–104.

Corrado, Carol, Charles Hulten, and Daniel Sichel. 2005. "Measuring Capital and Technology: An Expanded Framework," in *Measuring Capital in the New Economy*, edited by C. Corrado, J. Haltiwanger, and D. Sichel, Studies in Income and Wealth, no. 65 (University of Chicago Press).

Corrado, Carol, Charles Hulten, and Daniel Sichel. 2009. "Intangible Capital and U.S. Economic Growth." *Review of Income and Wealth* 55, no. 3, pp. 661–85.

Crass, Dirk, and Bettina Peters. 2014. "Intangible Assets and Firm-Level Productivity." ZEW—Centre for European Economic Research Discussion Paper 14-120 (Mannheim, Germany).

Demmou, Lilas, Guido Franco, and Irina Stefanescu. 2020. "Productivity and Finance: The Intangible Assets Channel—A Firm-Level Analysis." OECD Economics Department Working Paper 1596 (Paris: OECD Publishing). https://doi.org/10.1787/d13a21b0-en.

Doraszelski, Ulrich, and Jordi Jaumandreu. 2013. "R&D and Productivity: Estimating Endogenous Productivity." *Review of Economic Studies* 80, no. 4, pp. 1338–83.

Haskel, Jonathan, and Stian Westlake. 2018. *Capitalism without Capital: The Rise of the Intangible Economy* (Princeton University Press).

Industrie 4.0 Landkarte [Industry 4.0 Map]. n.d. Platform Industrie 4.0. www.plattform-i40.de/PI40/Navigation/DE/Angebote-Ergebnisse/Industrie-4-0-Landkarte/industrie-4-0-landkarte.html.

Levinsohn, James, and Amil Petrin. 2003. "Estimating Production Functions Using Inputs to Control for Unobservables." *Review of Economic Studies* 70, no. 2, pp. 317–41.

McGrattan, Ellen R. 2020. "Intangible Capital and Measured Productivity." *Review of Economic Dynamics* 37, pp. 147–66.

OECD. n.d. OECD's Going Digital Project. www.oecd.org/going-digital/project/.

OECD. 2013. *Supporting Investment in Knowledge Capital, Growth and Innovation* (Paris). http://dx.doi.org/10.1787/9789264193307-en.

OECD. 2019. *Measuring the Digital Transformation: A Roadmap for the Future* (Paris). https://doi.org/10.1787/9789264311992-en.

OECD. 2020. *OECD Economic Surveys: Korea 2020* (Paris). https://doi.org/10.1787/2dde9480-en.

OECD.Stat. n.d. ICT Access and Usage by Business Database. https://stats.oecd.org/Index.aspx?DataSetCode=ICT_BUS.

Statistics Korea. n.d. Survey of Business Activities. http://kostat.go.kr/portal/eng/surveyOutline/3/8/index.static.

Syverson, Chad. 2011. "What Determines Productivity?" *Journal of Economic Literature* 499, no. 2, pp. 326–65.

Wooldridge, Jeffrey. 2009. "On Estimating Firm-Level Production Functions Using Proxy Variables to Control for Unobservables." *Economics Letters* 104, no. 3, pp. 112–14.

FOUR

Harnessing the Promise of Fintech

THOMAS PHILIPPON

This chapter analyzes the opportunities and challenges created by technological innovations in the finance industry (Fintech). Fintech refers to digital innovations and technology-enabled business model transformations in the financial sector. Innovations such as the use of smartphones and digital platforms for a variety of banking and financial services, automatic underwriting, smart contracts, and robo-advising can disrupt existing industry structures, blur industry boundaries, facilitate strategic disintermediation, revolutionize how existing firms create and deliver products and services, provide new gateways for entrepreneurship, and democratize access to financial services. Fintech can also create significant privacy, regulatory, and law-enforcement challenges.

The most likely benefits of Fintech include a lower cost of financial services, improved financial inclusion, and reduced discrimination. The most likely challenge is the adaptation of the current regulatory framework for consumer protection, regulation, and antitrust. The chapter concludes by offering three scenarios for the future of Fintech depending on the nature of returns to scale, the decision by big tech companies on whether to

provide financial services, and the degree of integration of Chinese intermediaries into the global financial system.

Background

The chapter examines Fintech in the context of the long-run evolution of
the finance industry and its regulations. To understand the risks and opportunities brought by Fintech, it is important first to analyze the state of
the finance industry.

I argue that lackluster productivity growth and tight regulations in the
industry have played an important role in the growth of Fintech. Financial
intermediation has remained costly and rather inefficient, creating room
for entry by Fintech firms. The regulations implemented in the aftermath
of the global financial crisis have put a brake on the expansion of global
banks and evened the playing field.

Efficiency, or Lack Thereof, in the Finance Industry

I start my analysis by showing that the current financial system is rather
inefficient and costly. Figure 4-1 shows the unit cost of financial intermediation in the United States, as defined in Philippon (2015). The raw measure is the ratio of the total cost of financial intermediation (the sum of all
payments from the nonfinancial sector to the financial sector in a given
year) to the value of intermediated assets (properly aggregated across all
markets and services, e.g., including liquidity services). Figure 4-1 shows
that this raw measure has been remarkably stable at around 200 basis points
for more than a century. In other words, it costs 2 cents per year to create
and maintain 1 dollar of intermediated financial assets. Equivalently, the
annual rate of return of savers is, on average, 2 percentage points below the
funding cost of borrowers. The updated series in figure 4-1 are similar to
the ones in the original paper. Bazot (2013) estimates unit costs for other
countries and finds convergence to US levels.

The raw measure, however, does not take into account changes in the
characteristics of end users (firms, households). These changes require quality adjustments to the raw measure of intermediated assets. For instance,
corporate finance involves issuing commercial paper for blue-chip companies as well as raising equity for high-technology start-ups. The monitoring requirements per dollar intermediated are vastly different between these

FIGURE 4-1. Unit Cost of Financial Intermediation, United States, 1886–2017

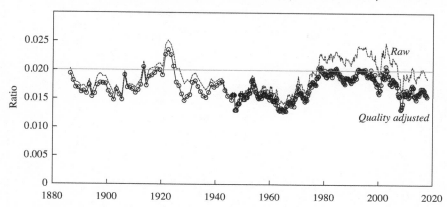

Source: Philippon (2015) and author updates.

Note: The quality-adjusted measure takes into account changes in firms' and households' characteristics.

two activities. Similarly, in the case of household finance, it is relatively more expensive to lend to poor households than to wealthy ones. Since relatively poor households have gained more access to credit in recent years, a raw measure of the unit cost of financial intermediation will be biased upward.[1] More generally, measurement problems arise when the mix of high- and low-quality borrowers changes over time.

Therefore, I perform a quality adjustment to the intermediated assets series, again following Philippon (2015). Figure 4-1 also shows the quality-adjusted unit-cost series. It is lower than the unadjusted series by construction, since quality-adjusted assets are (weakly) larger than raw intermediated assets. The gap between the two series grows when there is entry of new firms, and/or when there is credit expansion at the extensive margin (i.e., new borrowers). Even with the adjusted series, however, we see no significant decrease in the unit cost of intermediation until the mid-2000s. This observation, of course, is the major disappointment with the finance industry over the past forty years. We do not see the dramatic reduction in unit cost that one would have hoped after the advent of digital technologies.

The good news, however, is that our measure suggests some decrease in the unit cost of financial intermediation in the aftermath of the global financial crisis. The implied improvement in efficiency reflects a combination of

FIGURE 4-2. **Employment in Finance versus Other Industries, United States, 1998–2019**

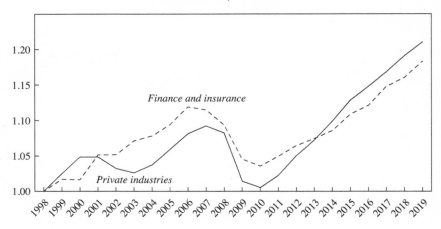

Source: Philippon (2015) and author updates.

Note: Employment is full-time equivalent, normalized to 1 in 1998.

cost cutting, productivity gains driven by technological progress, and competition from new entrants, including Fintech entities.

Figure 4-2 shows that employment grew faster in finance than in other private industries in the United States in the 2000s, but more slowly after the great financial crisis of 2008–2009. In 2013, relative employment in finance was back at its level of 1998. Since 2013, relative employment in finance has been lower than before. This happened as credit and equity markets recovered and expanded. It, therefore, suggests an improvement in labor productivity in the financial intermediation sector, consistent with the decreasing unit cost shown in figure 4-1.

The series in figures 4-1 and 4-2, unfortunately, do not isolate the role of Fintech. The direct impact of entry by Fintech firms is probably limited, as their market shares, albeit growing, are still rather small in the United States. There are at least two other possible channels to consider, however. One channel is the competition effect. To keep entrants at bay, incumbents are forced to cut prices and improve quality. In equilibrium, the market share of entrants might be small, but the threat of entry can have a meaningful impact on productivity. Another channel is the technology diffusion/transfer effect. Fintech firms can develop technologies that are useful for incumbents, and incumbents can access these technologies either directly or by acquiring the new firms.

Post-2009 Financial Reforms

In this section, we highlight some key regulations and their likely impact on the industry. The financial crisis of 2008–2009 was a watershed moment for financial firms and their regulators.[2] A major goal of the postcrisis reforms was to address the issue of financial institutions considered too big to fail (TBTF). The basic idea was that systemically important banks (SIBs) should have higher loss absorbency capacity than other banks. The consensus was that the minimum capital requirements in the Basel III framework were too low.[3] While it is difficult to fully assess the success of these reforms, it is clear that big banks are safer today than they were ten years ago, at least in rich countries.

Figure 4-3 shows the evolution of the capital ratio of global systemically important banks (G-SIBs). The Tier-1 risk-based capital ratio (core capital relative to risk-weighted assets) more than doubled between 2011 and 2019, from the 6–7 percent range to 14 percent or more. Over the same period, the leverage ratio (core capital relative to unweighted assets) also increased significantly. In Europe, for instance, it rose from about 2.5 percent to about 5 percent. G-SIBs still have lower capital ratios than other banks, however.

Another goal of the reforms was to reduce implicit TBTF subsidies for SIBs. If creditors of large banks anticipate a bailout in case of financial distress, they will be willing to lend to large banks at a lower cost than they would to small banks. This funding subsidy is a distortion that undermines the safety and efficiency of the financial system. Recent data show that TBTF reforms have reduced these funding subsidies.[4]

Higher capital and a reduction in funding cost subsidies have contributed to lower profitability of SIBs. The profitability of SIBs, and in particular of G-SIBs, has fallen relative to that of other banks.[5] This is in part due to increasing regulations focused on restoring a level playing field between systemically important banks and the rest.

At the same time, market shares of SIBs in their domestic markets have decreased since 2010. This is true for their shares of assets, loans, and deposits, as shown in figure 4-4. Interestingly, most of the decline

FIGURE 4-3. Capital Ratios of Global Systemic Banks, 2011–2019

Tier-1 risk-based capital ratio (percent)

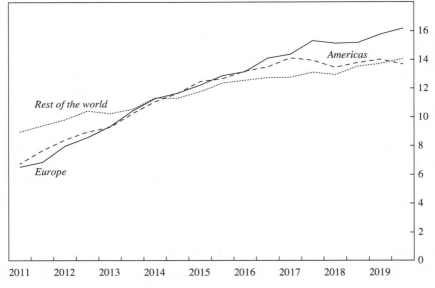

Source: Basel Committee on Banking Supervision (2020).

Note: The graph shows the fully phased-in initial Basel III framework up to and including end-2018 and the actual framework in place for end-June 2019.

happened during the implementation of the postcrisis reforms, between 2012 and 2015.

Overall, postcrisis reforms seem to have had a meaningful impact on the finance industry. They have made it safer and more open to competition. The relative retreat of domestic systemically important banks (D-SIBs), however, is not happening in China, as we will discuss in the concluding section.

Growth of Fintech

Sahay and others (2020) discuss the promise of Fintech. They provide an excellent survey of the literature, in particular on the development of Fintech in emerging markets. They show that Fintech has improved financial inclusion and that this has been associated with higher GDP growth. They show that digital financial services are faster and often cheaper than tradi-

FIGURE 4-4. **Domestic Market Shares of Systemic Banks, 2010–2018**

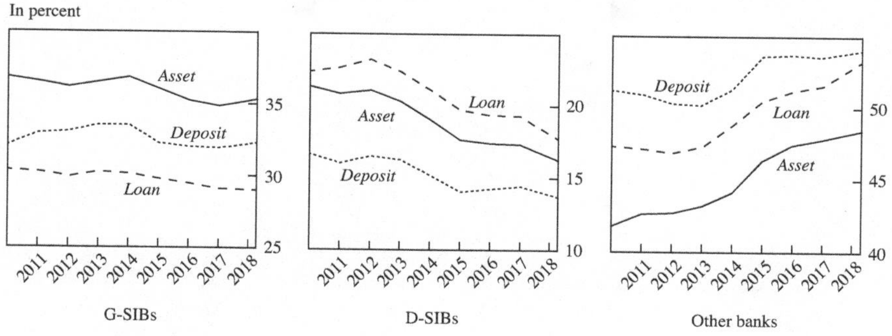

In percent

| G-SIBs | D-SIBs | Other banks |

Source: FSB (2020).

Note: Data are from a TBTF survey, which includes information by country on domestic loans to customers granted by domestic G-SIBs, domestic systemically important banks (D-SIBs), and other banks. The figure covers nineteen jurisdictions. Weighted averages. Composition changes are not adjusted.

tional financial services, and they argue that digital finance has been able to reach lower-income households and small and medium enterprises. Digital payments and lending have increased more where traditional financial services were less present. They also find that Fintech appears to be closing gender gaps in access to financial services.

Funding and Other Key Trends

Fintech funding activity was affected by the COVID-19 crisis, and some deals have been delayed, but the slowdown predated the pandemic after a period of strong growth (figure 4-5). Several important Fintech trends are highlighted in a recent KPMG report.[6] One trend is the growth in the use of application programming interfaces (APIs) and the importance of open data, discussed later in the chapter. Another trend is the growing connection between Fintech and big tech.[7] Regtech (the use of fintech solutions to satisfy regulatory requirements) is growing steadily, and the deployment of fully remote digital solutions will increase the need for fraud prevention, digital identity management, and cybersecurity.

Overall, if we look at the Fintech landscape, we see that payment firms are dominant. To better assess these developments, it is helpful to understand some of the "plumbing" of payment systems. Payment providers can deliver payment services either by accessing existing payment systems (i.e., using an

FIGURE 4-5. **Funding of Fintech**

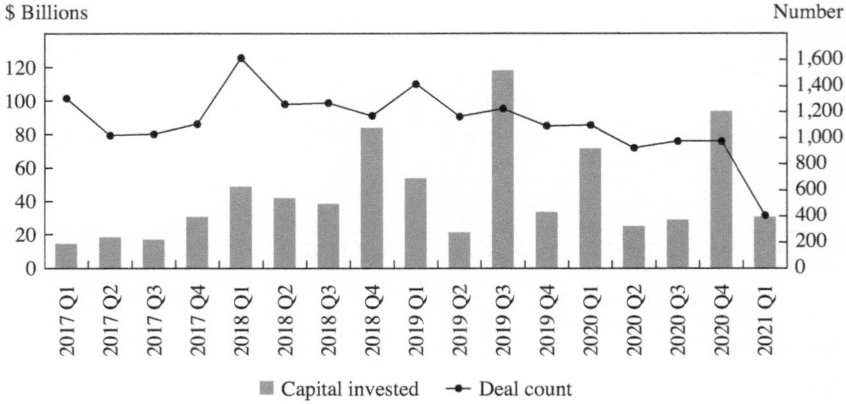

Source: Based on data from KPMG (2020) and PitchBook Data (n.d.).

Note: Total global investment activity (venture capital, private equity, and mergers and acquisitions) in Fintech.

overlay system) or by creating a stand-alone system. Overlay systems build a mobile or web interface that improves the ease with which customers can send and receive payments. These systems then use existing payments infrastructure, such as credit card or retail payment systems, to process and settle payments. Apple Pay and Google Pay are examples of such systems. They allow users to store debit and credit card information on their mobile devices, and allow payments using the device rather than the physical card. They are not fundamental, disruptive innovations. They are front-end services providing an improved user interface, but the payments are transferred using traditional systems. These services typically are not regulated because they provide the customer interface or point-of-sale payment instructions to allow customers to initiate payments. Meanwhile, the back end of the system is unchanged.

Stand-alone payment providers, on the other hand, offer closed-loop systems that do not depend on the existing payments infrastructure (except when they require a bank account to withdraw or top up funds). Alipay in China and M-Pesa in Kenya are examples.[8] In these arrangements, payments are processed, cleared, and settled by the platform provider independently of any other system. In contrast to the examples of Apple Pay and Google Pay, stand-alone providers are providing services similar to what a bank offers (i.e., a correspondent bank). Therefore, in most jurisdictions, stand-alone payment providers would be regulated or overseen by banking authorities. Alipay and M-Pesa are truly innovative payment systems, but they tend to remain mostly domestic.

What Fintech Does Well

The entry of Fintech lenders has brought innovations and improved efficiency. Buchak and others (2018) study Fintech lenders in the market for residential mortgages. They argue that the growth in their market share can be explained by differences in regulation and technological advantages. They find that Fintech lenders serve more creditworthy borrowers (relative to shadow banks) but charge higher interest rates (14–16 basis points), which is consistent with the idea that consumers are willing to pay for better user experience and quicker decisions. Fuster and others (2019) study the differences between Fintech and traditional lenders in the mortgage market and find that Fintech lenders process applications 20 percent faster, without increasing loan risk. They also provide evidence that Fintech lenders adjust supply more elastically to demand shocks, and that they increase the propensity to refinance, especially among borrowers who are likely to benefit from it.

Overall, these results suggest that Fintech firms have improved the efficiency of financial intermediation in credit markets. As one would expect, they are gaining market shares. In its 2019 report on Fintech marketplace trends in the United States, Experian (2019) finds that Fintech firms more than doubled their share of unsecured personal loans, from 22.4 percent in 2015 to 49.4 percent in 2019. Fintech loans tend to be smaller ($5,548) than those of traditional lenders ($7,383).[9] The composition of the loan portfolios is also interesting. Fintech lenders seem to specialize in the middle of the distribution of credit risk: prime and near prime. They have more near-prime borrowers than do traditional lenders (33.6 percent compared to 27.8 percent), while they have about the same ratio of prime borrowers. Traditional lenders, on the other hand, tend to lend more to the extremes: they have more super-prime borrowers (6.8 percent compared to 5.5 percent for Fintech firms), but they also have more subprime borrowers (26.5 percent compared to 24.6 percent for Fintech firms) and deep subprime borrowers (2.9 percent compared to 1 percent for Fintech firms). Younger generations (Generations X, Y, Z) are increasingly likely to borrow from Fintech lenders.

Fintech and Banking

The entry of Fintech firms into banking is particularly relevant because banks offer large bundles of financial services. A crucial question, then, is whether these services can be unbundled by Fintech firms. To understand the issue, we must have a theory of banking services. What is a bank?[10] There are two traditions in the banking literature. One tradition focuses on the asset side and proposes the following answer: banks make loans. More precisely, banks have a particular expertise in the screening and monitoring of borrowers, as well as in the risk management of pools of loans. The other tradition focuses on the liability side and answers as follows: banks take deposits. This tradition argues that banks are defined first and foremost by their deposit-taking franchise and their ability to provide liquid savings to their depositors. Both traditions can be challenged by Fintech.

The "banks make loans" tradition emphasizes banks as delegated monitors of borrowers, as in the model of Diamond (1984). Banks have information-processing abilities that are not available to the general public. They can screen and monitor borrowers. This theory relies on returns to scale in information processing. It does not rely on banks being able to issue deposits. In that view, one could argue that all financial firms making loans should be treated as banks. This view is consistent with the long history of merchant banking.

The "banks take deposits" view argues that the defining feature of banks is their ability to engineer safe and liquid liabilities that are valued by savers. These liabilities also facilitate transactions, as in the model of Gorton and Pennacchi (1990). According to this view, money market funds are (narrow) banks. This view is consistent with the fact that essentially all banks are predominantly financed by deposits. Over the past century, deposits have accounted for about 80 percent of bank assets. Other financial firms do not have the same stability over time and across firms.

A synthesis of these two views emphasizes the complementarities between loan making and deposit taking. It seeks to explain the connections between the structure of assets and the structure of liabilities. According to this view, a bank is an institution that makes loans, takes deposits, and benefits from the synergies between the two activities. Hanson and others (2015) emphasize that banks hold both loans and securities. These securities are (mostly) non-Treasury bonds. They tend to be relatively illiquid and volatile, such as mortgage-based securities and collateralized mortgage obligations. On the liability side, they show that deposits are a stable source of funding. On balance, they argue that the deposit franchise defines banks to a larger extent than the loan franchise. While all banks rely heavily on deposits, these researchers estimate that, in the United States on average over the past forty years, a bank at the 10th percentile of the distribution had a ratio of securities to assets of 6.9 percent, whereas for a bank at the 90th percentile, the ratio was almost six times higher, at 40.7 percent. Although lending is a core banking activity, it does not determine the size and scope of banks. The mix of loans and securities varies a lot across banks. Hanson and others argue that the deposit-taking franchise is more important: a bank with a large deposit franchise will be large, but not necessarily by making a lot of loans. It could instead be holding securities.

This discussion is not academic or theoretical; it goes to the heart of the regulation of Fintech. For example, in a recent case in front of the US Second Circuit Court of Appeals, the New York State Department of Financial Services superintendent argued that only deposit-taking institutions are banks. As a result, New York and other states want to prevent the Office of the Comptroller of Currency from issuing national banking charters to institutions that only make loans or process payments, activities that predominantly define the current Fintech landscape.[11]

Two Issues

What role will Fintech play in the future? There are two important issues here. The first is whether Fintech will democratize access to financial services. Fintech uses digital technologies, and many have argued that these technologies have a tendency to create "winner takes all" outcomes.[12] The fundamental economic issue is that of fixed versus marginal costs. Digital technologies have relatively high fixed costs and low marginal costs. I will study this issue in the next section and conclude that Fintech is likely to improve access to financial services. I will also discuss the risk of new inequalities and biases.

The second issue, discussed in section 4 of the chapter, is what regulatory challenges are created by Fintech and how they should be managed. One set of challenges revolves around fraud and regulatory arbitrage. These challenges are not specific to Fintech. All disruptive technologies create them. What is specific here is that financial regulations are particularly heavy, so the scope for arbitrage is larger. Another challenge revolves around the regulation of algorithms. Regulating algorithms is not the same as regulating behavior, and the approach to regulation must be adapted.

Fintech and Access to Financial Services

Sahay and others (2020) introduce a "digital" financial inclusion index that aggregates digital payment services provided through mobile phones and the internet, and compare it to a "traditional" financial inclusion index for services provided by traditional financial institutions. Their sample covers a diverse group of fifty-two countries, including emerging markets and developing economies, over the period 2014–2017. They find that digital inclusion increased over the period while traditional inclusion remained stable.

Philippon (2019) analyzes two features of new financial technologies that have stirred controversy: returns to scale and the use of big data and machine learning. I argue that the nature of fixed versus variable costs in robo-advising is likely to democratize access to financial services. Big data is likely to reduce the impact of negative prejudice in the credit market, but it could reduce the effectiveness of existing policies aimed at protecting minorities.

The Bright Side: Lower Cost Per Client

Philippon (2019) models increasing returns in the context of asset management and robo-advising. Search costs imply that wealthy households have access to better advice. I find that robo-advising and related technologies will change the nature of fixed costs in a way that is likely to improve access to financial services. The main intuition is that fixed technological costs are spread among all users, and thus, in equilibrium, the bulk is paid by wealthy households. To the extent that it is cheaper to offer the same technology to all clients, this amounts to a cross-subsidy from wealthy to less wealthy households. A good example is the development of an online banking app, which represents a large fixed cost. Banks are willing to invest in the app because their wealthy clients demand this service. But once the app is constructed, it is offered to all clients because it would be costly and inefficient to maintain two different apps. Less wealthy households, therefore, also benefit from the high-quality app. The cross-subsidy is limited only by the possibility to charge separately for some advanced features. While this will certainly happen, it will not be as prevalent as it was with human-based personalized advising.

Indeed, Abraham, Schmukler, and Tessada (2019) show that robo-advisers, because they save on fixed costs (such as salaries of financial advisers or maintenance of physical offices), can reduce minimum investment requirements and lower fees. This is exactly the prediction of my theoretical analysis in Philippon (2019). The key takeaway from this analysis is that, by lowering the fixed cost per relationship, Fintech allows more households to benefit from advisory services. The fact that Fintech might require higher up-front cost does not matter because the rich pay the lion's share of fees that serve to cover the fixed cost of setting up the robo-adviser. Once this cost is paid, less wealthy households benefit from cheaper services.

An important lesson here is that the nature of fixed costs matters a great deal for welfare. The welfare properties of fixed "coding" costs are fundamentally different from those of fixed costs per client. Notice, however, that these cost dynamics may not reduce inequality among all groups. They simply lower the threshold for access to high-quality services, reducing the gap between the rich and the middle class. But they may increase the gap between the middle class and the poor if the latter are still priced out.

Big Data in Credit Origination

The second force is the use of big data and machine learning. In Philippon (2019), I illustrate how this force plays out in the context of consumer credit. I argue that this technology is likely to reduce unwarranted human biases against minorities, but it will probably decrease the effectiveness of existing regulations. I return to this issue in the next section on regulatory challenges.

The advent of Fintech is often seen as a promising avenue for reducing inequality in access to credit. Bartlett and others (2019) study this issue, analyzing the role of Fintech lenders in alleviating discrimination in mortgage markets. They find that all lenders, including Fintech, charge minorities more for the purchase and refinance of mortgages, but that Fintech algorithms discriminate 40 percent less than face-to-face lenders. Regarding the use of new technologies in credit markets, Berg and others (2019) analyze the information content of the "digital footprint" (an easily accessible piece of information for any firm conducting business in the digital sphere) for predicting consumer default. They find that the predictive power of these new data equals or exceeds that of traditional credit bureau scores. Their results suggest that new technologies and new data might bring a superior ability for screening borrowers. How valuable these new data really are, however, remains an open question.

A Pitfall: Targeting

An important caveat must be borne in mind. Financial innovation can increase the targeting of consumers based on their financial sophistication, and this can have negative consequences for inclusion and equity. Ru and Schoar (2020) find that less educated people are more likely to be offered credit cards with higher late- and over-limit fees, with more back-loaded fees, and with contracts that use shrouded language. Firms are aware of the interaction between rent extraction and credit risk, in particular the fact that shrouded language attracts borrowers who do not understand risk and might borrow too much. The authors find that banks are more likely to rely on shrouded fees, especially for less educated customers, when unemployment insurance is more generous, as that is seen to lower their credit risk.

The targeting of unsophisticated households makes consumer protection more difficult. For instance, the CARD Act of 2009[13] in the United States was meant to protect consumers, and while it is true that banks cut overdraft and late fees, they made up for those reductions with low introductory interest rates and increasingly back-loaded fees.

The rise of Fintech will affect these issues and create new ones. One primary issue is the regulation of algorithms. Will machine learning exploit behavioral biases?

Takeaway and the Fintech Promise for Emerging Markets

Broadly speaking, then, my analysis is complementary to that of Sahay and others (2020). My analysis provides a theoretical justification (returns to scale, big data, machine learning) for the success of Fintech in reaching more individuals and firms. Sahay and others provide evidence on increasing financial inclusion in a large sample of countries in recent years, triggered by digital services. They show that democratization of financial services is indeed happening. They document a number of benefits: accessibility (including mobile phones), lower cost of intermediation, flexibility (you can sit at home in the middle of the night and pay your bills and apply for loans), user friendliness, greater customization, and higher efficiency.

There are several risks, however, some of which are more salient in emerging markets. Fintech could increase the risk of financial fraud. While Fintech per se does not create new types of financial stability risks, regulators must ensure that Fintech firms satisfy prudential requirements for capital and liquidity. A risk that is more specific to Fintech is that it could create new sources of financial exclusion. Regulators are rightly concerned about digital and financial literacy, which can create a large divide between high- and low-income households, men and women (notably in emerging markets and developing economies), and big and small nonfinancial firms. Finally, biases can exist in historical data and/or algorithms that can perpetuate discrimination, as discussed later.

Another broad issue is access to human and physical capital. Fintech firms can only fulfill their promise if they can rely on efficient electricity grids and digital infrastructure. Upgrading and maintaining these infrastructures could be a challenge in some poor countries. Perhaps even more important, Fintech relies intensively on human capital. The shortage of coders is affecting lower-income countries much more than countries such as the United States or China, and addressing this shortage should be a priority for policymakers.

Regulatory Challenges

Some key regulatory challenges are associated with the rise of Fintech. I address them here, and I make the case for new types of regulations to address the new challenges.

Fraud and Arbitrage

Innovative firms succeed because they do not play by the same rules as older firms. This fact, however, has markedly different implications depending on which set of rules is being challenged. New firms always challenge old technology and old ways of doing, and this is overwhelmingly a good thing.

New firms also engage in regulatory arbitrage. The successes of Uber and Airbnb are clear examples of both kinds of disruptions. New firms in finance are no different. They introduce technological innovations, and they engage in regulatory arbitrage.

What is different in finance, however, is the size and complexity of existing regulations. For better or for worse, finance is one of the most regulated industries. This creates barriers to entry as well as large opportunities for regulatory arbitrage.

A light-touch approach to regulation for Fintech firms is useful. British regulators have pioneered the idea of a sandbox—a lighter framework that allows young firms to grow—and the idea has caught on around the world, particularly in Asia. The framework released by the Hong Kong Securities and Futures Commission in 2019 allows digital asset exchanges to be licensed and regulated under a new sandbox-style approach, although it is limited to providers with at least one virtual asset considered to be a security.

There can be a fine line, however, between sandboxing and complacency. The case of the German Fintech Wirecard provides a striking reminder of this tension.

Wirecard

Wirecard, based in Munich, was a payment-processing company listed on the Frankfurt Stock Exchange and included in the Deutscher Aktien Index (DAX) from September 2018 until its demise in 2020. Figure 4-6 shows the spectacular rise in Wirecard's stock price from 2015 to September 2018. Starting in 2019, a series of investigations, notably by the *Financial Times* (FT), challenged the company's reported performance.[14] In June 2020, following an audit by Ernst & Young, Wirecard admitted that it had "misplaced" €1.9 billion. The money was supposed to be located in two banks in the Philippines. In fact, it never existed. The chief executive officer (CEO) was fired and later arrested, and the company went bankrupt.

The rise and fall of Wirecard illustrates many key aspects of financial fraud: innovation, rapid growth, complexity, and regulatory failures, as well as the crucial importance of journalists and whistleblowers. The success of Wirecard was based on rapid geographic expansion and the introduction of new products, such as virtual prepaid cards and fraud prevention software. Wirecard Asia Pacific was launched in Singapore (2007), and the company expanded to Australia, New Zealand, South Africa, and Turkey (2014), and to the United States (2016).

The Wirecard case is also an illustration of the important role of a free press. The FT's Dan McCrum published his first piece on the Wirecard saga in 2015 on *Alphaville*, the famous financial blog of the FT.[15] He argued that Wirecard's numbers did not seem to add up. Following a new piece in 2016, motivated by a report written by investors (the Zatarra report), Wirecard and its chief operating officer (COO) tried to intimidate the FT's reporters.[16]

As in most cases of fraudulent accounting, important breakthroughs came from whistleblowers. At Enron, for instance, in the summer of 2001, Vice President Sherron Watkins wrote a memo to the CEO, Kenneth Lay,

FIGURE 4-6. **Wirecard Stock Price History**

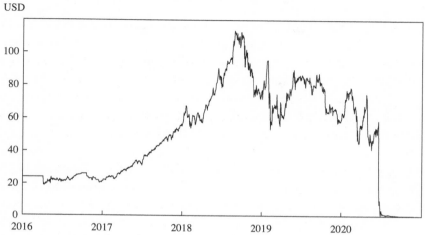

Source: Yahoo Finance.

showing that the company's accounts were fraudulent. She maintains that she is the "only whistleblower in any kind of modern history that has a positive story," because Enron imploded before the company had time to pursue its retaliatory plans.[17] For her whistleblowing, she was named one of *Time*'s Persons of the Year in 2002. In the Wirecard case, Dan McCrum and his colleague Stefania Palma met with whistleblowers in Singapore in the fall of 2018 and learned the details of the fraud, leading to a series of articles in 2019 that revealed in particular the construction of fictitious money flows using nonexistent business partners.

The Wirecard case is also, and perhaps most important, the story of a massive failure by German regulators. If it had ended in 2019, the Wirecard story would have been just another accounting-fraud scandal revealed by courageous journalists and whistleblowers. But German regulators decided to add insult to injury. Instead of promptly investigating and shutting down Wirecard, thereby limiting the eventual losses for investors, the Federal Financial Supervisory Authority (BaFin) decided to ban short selling and to investigate the journalists.

Going after short sellers is not exactly new. It happens all the time. For instance, it happened recently in the case of the French retailer Casino, whose parent company was bankrupt and was an early adopter of creative accounting. The French regulator also opened investigations into short sellers.[18] But that did not include opening a criminal investigation against journalists.

Intimidation tactics are not new either. But in the case of Wirecard, the magnitude and styles were somewhat new and might be a preview of what can be expected in the future. For instance, Wirecard reportedly hired hackers, including the Indian company BellTroX InfoTech, to go after its critics.[19]

The Wirecard fiasco contains a couple of lessons for regulators and market participants.[20] One obvious lesson is that, precisely because financial regulations are quite heavy, a company that manages to get around the regulations gains a significant advantage. Another lesson is that Fintech founders are digital natives, and some come from a hacking culture. They may thus be more likely to use digital tools to commit fraud and intimidate whistleblowers and journalists who are an important source of information for regulators.[21]

Data Ownership and APIs

The growth of Fintech also increases the salience of the data-ownership issue. A successful open-banking ecosystem requires a good protocol for application programming interfaces. In an open-banking framework, third-party financial service providers have access to consumer financial transaction data from banks through the use of APIs. APIs define standardized methods of interactions that govern and execute data flows between different systems. A single interoperable technology and data-sharing protocol enables entrants to focus on customer-facing innovations instead of on the "plumbing" of transactions. It also improves audit and regulatory compliance.

Clear and consistent customer data ownership needs to be at the core of any open-banking model. Jurisdictions differ in how close they are to meeting this requirement. The European Union's Second Payment Services Directive (PSD2)[22] is relatively clear, but the situation in the United States is more confused. The Dodd-Frank Act,[23] Section 1033, introduces the notion that consumers own their financial data, and a 2018 US Treasury report recommends that the government clarify that "access" to a consumer's financial data includes third-party access permitted by the consumer.[24] The US Consumer Financial Protection Bureau agrees, but its data-sharing principles are nonbinding.

Agreeing on a model for liabilities has been one of the more contested and difficult issues for policymakers across jurisdictions. The liability framework drives a significant portion of the economic risk that banks and nonbanks must bear in a third-party data-sharing arrangement. A prerequisite to a clear, evenly applied apportionment of liability is the concept of traceability. Traceability means the ability to track—using registries, encoded headers, and other tools—the path taken by users' data after the consumer's consent to using a third party. With traceability, regulators are able to assign a higher degree of certainty for fault through a kind of forensic ledger that allows them to appropriately assign liability for a data breach. The concern from incumbent financial institutions is that third-party Fintech firms are new and often untested. As a result, they might not be able to pay in case the liability is large.

An open issue for regulators and market participants is to provide a solution that protects the customer and the soundness of the original custodian, while ensuring that customers have competitive products. If a third party cannot pay under PSD2, the liability for making the customer whole rests as a contingent liability on the balance sheet of the cyber risks insurance market that has provided coverage to the third party. Understanding the extent of the various types of claims and situations of fault remains an outstanding issue in the European Union, and requires additional work to limit circumstances where a customer suffers a loss and requires compensation yet the insurer is not compelled to act.

Regulating Algorithms: Liabilities, Prejudice, and Statistical Discrimination

Regulatory institutions need to be upgraded to deal with the regulation of algorithms, as doing so is much different from regulating human actors. Regulators will need new technology, data, and flexibility to run experiments and learn.

The traditional approach, based on human compliance, is to follow pre-specified steps. Digital compliance is different. The codification of actions and regulation has three effects: (1) it makes the actions (the code) more observable, which is good for monitoring and reduces moral hazard, but (2) it might increase existing biases (e.g., machine learning exploiting behavioral biases), and (3) it creates unknown liabilities. Suppose, for instance, that an artificial intelligence (AI) system identifies a group in the data—say, "alcoholic." Can it use that information? Lend less and be liable for discrimination? Lend more and be potentially liable for exploiting an observable weakness? There is no guidance today, but maybe there will be in the future and the lines of code could make the lender liable.

Regulators will also need to monitor how machines learn. In this process, AI can be used in two ways. First, it can be used to replicate human decisions. If there is no direct outcome measure, human biases will persist and in fact will get worse as machines learn to perfect human biases. Second, AI can be used to optimize an objective outcome; in that case, the machine will eventually learn the unbiased signal and be likely to improve welfare.

The key point here regarding discrimination is to make sure that algorithms are trained on actual outcome variables. In other words, we would not want to train the machines to simply replicate existing human choices.

The improvement one can expect from AI depends on the underlying model of discrimination: AI can successfully fight discrimination based on prejudice (as defined in the work of Becker, 1957), but can reinforce statistical discrimination (discrimination based on biases resulting from imperfect information, as defined in the work of Arrow, 1973, and Phelps, 1972).

Conclusion: Fintech, Big Tech, and the Future of Competition in the Finance Industry

One way to conclude this chapter is to envision how the finance industry will evolve over the next five or ten years. There are now three sets of players in the finance industry: traditional intermediaries such as banks, insurance companies, and funds, which are all expanding their IT spending; Fintech firms, which are trying to expand their reach beyond their niche markets; and big tech firms that are becoming more involved in finance, such as Alipay and Ant Financial in China, and Apple Pay and Amazon Pay in the United States. Cornelli and others (2020) find that Fintech and big tech credit reached about $225 billion and $575 billion globally, respectively, in 2019. Big tech credit has grown particularly quickly in Asia (China, Japan, Korea, and Southeast Asia), and in some countries in Africa and Latin America. An open question is how competition between these players is going to shape the evolution of the industry.

What, then, are the possible scenarios for the future? And what are the key factors? We can distinguish three main forces at play:

1. Returns to scale and network effects: how large are they really?
2. China: to integrate into the global financial system or not to integrate?
3. Big tech: to enter more segments of the financial market or not to enter?

Returns to Scale

Technological returns to scale and network effects will influence the degree of concentration in the industry. The increasing application of new technologies in finance can democratize access to financial services for consumers, as discussed earlier, but at the same time they can increase concentration among providers.

The degree of returns to scale and network effects will influence the relationships between Fintech firms and traditional banks, in particular the extent to which they compete or collaborate. They will also influence the entry of big tech in finance. Some small Fintech firms cater to niche markets and fill gaps left by traditional banks, while digital banks compete more directly with traditional banks. In between these extremes lies a continuum of collaboration and competition. For instance, Fintech firms pay a service fee and let traditional banks deal with compliance issues related to anti-money laundering and combating the financing of terrorism. Some traditional banks in turn buy specific services from Fintech companies to modernize their digital platforms.

The growth of Fintech firms will depend importantly on their access to data. Data sharing matters for consumer protection but also for competition. We need smart regulation of data sharing, because simply limiting data sharing across firms might reinforce the market power of incumbents. Note, however, that it is not the data per se that give market power. It is the control of bottlenecks, or the control of consumers' intentions (such as through digital platforms that exercise control over apps on smartphones, over maps, or over search links). Data provide a way to keep control of these bottlenecks. The policy implication is that regulatory efforts should have an important focus on digital platforms that act as bottlenecks and gatekeepers.

China

Today, China is commercially integrated into the global economy, but financially it is still mostly isolated. This is the case despite the rapid growth of Chinese banks over the past fifteen years. American banks were globally dominant at the end of the Bretton Woods era in the 1970s. Japanese and European banks later increased their market shares, so that by the 1990s Japan and Europe accounted for about 70 percent of big banks' assets. In 2018, large Chinese banks accounted for around 25 percent of global banking assets, which was higher than China's share of global GDP (slightly less than 17 percent). Even though some Chinese banks are among the largest in the world today, most of their assets and liabilities are domestic. Chinese banks are not integrated into the global financial system to the extent one would expect given the size of the Chinese economy and its dominance in global trade.

When we consider Fintech, China is arguably the most advanced and innovative country in the world. As in the case of traditional banking, however, its achievements in Fintech are so far mostly domestic.

A crucial question facing Chinese policymakers is whether to let China's financial system become more globally integrated. The answer remains highly uncertain as it depends on how Chinese leadership perceives its economic and political interests. What is clear, however, is that their choices will have global consequences. China is forecast to reach 21 percent of global GDP by the mid-2020s. Assuming that its ratio of banking assets to GDP remains what it is, China could by then account for more than 30 percent of global banking assets. Given their rapid growth, Chinese Fintechs could hold a significant fraction of these "banking" assets.

Big Tech

Big tech firms are also challenging incumbent banks. They are rapidly gaining traction in the provision of financial services in China, and they are also becoming active in other regions, including in other parts of Asia and in Africa and the Americas.[25] These firms have large, developed customer networks established through e-commerce platforms or messaging services, and they can apply their unique technological expertise to the provision of financial services. Their collection of proprietary data and use of technology, increasingly including advanced practices such as AI and machine learning, allow these firms to gather significant information on their users to help tailor their offerings to individual customers' preferences. These advantages give these firms the potential to become significant players in the finance industry.[26]

COVID-19 is accelerating the transition to the digital economy, but in doing so it is deepening inequality between firms. It is increasing the clout of big tech firms as they expand market shares. Tech firms in general are doing well. Gompers and others (2020) find relatively small negative effects on investments by venture capitalists, who report that 52 percent of their portfolio companies are positively affected or unaffected by the pandemic, and only 10 percent are severely negatively affected. This stands in sharp contrast to other small businesses. Alekseev and others (2020) find that 61 percent of small businesses in the United States experienced a negative shock and lost, on average, over half their business. Only about 56 percent of small businesses expected to survive if the conditions in late April 2020 were to continue longer than six months.

It is far from clear, however, that big tech firms intend to offer standard banking and insurance services. Several reasons can explain their reluctance. The first reason is the weight of traditional banking regulations. In addition, antitrust regulators are already worried about the footprint of big tech firms, and they would carefully monitor their entry into financial services. The comparative advantage of big tech lies in its use of big data, but privacy concerns are growing and might prevent big tech companies from leveraging their technological advantage. Finally, the entry of big tech will depend on the extent to which banking services can be unbundled. Big tech firms are unlikely to become universal banks, but they might want to offer some banking services. They would become significant players only if these services could be unbundled from the rest.

Scenarios and Regulatory Response

By combining the above factors, we can imagine a set of scenarios for the finance industry. If returns to scale and network effects are moderate, one would expect an "enhanced status quo" scenario whereby traditional banks and Fintech continue to engage in a balanced mix of collaboration and competition. Big tech firms would mostly stay out of mainstream finance and only provide certain specialized services, such as payment apps. The role of regulators would then be to ensure compliance with data protection and financial integrity/accountability, and to avoid control of bottlenecks by firms that would give them excessive market power and capacity to charge high transaction fees.

If returns to scale are large, a "concentration" scenario becomes likely. The finance industry would presumably attempt to consolidate. Regulators would then need to avoid excessive consolidation that would lead to market dominance by a few providers.

If network effects are large, a "big tech entry" scenario cannot be excluded. The resulting competition with other financial services providers could enhance consumer welfare, but regulators would need to carefully monitor data privacy and market dominance by a few digital gatekeepers. With network effects and returns to scale, Chinese financial intermediaries could also play a key role in the evolution of the global finance industry.

NOTES

I am grateful to Ratna Sahay for her comments. All mistakes are mine.

1. Using the Survey of Consumer Finances, Moore and Palumbo (2010) document that, between 1989 and 2007, the fraction of households with positive debt balances increased from 72 percent to 77 percent. This increase is concentrated at the bottom of the income distribution. For households in the 0 to 40 percentiles of income, the fraction with some debt outstanding went from 53 percent to 61 percent between 1989 and 2007. In the mortgage market, Mayer, Pence, and Sherlund (2009) show that subprime originations accounted for 15 to 20 percent of all Home Mortgage Disclosure Act (HMDA) originations in 2005.

2. For discussion and references, see Acharya and others (2016).

3. The Basel framework is a set of global standards for banking regulations. See Bank for International Settlements (n.d.).

4. FSB (2020).

5. FSB (2020).

6. KPMG (2020).

7. Petralia and others (2019).

8. McGath (2018).

9. Experian (2019).

10. For an illuminating discussion, see Hanson and others (2015).

11. See Brooks and Calomiris (2020).

12. See, for example, Stafford (2019).

13. The Credit Card Accountability Responsibility and Disclosure Act of 2009.

14. See McCrum (2020).

15. See McCrum (2015).

16. See Zatarra Research and Investigations (2016). Wirecard's COO, Jan Marsalek, was a shadowy character with contacts in Russian secret services who hired private investigators in several countries and used wide-ranging social media misinformation and surveillance tactics.

17. National Whistleblower Center (n.d.).

18. See Smith and Fletcher (2019).

19. See Scott-Railton and others (2020).

20. See also Langenbucher and others (2020).

21. Dyck, Morse, and Zingales (2010).

22. The PSD2, which came into effect in January 2018, is an EU directive to regulate payment services and payment service providers.

23. The Dodd-Frank Wall Street Reform and Consumer Protection Act is financial regulatory system reform legislation enacted in January 2010 in the aftermath of the financial crisis.

24. US Department of Treasury (2018).

25. See Frost (2020).

26. BIS (2019) and FSB (2019).

REFERENCES

Abraham, Facundo, Sergio Schmukler, and Jose Tessada. 2019. "Robo-Advisors: Investing Through Machines." World Bank Research and Policy Briefs (Washington, DC: World Bank). https://ssrn.com/abstract=3360125.

Acharya, Viral V., Lasse Heje Pedersen, Thomas Philippon, and Matthew Richardson. 2016. "Measuring Systemic Risk." *Review of Financial Studies* 30, no. 1, pp. 2–47.

Alekseev, Georgij, Safaa Amer, Manasa Gopal, Theresa Kuchler, J. W. Schneider, Johannes Stroebel, and Nils Wernerfelt. 2020. "The Effects of COVID-19 on U.S. Small Businesses: Evidence from Owners, Managers, and Employees." NBER Working Paper 27833 (Cambridge, MA: National Bureau of Economic Research).

Arrow, Kenneth. 1973. "The Theory of Discrimination," in *Discrimination in Labor Markets*, edited by Orley Ashenfelter and Albert Rees (Princeton University Press).

Bank for International Settlements. n.d. "Basel III: International Regulatory Framework for Banks." www.bis.org/bcbs/basel3.htm.

Bank for International Settlements. 2019. *Big Tech in Finance: Opportunities and Risks.* Annual Report. www.bis.org/publ/arpdf/ar2019e3.pdf.

Bartlett, Robert, Adair Morse, Richard Stanton, and Nancy Wallace. 2019. "Consumer-Lending Discrimination in the FinTech Era." NBER Working Paper 25943 (Cambridge, MA: National Bureau of Economic Research).

Basel Committee on Banking Supervision. 2020. *Basel III Monitoring Report* (Basel, Switz.).

Bazot, Guillaume. 2013. "Financial Consumption and the Cost of Finance: Measuring Financial Efficiency in Europe (1950–2007)." Unpublished manuscript.

Becker, Gary. 1957. *The Economics of Distribution* (University of Chicago Press).

Berg, Tobias, Valentin Burg, Ana Gombović, and Manju Puri. 2019. "On the Rise of FinTechs: Credit Scoring Using Digital Footprints." *Review of Financial Studies* 33, pp. 2845–97.

Brooks, Brian P., and Charles W. Calomiris. 2020. "Fintech Can Come Out of the Shadows." *Wall Street Journal*, September 9.

Buchak, Greg, Gregor Matvos, Tomasz Piskorski, and Amit Seru. 2018. "Fintech, Regulatory Arbitrage, and the Rise of Shadow Banks." *Journal of Financial Economics* 130, pp. 453–83.

Cornelli, Giulio, Jon Frost, Leonardo Gambacorta, P. Raghavendra Rau, Robert Wardrop, and Tania Ziegler. 2020. "Fintech and Big Tech Credit: A New Database." BIS Working Paper 887 (Basel, Switz.: Bank for International Settlements).

Diamond, Douglas W. 1984. "Financial Intermediation and Delegated Monitoring." *Review of Economic Studies* 51, pp. 393–414.

Dyck, Alexander, Adair Morse, and Luigi Zingales. 2010. "Who Blows the Whistle on Corporate Fraud?" *Journal of Finance* 65, pp. 2213–53.

Experian. 2019. "Fintech vs. Traditional FIs: Trends in Unsecured Personal Installment Loans." https://www.experian.com/blogs/insights/2019/09/fintech-vs-traditional-fis-latest-trends-personal-loans/.

Financial Stability Board. 2019. *FinTech and Market Structure in Financial Services: Market Developments and Potential Financial Stability Implications* (Basel, Switz.).

Financial Stability Board. 2020. *Evaluation of the Effects of Too-Big-to-Fail Reforms: Consultation Report* (Basel, Switz.).

Frost, Jon. 2020. "The Economic Forces Driving Fintech Adoption across Countries." BIS Working Paper 838 (Basel, Switz.: Bank for International Settlements).

Fuster, Andreas, Matthew Plosser, Philipp Schnabl, and James Vickery. 2019. "The Role of Technology in Mortgage Lending." *Review of Financial Studies* 32, pp. 1854–99.

Gompers, Paul, Will Gornall, Steven Kaplan, and Ilya Strebulaev. 2020. "Venture Capitalists and COVID-19." NBER Working Paper 27824 (Cambridge, MA: National Bureau of Economic Research).

Gorton, Gary, and George Pennacchi. 1990. "Financial Intermediaries and Liquidity Creation." *Journal of Finance* 45, pp. 49–72.

Hanson, Samuel G., Andrei Shleifer, Jeremy C. Stein, and Robert W. Vishny. 2015. "Banks as Patient Fixed-Income Investors." *Journal of Financial Economics* 117, pp. 449–69.

KPMG. 2020. *Pulse of Fintech H1'20.* September. https://assets.kpmg/content/dam/kpmg/xx/pdf/2020/09/pulse-of-fintech-h1-2020.pdf.

Langenbucher, Katja, Christian Leuz, Jan Pieter Krahnen, and Loriana Pelizzon. 2020. *What Are the Wider Supervisory Implications of the Wirecard Case?*

European Parliament Study. www.europarl.europa.eu/RegData/etudes
/STUD/2020/651385/IPOL_STU(2020)651385_EN.pdf.

Mayer, Christopher J., and Karen Pence. 2008. "Subprime Mortgages: What,
Where, and to Whom?" NBER Working Paper 14083 (Cambridge, MA:
National Bureau of Economic Research).

Mayer, Christopher, Karen Pence, and Shane M. Sherlund. 2009. "The Rise
in Mortgage Defaults." *Journal of Economic Perspectives* 23, pp. 27–50.

McCrum, Dan. 2015. "The House of Wirecard." *Financial Times*, April 27.

McCrum, Dan. 2020. "Wirecard and Me: Dan McCrum on Exposing a Criminal Enterprise." *Financial Times*, September 2.

McGath, Thomas. 2018. "M-PESA: How Kenya Revolutionized Mobile Payments." *N26 Magazine*, April 9.

Moore, Kevin B., and Michael G. Palumbo. 2010. "The Finances of American
Households in the Past Three Recessions: Evidence from the Survey of Consumer Finances." Unpublished manuscript.

National Whistleblower Center. n.d. "How Whistleblowers Changed the
World." www.whistleblowers.org/how-whistleblowers-changed.the world/.

Petralia, Kathryn, Thomas Philippon, Tara Rice, and Nicolas Véron. 2019.
*Banking Disrupted? Financial Intermediation in an Era of Transformational
Technology.* 22nd Geneva Report on the World Economy (Geneva: Centre
for Economic Policy Research).

Phelps, Edmund. 1972. "The Statistical Theory of Racism and Sexism." *American Economic Review* 62, no. 4, pp. 659–61.

Philippon, Thomas. 2015. "Has the US Finance Industry Become Less Efficient? On the Theory and Measurement of Financial Intermediation."
American Economic Review 105, pp. 1408–38.

Philippon, Thomas. 2019. "On Fintech and Financial Inclusion." NBER
Working Paper 26330 (Cambridge, MA: National Bureau of Economic
Research).

PitchBook Data. n.d. https://pitchbook.com/data.

Ru, Hong, and Antoinette Schoar. 2020. "Do Credit Card Companies Screen
for Behavioural Biases?" BIS Working Paper 842 (Basel, Switz.: Bank for
International Settlements).

Sahay, Ratna, Ulric Eriksson von Allmen, Amina Lahreche, Purva Khera,
Sumiko Ogawa, Majid Bazarbash, and Kim Beaton. 2020. *The Promise of Fintech: Financial Inclusion in the Post COVID-19 Era* (Washington, DC: International Monetary Fund).

Scott-Railton, John, Adam Hulcoop, Bahr Abdul Razzak, Bill Marczak, Siena
Anstis, and Don Deibert. 2020. *Dark Basin: Uncovering a Massive Hack-for-
Hire Operation.* Citizen Lab (University of Toronto).

Smith, Robert, and Laurence Fletcher. 2019. "Casino Affair Raises Tough
Questions for French Regulator." *Financial Times*, June 6.

Stafford, Philip. 2019. "Winner-Takes-All Digital Economy Poses Risks for Capital Markets." *Financial Times*, December 9.

US Department of Treasury. 2018. *A Financial System That Creates Economic Opportunities: Nonbank Financials, Fintech, and Innovation.*

Zatarra Research and Investigations. 2016. *Wirecard's Underhand Practices and How It Incriminated Itself.* www.yumpu.com/en/document/read/56361488/wwwzatarra-researchcom.

FIVE

Automation, Jobs, and Wages

Should Workers Fear the New Automation?

HARRY J. HOLZER

At least as far back as two centuries ago, when the Luddites were sabotaging factory equipment in Britain, workers in industrial countries have periodically feared that their jobs were threatened by automation. In the United States, the automation scare of the late 1950s and early 1960s—soon after the public became aware of the rising power of mainframe computers—was one more recent episode of widespread fear regarding automation and jobs.

At some level, these fears have been misplaced. A few centuries of industrialization and automation in more developed economies have generated no sign of permanent large-scale reductions in employment; to the extent that automation displaces some workers from their jobs, enough new jobs have always been created to generate relatively full employment over time.[1]

On the other hand, there are often some workers left worse off by this process—not just those directly displaced, but also others whose earnings are lowered by the machines with which they have to compete. The COVID-19 pandemic has likely accelerated the speed with which digital technology will displace less-educated workers in industries like retail trade or leisure and hospitality, where online shopping and telecommuting will now more rapidly replace sales workers in brick-and-mortar retail, or those serving food or coffee to office workers in the downtown areas of major cities.

In the current environment, at least some analysts[2] fear that "this time is different"—in other words, that the unprecedented power of the coming generation of robotics and artificial intelligence (AI) will create job losses large enough to overwhelm the adjustment process. These fears have driven new policy proposals such as a "robot tax," as well as calls for a publicly provided universal basic income for all workers.[3] And the pace of such automation, along with fears about its impacts, will likely accelerate as the COVID-19 pandemic increases the use of online shopping in retail and telecommuting in many industries.

This chapter reviews the economics of automation and the labor market, and then describes the "new automation" and how it will likely play out in terms of employment, wages, and inequality. It also reviews some implications for public policy. The discussion is relevant for all industrialized economies, though the chapter's particular focus is on the United States.

The Economics of Technological Change and the Labor Market

As MIT economist David Autor asked in a 2015 paper, if automation replaces workers, and it has occurred so continuously for a few centuries, why are there still so many jobs?

Economists have a fairly standard set of answers to this question. They go roughly as follows:

- Automation raises productivity and reduces the costs of producing goods and services.
- Lower production costs generate lower consumer prices on those goods and services.
- Price decreases raise consumers' real income and cause them to spend more overall.
- Price decreases on these particular goods and services (relative to others) also raise consumers' purchases of them.

As a result, consumer spending rises both within the industry being automated and elsewhere. The extent of such higher spending depends on the magnitudes of what economists call income and price elasticities of demand. The income elasticity of a product is the extent to which purchases of it rise when consumer income rises, while the price elasticity is the extent to which purchases of the product rise when its price declines.

Automation can thus potentially raise employment in a given industry, even while it reduces the labor needed per unit of production, if it reduces prices sufficiently to generate large increases in overall product demand; in such cases, the percentage increase in production outweighs the percentage decline in labor needed per unit. This famously happened when Henry Ford created the first assembly line early in the twentieth century to produce his Model T. Price reductions were so substantial that middle-class Americans of that era could afford purchases of automobiles for the first time, generating enormous growth in jobs in auto production. Another such episode occurred in the 1980s and 1990s, when the prices of personal computers dropped dramatically and purchases of them became very common; the same happened for cellular phones in the early 2000s.

On the other hand, if price reductions and income elasticities are not sufficient to generate enough new product demand to offset per-unit reductions in labor demand, then employment in the automating industry might decline, but the higher real incomes generated should still raise demand for other goods and services, and employment should rise as production rises to meet that new demand. This process should continue until sufficient new demand has occurred to generate new jobs for all in the labor market who might need them.[4]

Of course, even if overall employment remains constant over time despite automation, and even if employment in the automating industry is rising, some workers could still be worse off than they were before the automation was implemented. Indeed, two groups of workers are likely hurt: those directly displaced by the new machines, and those with skills similar to those displaced, in the same or other industries, who now face lower demand for their labor, thus facing lower wages and/or employment.

For any new technology embodied in some new form of equipment (or capital, in the lingo of economists), most workers can be considered either complements or substitutes for that technology. The complements are those who face rising demand for their services after the new technology is implemented; the most obvious example would be the engineers who create and improve the new technology and the technicians who maintain it. The substitutes, however, are those workers who do (or have done) what the machine now does more efficiently, and who consequently face falling demand for their labor services.

Those substitutes who are directly displaced by the machines suffer large employment losses in the short term, and often have relatively lower wages if and when they are reemployed.[5] Others in the same or other industries face no such immediate declines, but may suffer stagnant or falling wages for years afterward. Indeed, one of the primary explanations for the declining relative earnings of less-educated workers in the United States during the past four decades has been that digital technologies have generated skill-biased technical change (SBTC), in which automation has reduced the demand they once faced in the labor market. The owners of the capital in which the new technologies are embedded have likely benefited from this automation as well.[6]

Though other forces have no doubt also been at play in raising labor market inequality, including institutional factors (like declining unionism and minimum wage levels), many mainstream labor economists regard SBTC as the most prominent explanation of recent increases in labor market inequality in the United States and other industrial countries.[7] Indeed, the most negative impacts of digital technologies have been suffered by those performing routine manual work such as manufacturing on assembly lines and office clerical work, while the same technologies have raised the demand and relative earnings of college-educated workers as well as those performing more social tasks (which cannot be so easily digitalized) in low-wage service jobs.[8]

The resulting "polarization" in the labor market, and declines in both wages and employment for less-educated middle-skill workers, has been a major contributor to the increases in labor market inequality since 1980.[9] And a recent paper by Acemoglu and Restrepo (2020) finds that the wave of digital automation that started in the 1980s generated relatively few new jobs over time for the unskilled workers it displaced.

It is also worth noting that substitutability or complementarity with new automation is not usually an either/or proposition; a given group of workers may be substitutable in some ways and complementary in others. In this case, the degree of substitutability will depend on the exact set of tasks performed by the worker before and after the automation has been implemented. If the majority of their working time has been spent on tasks that the automation completes more efficiently, they are likely more substitutable than complementary—unless they can fairly easily switch to a new set of tasks, like machine maintenance or quality control, which can turn them into complements.

Of course, if employers feel that their incumbent workers have underlying skills that they still value—whether general or specific to the occupation or industry—or that the recruiting and training costs of replacing them are high, they might choose to invest in some on-the-job retraining to help the workers become more complementary to the new automation, thereby avoiding permanently laying them off. But in other cases, employers might decide that they are better served by hiring new workers who already have the complementary skills the employer seeks, or who can be more efficiently trained to become such complements.

More broadly, workers can make a set of adjustments to become more complementary to automation, either at the same firm, at a different firm in the same industry, or in a new industry. For instance, they can invest in their own education or training to learn a new skill set, or they can relocate to a new region of the country where their skills are in higher demand. Of course, making these investments can be costly, without any guarantee that the worker will accrue the expected rewards. And the new investments are made more easily by some workers—often those who are younger or already more educated—than others who are older and less educated.

Thus, displaced manufacturing or clerical workers who are middle-aged and have only a high school education or less are more likely to be permanently displaced and suffer large earnings losses than those who are younger or more educated. The latter will generally find it easier to obtain some additional education and a credential that is now in higher demand.[10] Similarly, younger and more-educated workers will more easily relocate to a new state or region than those older and less educated; the former will more frequently obtain the necessary information and bear the costs and risks of the geographic move.[11]

As an example, recent evidence suggests that imports of manufacturing goods from China, in the wake of their being admitted to the World Trade Organization (WTO) in 2001, generated large employment losses for less-educated workers in the United States,[12] especially those residing in smaller metropolitan areas of the Midwest (in states like Pennsylvania, Ohio, Michigan, and Wisconsin). These geographically concentrated job losses have generated large employment disparities across US regions, with large and growing numbers of workers who do not relocate in response to such dis-parities.[13] This clearly indicates the high perceived costs of adjusting for less-educated workers in the distressed regions.[14] And the worker discontent generated in those regions and elsewhere has contributed to growing political populism, in the United States and many other industrialized countries.

The New Automation: Is This Time Different?

While industrial economies in the past and present have always shown an ability to create enough new jobs to replace those that have become auto-mated, some commentators fear that the coming wave of robotics and AI—especially when combined with globalization—will be much more power-ful than any forms of automation that we've observed to date, and will therefore hurt more workers over time.

For instance, technology entrepreneur Elon Musk predicts that "robots will be able to do everything better than us. . . . It is the biggest risk we face as a civilization. . . . There will certainly be a lot of job disruption."[15]

Somewhat less fatalistic but still alarming is the perspective of econo-mist Richard Baldwin (2019). Writing about the interplay of globalization and robotics (which he calls "globotics"), he argues that "globotics is dif-ferent for two reasons: It is coming inhumanly fast, and it will seem unbe-lievably unfair. . . . [It] is advancing at an explosive pace . . . injecting pres-sure into our socio-politico-economic system (via job displacement) faster than our system can absorb (via job replacement)." Economist Frank Levy and political scientist Darrell West similarly argue that job displacement in major industries will soon generate major economic disruption that will fuel even greater political polarization and antidemocratic populist responses.[16]

These predictions are based on the notion that robotics and AI will gain the power relatively soon to do vastly more human functions than has ever been true in the past. The Massachusetts Institute of Technology (2019) report *The Work of the Future* argues, "As robots gain flexibility and situa-tional adaptability, they will certainly take over a large set of tasks in ware-houses, hospitals, and retail stores—such as lifting, stocking, transporting, cleaning, as well as awkward physical tasks that require picking, harvest-ing, stooping and crouching."

But the reach of AI, embodied in robots as well as other forms of automation, will go far beyond such physical tasks. By using machine learning and algorithms to process vast quantities of data and continuously update its analytical and predictive power, AI will increasingly be able to recognize complex patterns in such data and make judgments on actions to take in a wide range of circumstances and environments.[17] These environments will include unregulated traffic situations, financial markets, and human health care; in each, machine learning will enable AI to quickly analyze data, predict outcomes, and choose how to respond in ways that outpace what many millions of workers now do. And, according to Baldwin, machines abroad as well as domestically will be able to participate in such functions and contribute to job displacement.

At the same time, the speed with which these new technologies are implemented can be overstated. For one thing, a physical and human infrastructure will be needed to implement and maintain new forms of automation like autonomous vehicles. Organizations may need years to adapt to these changes and to reorganize workplaces in ways that maximize the productive use of the new automation.[18]

Accordingly, the productivity gains and cost reductions associated with robotics and AI may be small for some time, perhaps reducing the incentives of many firms to quickly implement them—especially if the costs of firms buying and implementing the new technology are relatively high for a while. And even when such automation is implemented, a newer version of the "Solow paradox" of the 1980s and early 1990s—in which evidence of productivity gains was very limited for about fifteen years, despite ongoing adoption of digital automation in workplaces—may once again be observed, further inducing firms to adopt such technologies relatively slowly.[19]

Even after firms have implemented the new automation, their need for complementary human workers to make a range of judgments that robots or AI will not be able to make—such as those involving "ethical judgment, emotional intelligence, artistic taste and the ability to define tasks well"[20]—will no doubt remain, though in an evolving form. And workers will then face incentives to adapt by learning to perform new tasks as much as possible, and their employers will have some incentives to help them do so.

Still, implementation of new robots and AI may be rapid enough to displace workers and generate rising inequality over the next few decades.[21] Implementation in industries such as advanced manufacturing, transportation and warehousing, retail, and leisure/hospitality could lead to large job losses among less-educated workers, while in health care, accounting, finance, and the legal professions it could lead to displacements among more highly educated workers too.

To empirically assess the potential of the new robotics and AI to displace humans and generate new jobs, we can review two very recent empirical literatures: the latest estimates of the extent to which robots and other forms of new software have very recently displaced workers in manufacturing and some services; and predictions regarding future displacements based on data on occupational tasks and their automatability.

The most recent empirical evidence regarding employer adoption of robots appears in Acemoglu and Restrepo (2017) and Borjas and Freeman (2019). Their data begin in 1990 and 2004, respectively, but track the implementation of robots and their impacts on employment and earnings well into the last decade (2010–2019). Acemoglu and Restrepo find that each extra robot per 1,000 workers reduces employment by 0.18–0.34 of a percentage point and wages by 0.25–0.50 percent among workers in affected industries. The magnitudes of impacts estimated by Borjas and Freeman are relatively similar, and are largest for the least-educated workers—clearly indicating that SBTC remains a strong feature of recent robotics.

Similarly, Webb (2020) finds negative impacts on employment and earnings of the least-educated workers in occupation/industry combinations that faced relatively greater exposure to robots in the period 1980–2010—using a very different statistical methodology from that used by Acemoglu and Restrepo or Borjas and Freeman to measure occupation and industry exposure to robots (more on this later).

Of course, all three of these studies focus primarily on manufacturing industries, where the penetration to date of robots has been the highest. But Webb also estimates the impacts of new kinds of computer software in a range of occupations and industries—like parking lot attendants, plant or equipment operators, and packers and packagers. Again, he finds displacement associated with software implementation and negative impacts on worker employment and earnings, though with smaller differences across education groups than he observes from robotics.

While all of these papers are convincing, they only estimate short-run impacts on employment and earnings of workers; any subsequent positive impacts on employees, especially after firms and workers have had time to adjust to them, are not captured there. But in contrast to the pessimistic findings of Acemoglu and Restrepo (2020) cited above, a few new papers estimate such positive effects.

For instance, using company-level data in manufacturing between 2003 and 2015, Chandler and Webb (2020) show that British firms that automated their machine tooling enjoyed higher rates of survival in response to low-price Chinese imports, and that employment increased both within these firms and in their local labor markets. Bessen and others (2019), using Dutch data on a wider range of industries from 2000 onward, similarly find that firm-level employment grows in firms that automate and declines in those that do not.

Together, these papers imply that less-skilled workers face displacement risks when firms automate, but that employment subsequently grows in these firms, presumably for workers performing different tasks from those displaced.[22] Furthermore, the rate of technological implementation and displacement is not fixed ex ante but responds to a range of different economic factors—such as pressure from low-wage imports (as in Chandler and Webb) or rising costs due to recent minimum wage increases.[23]

Institutional factors matter as well—for instance, technological displacement is lower for union than for nonunion workers.[24] More broadly, when workers have some "voice" in their workplaces, new technology is implemented in more worker-friendly fashions,[25] and workers are more likely to receive training to perform tasks that are complementary to the new machines.

Of course, as all these papers use data from recent decades, they remain more backward looking than forward looking. A different group of papers is more directly predictive of future automation and its employment impacts. They begin with data on the task content of occupations—such as the Occupational Information Network (O-NET) data of the US Department of Labor, or the Programme for the International Assessment of Adult Competencies (PIAAC) survey data of the Organization for Economic Cooperation and Development (OECD).[26] They then match the occupational task data with other data on the extent to which various tasks will be automatable in the near future, where the latter are drawn from surveys of computer scientists or patent applications.

Together, these data are used to infer which occupations, and therefore which workers, face varying risks of displacement. Such a methodology was first used by Frey and Osborne (2013) and Arntz, Gregory, and Zierahn (2016). It has been more recently applied to the entire range of occupations in OECD countries by Nedelkoska and Quintini (2018), who estimate that approximately 9 percent of workers in current occupations in the United States face "high risk" of displacement in the next few decades (with relatively similar rates in most other OECD countries). *High risk* refers to those in occupations where more than 70 percent of tasks will be automatable. About another 30 percent face at least "moderate risk" of displacement, defined as 50–70 percent of tasks being automatable. The least-skilled workers in occupations such as food preparation assistant, cleaner and helper, assembler, and vehicle/plant operator face the highest average risk of displacement—around 60 percent. Those in the health, legal, and accounting professions face 30–35 percent risk, implying that they might more easily gain new skills to replace the ones made obsolete by automation. In these analyses, future automation is still clearly regarded as being skill biased.

But Webb's (2020) predictions regarding AI specifically are different from these, and are also different from his own predictions regarding past robotics or software implementation. In a new methodology that he applies retrospectively (and convincingly) to robotics and software employment but prospectively to AI, he uses text analysis of recent patent applications and measures correlations between word pairs found there and in the O-NET occupational task descriptions. These correlations imply greater risk of task displacement among workers with more education, which peak at the 90th percentile of educational attainment across occupations before falling off. The fact that he gets results that are very similar to those of other researchers on robotics, but very different results for AI, suggests that these technologies have very different impacts from each other on workers by educational category, potentially putting most workers at risk of displacement one way or the other. His results are also consistent with more qualitative predictions by Baldwin (2019), who argues that white-collar services will become much more internationally tradable than before, placing white-collar workers at much greater risk of displacement in the future than has been the case so far.

But even if AI and other forms of coming automation generate greater risks of task displacement for more-educated workers than for less-educated ones, the ability of the former to adapt by learning new skills that complement the new automation will no doubt be higher as well, especially among younger more-educated workers.

This will likely be true for a number of reasons. First, American employers invest vastly more in on-the-job training for their professional and managerial employees than for all others.[27] This is likely because on-the-job training is essentially an investment by the firm in its "human capital," and such investments pay off more for employees with stronger basic skills and work performance, who are also more likely to stay longer with any given firm.[28] Of course, as noted above, these factors are not carved in stone and will vary with institutional characteristics such as worker "voice" and unionism.

But there is also a second reason why highly educated employees will adjust better to displacement risks: they will likely choose to reinvest in postsecondary education much more frequently than less-educated workers facing similar displacement risks. All else constant, highly educated workers will have much more knowledge of and positive experiences with postsecondary education, more information about coming displacement risks and new skills for which demand will remain high, and more resources with which to pay for such education.

A third reason for the likelihood of better adjustments to automation among more-educated workers can be found in evolving institutional changes in many workplaces. Not only is it true that "voice" mechanisms such as unions are declining rapidly among the less-educated employees whom they have traditionally helped the most (at least in the private sector); there is also a growing tendency of firms to outsource the employment of their nonprofessional and nonmanagerial employees to outside contractors, a phenomenon labeled "fissuring" by David Weil (2014, 2019). While hard data on the incidence of fissuring are still scant, it appears to have risen quite a lot in Weil's anecdotal data.

The implications of fissuring for the ability of workers to adapt to automation could be profound. For instance, it is much less likely that firms will invest in training employees who actually work for another company. Furthermore, employees in fissured workplaces are much less likely to share in the product market gains of successful companies than are regular employees; they therefore have even less reason to prolong their tenure at these firms if they are not treated as long-term assets worthy of investment.[29]

Fissuring is just one dimension of a broader trend in which the quality of jobs available to US workers seems to be declining, even controlling for their skills. Some analysts worry about the disappearance of regular full-time work as employers turn their workers into independent contractors and perhaps will increasingly rely on the "gig" or "app" economy for their workers. To date, these trends look relatively small, and the new types of jobs at least sometimes provide the flexibility and self-management that many workers enjoy.[30] But these trends may grow a great deal more over time.[31]

There is also separate evidence that employers are increasingly choosing low labor costs as their dominant mode of competing, rather than "high-road" strategies where they invest more in the skills of their workers and compete on the basis of quality rather than only low cost. Research finds that employers can, at least sometimes, compete effectively through a "good-jobs" or high-road strategy,[32] and such strategies would enable workers to share more of the benefits of technical innovation. But there is little evidence that many employers are choosing this road.[33]

Overall, then, the above analysis implies that future automation and even AI will likely continue to be skill biased and, therefore, contribute to growing labor market inequality. Does this necessarily mean that less-educated workers will be worse off in the future? And what other labor market trends will interact with automation to generate positive or negative outcomes for workers?

The brightest prospect associated with future automation is that, all else equal, it should raise average worker productivity, which in turn should result in higher average compensation for workers.[34] Of course, the extent to which productivity will really rise, rather than reflect what Acemoglu and Restrepo call "so-so" technologies that simply reduce employer labor costs rather than raise productivity, is an open question.[35] And the extent to which rising productivity actually increases median wages is another.[36]

But a few other labor market trends that affect the labor market context in which automation will advance are also relevant here. First, demographers project a rise in the nonwhite fraction of the US population, with likely lower educational attainment than those of native-born whites. Of course, the exact magnitude of these changes depends on immigration rates, which have declined in the United States in recent years, especially among those from Latin America, who often arrive with lower attainment than those from other origins.[37] If these projections are true, then the postsecondary education levels of Americans will be lower and more unequal as well, impeding the ability of a larger proportion of workers to adapt to automation.

Second, rising inequality along with high rates of job displacement and limited adjustments will likely cause many workers to withdraw from the labor market rather than accept the prospect of lower wages. Indeed, labor force participation among less-educated men in the United States has already declined in recent years.[38] This has likely been caused, at least partly, by their declining wage prospects.[39] But other developments, such as criminal records, disability, and opioid dependency, have also contributed to these trends.[40] And an aging population will be one more source of lower labor force participation, especially if immigration does not rebound from its recently lower levels.

Third, if labor force participation continues to drop and firms experience a new set of skill demands after they automate, shortages in such skills might well become more commonplace in the labor market.[41] This could lead to more disruption in production, unless it motivates employers and educational institutions to invest more in adapting to these conditions.

Overall, automation in the United States, and more generally in industrialized economies, not only will be disruptive, but will occur in the context of other demographic and labor market changes that will perhaps magnify the challenges it creates.

Policy Implications

Given the challenges that many workers will face over time from automation—especially those without college degrees—we need a robust policy agenda in the United States and other industrialized economies to help them adjust to this reality.

An appropriate policy agenda would include the following elements:

- improvements in education and workforce development systems, so workers at risk of displacement or lower wages can become more complementary to automation;
- encouragement to employers to use automation to create good jobs;
- "making work pay" with wage subsidies or tax credits to enhance the value of the many low-wage jobs that automation will likely generate; and
- sensible retirement and immigration policies to adjust to the realities of a changing labor market.

The policy details discussed below focus primarily on the United States, but a similar agenda could be developed in virtually any industrialized

economy where automation poses potentially large benefits to some workers and large risks to others.

Education and Workforce Development

There are a variety of ways in which we can improve the abilities of workers to develop skills that are more complementary with, and less substitutable by, the coming automation. These approaches include providing more
instruction in "twenty-first-century skills" for children and youth; enabling
more workers to update their skills, either before or after a potential layoff
from automation; and encouraging employers to retrain incumbent workers whenever possible, rather than displace them.

TWENTY-FIRST-CENTURY SKILLS. Scholars have identified a set of skills that
are likely to remain complementary with automation, even in the era of AI.[42]
These include critical thinking, creativity, communication, and other social
skills that can be used with coworkers as well as clients and customers.

Of course, these are general cognitive and socio-emotional skills that
can be useful in almost any work context, and that will also help workers
adapt to new automation and reskill if/when they must. They are the skills
most frequently developed in general K–12 education as well as liberal arts
programs at two-year and four-year colleges, rather than those that are
more specific to an occupation or industry. Indeed, specific training may
carry a higher risk of becoming obsolete in a more dynamic labor market
with a lot of technological change, where automation might come to perform the specific tasks now done by welders, machinists, drivers, health
technicians, and the like.

But does this imply that we should discourage such specific training,
and turn everyone into a liberal arts major in college? Not at all. While the
average return to a four-year degree in liberal arts appears to be higher in
the long run than that in science, technology, engineering, or mathematics
(STEM), according to David Deming (2019), this is not likely true for each
student/worker, and likely not for those in two-year programs. Indeed, the
labor market value of the terminal associate in arts degrees is very low,
while certificates in technical and some other high-demand fields have rea-
sonably good market value.[43] And digital or information technology (IT)
skills are growing increasingly important in a wide range of nontechnical
occupations (like those in retail and warehouse, as well as communications

and finance), regardless of whether they require four-year college degrees or not.[44]

In addition, the evidence suggests that sector-based training programs—where community colleges work with employers to train workers for high-demand fields—can have very high returns for low-income workers.[45] The same can be said about apprenticeships,[46] which have been successfully used to enhance the skills and earnings of noncollege workers in Germany, Switzerland, and many other European Union (EU) countries.

So we should continue to support workers who can obtain these kinds of training, despite their specificity; we can do this with more support for community colleges and for workforce training, along the lines that I have outlined elsewhere.[47] If the specific skills these workers obtain then become obsolete, we should help them retrain, with some of the additional approaches noted below.

ENABLING WORKERS TO UPDATE SKILLS. How can we help workers whose skills become (or are likely to be) obsolete because of automation reskill? One approach is through lifelong-learning accounts, in which workers can set aside a bit of their payroll each month that they can use if/when they need to retrain.[48] Among other industrialized countries, France has recently created individual lifelong-learning accounts to address labor shortages in higher-skilled occupations experiencing rising demand.[49] Of course, training programs in higher-education institutions also would need to scale up and become more accessible to working older students for these efforts to truly be successful.

In addition to funding, workers who retrain will also need a broad range of supporting workforce services, such as labor market information and career guidance, along with help reconnecting to community colleges and other postsecondary institutions. Better career guidance for students at community colleges is sorely needed,[50] whether it is provided directly on campus or at the One Stop centers (now called American Job Centers) funded by the Workforce Innovation and Opportunity Act (WIOA). More financial support for these services should be explicitly provided in the Higher Education Act or WIOA or both. And while the track record of online higher education to date is mixed at best,[51] the kinds of online education that would make it easier for working adults to retrain should be further developed. The COVID-19 pandemic has dramatically demonstrated the scope for scaling up online learning tools. New digital platforms like Task Rabbit and Amazon Mechanical Turk, which improve the matching of workers with particular skills to jobs where they are needed, can help as well.

ENCOURAGING EMPLOYERS TO RETRAIN RATHER THAN DISPLACE. For workers at high risk of layoff due to automation, perhaps we can offer tax credits plus technical assistance that encourage employers to retrain the workers instead. The history of state tax credits or subsidies for incumbent worker training has some success stories,[52] though political support for them has always been limited. In light of public fears over displacement from automation, these programs deserve new scrutiny and support.

A complementary approach to subsidizing retraining might be to modestly tax worker displacement associated with new automation. Arguments for a general "robot tax" (which Elon Musk and Bill Gates have sometimes recommended) do not seem persuasive, given that such a tax could discourage productivity-enhancing investments. But a displacement tax makes more sense, given the broader social costs created when workers are displaced.[53] Indeed, the US unemployment insurance system already imposes higher taxes on employers who frequently lay off workers (a practice known as "experience rating"); adding an additional modest displacement tax at the federal level could be viewed simply as an attempt to strengthen that system in the face of likely rising displacements associated with automation.

Together, taxes on displacement along with subsidies for on-the-job training might incentivize firms to implement automation in a more worker-friendly way, with less displacement and more adjustment for incumbent workers.

Encouraging the Creation of Good Jobs

There is an argument for rewarding employers who create "good" (or well-paying) jobs, especially for employees without college degrees, even in the absence of automation, since those employers create a "public good."[54] But in a world where automation might raise the rewards both for the owners of capital and for highly skilled workers, while decreasing them for the less skilled, the argument to support more good-job creation becomes even more compelling.

A variety of mechanisms are in place that federal, state, or local governments could use to encourage more good-job creation in an automating labor market. These could include tax credits[55] or grants, technical assistance, preference in public procurements and contracts, and even the bully pulpit. Absent a strong base of evidence on exactly what works cost effectively in this area, experimentation and evaluation of approaches that cities or states might adopt to encourage the creation of good jobs should be high on the agenda.

And given the evidence cited above—that, all else equal, unions lead to more worker-friendly implementation of automation by employers—the need for American workers (and those elsewhere) to have some voice in the workplace, whether through unions or via other mechanisms (like work councils in the EU), remains strong.[56] The near disappearance of unions in the private sector in the United States has likely made the effects of new technologies on incumbent workers more negative than it otherwise would have been.

Making Work Pay

The idea of expanding wage subsidies for low-wage workers, as a way to both improve their incomes and incentivize more work, has been recommended for decades.[57] In the United States, the Earned Income Tax Credit, which provides a nearly 50 percent subsidy for workers in low-income families, has become the largest cash-assistance program to the poor. Ideas for strengthening this program, and making it more supportive for groups who now receive fairly little (like childless adults), are a high priority.[58]

A similar idea designed to support dislocated rather than poor adults is wage insurance. Under this proposal, workers who are displaced from a better-paying job—for example, one that pays $20 per hour—and who can now only earn $10 per hour would receive a cash payment from the government that makes up perhaps half the difference (or $5 an hour) for some number of years. This would incentivize displaced workers to remain in the labor force at lower-wage jobs, rather than simply to drop out. Unemployment insurance reforms that rationalize the amount and duration of benefits, such as those recently implemented in France, could also potentially encourage greater job search and offer acceptance among the unemployed.[59] The US unemployment insurance system is already more stringent (in terms of worker eligibility, wage replacement, and duration of coverage) than those in most EU countries.[60]

In addition, other policies might also help workers remain attached to the workforce when their only options are low-wage jobs. For instance, providing paid family leave to workers who care for newborns or other family members might enable those workers to remain attached to jobs instead of leaving the labor force altogether;[61] improved subsidies for child care for low-income workers would likely do the same.

Of course, these options, as well as some of those mentioned earlier, entail fiscal costs. At least in the United States, where one political party (the Republicans) has mostly pledged to never raise taxes at the federal level, generating increases in revenue seems difficult. A broad-based effort, spanning taxes and expenditures, to restore fiscal sanity should be a high priority as well—not least to fund the labor market services that are needed for an era of high automation and displacement.

Retirement and Immigration Policies

As the native-born population ages and labor force participation declines—at least partly due to displaced workers leaving the labor force—there is a strong case to be made for policies that discourage early retirement and replenish the labor force with more immigrants.[62] These policies would bolster labor force and economic growth, and also help deal with the federal fiscal crisis that Baby Boomer retirements are already beginning to create.[63]

We could discourage earlier retirements simply by raising the retirement age, especially in an era of improving longevity overall. On the other hand, given recently observed decreases in longevity and increases in "deaths of despair" among working-class Americans,[64] this alone might not now be the best approach. Other, complementary measures have been widely discussed, including efforts to make workplaces more friendly to senior workers.[65]

As for immigration, policies should encourage higher rates of immigration to the United States, rather than the decreases now occurring.[66] The benefits of high-skill immigration to the US economy are quite obvious, and include benefits like more innovation and more business start-ups.[67] At the same time, there is sufficient evidence that low-skill immigrants might substitute at least a bit for noncollege native-born workers. So some tilting of the immigration system toward more higher-educated workers is warranted, which to some extent is already happening.[68] On the other hand, the economic benefits of even low-skilled immigrants should not be discounted. And the elements of comprehensive immigration reform that have been defined in previous legislative efforts in the United States—such as more legal immigrants, enforcement against illegal immigrants, and a path to legality and even citizenship for those already here—remain compelling.

One policy that has recently been much debated is universal basic income, or UBI.[69] The case for it does not seem very persuasive. It makes much more economic sense to help workers adjust to automation rather than pay them to withdraw from the labor market. In a world where the population is aging in many industrialized countries, and the fiscal costs of paying for retirement programs are already so high, UBI would exacerbate problems. The policy options discussed above are more practical, both economically and fiscally.

Conclusion

The labor market effects of automation, in the United States and other industrialized countries, will likely be somewhat similar to what we have seen in the past several decades—with both displacements and rising inequality—only more so. The pace of such developments could well accelerate, as the COVID-19 crisis has increased our reliance on digital shopping, remote work from home, and other automated efforts. And there is some evidence that AI could displace workers much higher in the skill distribution than those previously affected.

But there are also a range of investments that can make workers more complementary with new automation, and public policies should encourage that. We can make twenty-first-century skills more central in K–12 education systems, complementary skills (or high-demand sector-based) training at community or four-year colleges more accessible, and employer retraining (rather than displacement) more attractive. Other policies—such as rewards for creation of good jobs, wage subsidies to make work pay, and updated immigration and retirement policies—can address some of the unintended consequences of automation, at the same time that changing demographics and labor market institutions complicate its effects.

It is possible that the benefits of the new automation will mostly accrue to the owners of capital, or to those with the most technical (or other) skill sophistication, while millions of other workers face more threats from automation than gains. But the approaches outlined above could help ensure that whatever productivity gains AI and robotics generate—and they should be substantial—are widely shared by workers in all educational groups.

NOTES

I would like to thank Simeon Djankov, François Bourguignon, and other participants in the Brookings-KDI conference that generated this volume for helpful comments on an earlier draft.

1. This chapter abstracts from issues related to business cycles, including those generated by the COVID-19 crisis of 2020, which I assume to be mostly resolved over the next few years.

2. For example, Avent (2016).

3. Lowery (2018).

4. See Autor and Salomons (2018) for more evidence on these forces in the United States.

5. Farber (2017).

6. Autor and others (2017).

7. See Autor, Katz, and Kearney (2008) and Autor, Goldin, and Katz (2020) for evidence in favor of SBTC, while Card and Dinardo (2002) and Fortin, Lemieux, and Lloyd (2018) argue that institutional factors have been as or more important.

8. Autor (2010).

9. Holzer (2015) argues that there are "two middles" in the labor market: an older set of middle-paying jobs consisting mostly of clerical and production jobs that paid high school workers relatively well; and a "new middle" that requires some postsecondary education and credentials, as in health care or advanced manufacturing. The former has declined more rapidly than the latter has grown, leading to the appearance of a shrinking middle sector.

10. Jacobson, Lalonde, and Sullivan (2005).

11. See Bound and Holzer (2000).

12. Autor, Dorn, and Hanson (2016).

13. Austin, Glaeser, and Summers (2018).

14. Molloy and others (2016) provide evidence indicating a labor market that has generally grown more sluggish, where workers move less across geographic regions and between jobs.

15. West (2018).

16. Levy (2018) and West (2018).

17. Agrawal, Gans, and Goldfarb (2017).

18. Button (2019).

19. Nobel laureate Robert Solow famously argued that, in the late 1980s and early 1990s, we saw evidence of technological change everywhere but in the productivity numbers. But productivity growth then rose more substantially

between the mid-1990s and the mid-2000s before declining again. Questions about whether we are measuring productivity well enough to capture these gains have arisen as well. See Baily and Montalbano (2016). On the other hand, Acemoglu and Restrepo (2020) argue that even "so-so" technologies that have only mild positive impacts on productivity can be implemented rapidly enough by employers to generate substantial displacement.

20. Agrawal, Gans, and Goldfarb (2017).

21. Massachusetts Institute of Technology (2019).

22. Acemoglu and Restrepo (2018).

23. Aaronson and Phelan (2019).

24. Parolin (2020).

25. Helper, Martins, and Seamans (2019) and Kochan and Kimball (2019).

26. PIAAC is administered by the OECD in all its member countries to assess the performance of skilled tasks in the workplace. O-NET, provided by the US Department of Labor, supplies data on task performance in specific occupations. It has replaced the Dictionary of Occupational Titles from previous decades.

27. Lerman, McKernan, and Riegg (2004).

28. Mincer (1974) and Jovanovic (1979) were among the first economists to argue that employers will invest more in workers with higher predicted tenure with the firm; of course, investment in such training makes it more likely that the workers will stay, especially if the training is relatively more specific to a firm or industry and, therefore, less likely to be rewarded by employers in other jobs.

29. Weil (2019).

30. See Katz and Krueger (2019) for evidence on trends in workers becoming independent contractors, and Collins and others (2019) for evidence on app workers and the gig economy.

31. Sundarajan (2016).

32. Ton (2014) and Osterman (2018).

33. Ton (2014) presents a number of case studies of companies that embrace a good-jobs strategy to raise worker performance and productivity; Walmart is a company that has recently undertaken such a strategy. But declining unions and declining wages among workers with high school or less education broadly suggest that relatively few firms are embracing such strategies.

34. Stansbury and Summers (2017).

35. Brown (2019).

36. Groshen and Holzer (2019).

37. Hanson (2017).

38. Eberstadt (2016).

39. Economists refer to the relationship between work effort and market compensation as the labor supply function. While in theory this relationship

could be either positive or negative (or neither), empirical evidence suggests positive correlations (or elasticities) for most groups (McClelland and Mok, 2012).

40. Abraham and Kearney (2019) and Binder and Bound (2019).

41. Exactly how to define and measure worker or skill shortages is somewhat controversial among economists. See Barnow, Trutko, and Schede Piatak (2013).

42. National Academy of Sciences (2014).

43. Backes, Holzer, and Dunlop Velez (2015).

44. Burning Glass Technologies (2019).

45. Maguire and others (2010) and Roder and Elliott (2019).

46. Lerman (2018).

47. Holzer (2020). In that piece, I argue that the occupational training available at America's community colleges could be more accessible and more effective with greater investments in career guidance, institutional incentives to strengthen subsequent student employment outcomes, and stronger ties with the business community.

48. Fitzpayne and Pollack (2018).

49. Hughes (2018).

50. Holzer (2020).

51. Bettinger and others (2017).

52. Holzer and others (1993) and Hollenbeck (2008).

53. For instance, any specific skills in which workers have previously invested become obsolete, generating the large drops in earnings that we observe for them. Costly public resources are also consumed, through programs like unemployment insurance and disability insurance.

54. Holzer (2019b). When either low-wage or high-wage employment can be equally profitable for a given firm, the high-wage jobs they might choose to create constitute a public good. Private markets underprovide such goods unless subsidized.

55. Holzer (2019c).

56. Kochan and Kimball (2019).

57. For example, Phelps (1997).

58. Arguments for how to strengthen the Earned Income Tax Credit appear in Nichols and Rothstein (2015).

59. Ekins (2017). The reforms implemented in France cap unemployment insurance benefits, in both amount and duration, while extending coverage to the self-employed. This is combined with expansion of worker-training opportunities, including through portable learning accounts. More broadly, a number of EU countries undertook reforms in the first two decades of the twenty-first century to increase market flexibility and worker incentives to accept available jobs, including the Hartz reforms in Germany and the "flexicurity" policies in Denmark.

60. Wandner (2018).
61. Black, Whitmore Schanzenbach, and Breitwieser (2017).
62. Holzer (2019a).
63. Congressional Budget Office (2020).
64. Case and Deaton (2020).
65. For example, Munnell (2007). Various ways to make retirement and other benefits (like health care) more portable than they are now might be important as well (Katz, Poo, and Waxman, 2018).
66. Frey (2019).
67. Holzer (2019a).
68. Hanson (2017).
69. Lowery (2018).

REFERENCES

Aaronson, Daniel, and Brian Phelan. 2019. "The Evolution of Technological Substitution in Low-Wage Labor Markets." Policy Brief (Brookings Institution).

Abraham, Katharine, and Melissa Kearney. 2019. "Explaining the Decline in the US Employment-to-Population Ratio: A Review of the Evidence." NBER Working Paper 24333 (Cambridge, MA: National Bureau of Economic Research).

Acemoglu, Daron, and Pascual Restrepo. 2017. "Robots and Jobs: Evidence from US Labor Markets." NBER Working Paper 23285 (Cambridge, MA: National Bureau of Economic Research).

Acemoglu, Daron, and Pascual Restrepo. 2018. "The Race between Man and Machine: Implications of Technology for Growth, Factors Shares and Employment." *American Economic Review* 108, no. 6, pp. 1488–542.

Acemoglu, Daron, and Pascual Restrepo. 2020. "Unpacking Skill Bias: Automation and New Tasks." *American Economic Association: Papers and Proceedings*, vol. 110 (May), pp. 356–61.

Agrawal, Ajay, Joshua Gans, and Ari Goldfarb. 2017. *Prediction Machines: The Simple Economics of Artificial Intelligence* (Cambridge, MA: Harvard Business Review Press).

Arntz, Melanie, T. Gregory, and U. Zierahn 2016. "The Risk of Automation for Jobs in the OECD." OECD Paper (Paris: OECD Publishing).

Austin, Gerald, Edward Glaeser, and Lawrence H. Summers. 2018. "Saving the Heartland: Place-Based Policies for the 21st Century." Policy Brief (Brookings Institution).

Autor, David. 2010. *The Polarization of Job Opportunities in the US Labor Market*. Hamilton Project (Brookings Institution).

Autor, David. 2015. "Why Are There Still So Many Jobs? The History and Future of Workplace Automation." *Journal of Economic Perspectives* 29, no. 3, pp. 3–30.

Autor, David, David Dorn, and Gordon H. Hanson. 2016. "The China Shock: Learning from Labor Market Adjustment to a Large Shock in Trade." NBER Working Paper 21906 (Cambridge, MA: National Bureau of Economic Research).

Autor, David, David Dorn, Lawrence F. Katz, Christina Patterson, and John Van Reenen. 2017. "The Fall of the Labor Share and the Rise of Superstar Firms." NBER Working Paper 23396 (Cambridge, MA: National Bureau of Economic Research).

Autor, David, Claudia Goldin, and Lawrence F. Katz. 2020. "Extending the Race between Education and Technology." NBER Working Paper 26705 (Cambridge, MA: National Bureau of Economic Research).

Autor, David, Lawrence F. Katz, and Melissa Kearney. 2008. "US Wage Inequality: Revising the Revisionists." *Review of Economics and Statistics* 90, no. 2, pp. 300–23.

Autor, David, and Anna Salomons. 2018. "Is Automation Labor-Displacing? Productivity Growth, Employment, and the Labor Share." Brookings Paper on Economic Activity No. 1 (Brookings Institution).

Avent, Ryan. 2016. *The Wealth of Humans: Work, Power and Status in the 21st Century* (New York: Macmillan).

Backes, Ben, Harry J. Holzer, and Erin Dunlop Velez. 2015. "Is It Worth It? Postsecondary Education and Labor Market Outcomes for the Disadvantaged." *IZA Journal of Labor Policy* 4, no. 1, pp. 1–30.

Baily, Martin, and Nicholas Montalbano. 2016. "Why Is US Productivity Growth So Low? Possible Explanations and Policy Responses." Brief, Economic Studies (Brookings Institution).

Baldwin, Richard. 2019. *The Globotics Upheaval: Globalization, Robotics, and the Future of Work* (New York: Oxford University Press).

Barnow, Burt, John Trutko, and Jaclyn Schede Piatak. 2013. *Occupational Labor Shortages: Concepts, Causes, Consequences and Cures* (Kalamazoo, MI: W. E. Upjohn Institute for Employment Research).

Bessen, James, Martin Goos, Anna Salomons, and Wiljan van den Berge. 2019. "Automatic Reaction: What Happens to Workers at Firms that Automate?" Working Paper (Boston University).

Bettinger, Eric, Lindsay Fox, Susanna Loeb, and Eric S. Taylor. 2017. "Virtual Classrooms: How Online Courses Affect Student Success." *American Economic Review* 107, no. 9, pp. 2855–75.

Binder, Ariel, and John Bound. 2019. "The Declining Labor Market Prospects of Less-Educated Men." NBER Working Paper 25577 (Cambridge, MA: National Bureau of Economic Research).

Black, Sandra, Diane Whitmore Schanzenbach, and Audrey Breitwieser. 2017. *The Recent Decline in Women's Labor Force Participation*. Hamilton Project (Brookings Institution).

Borjas, George, and Richard Freeman. 2019. "From Immigrants to Robots: The Changing Locus of Substitutes for Workers," in "Improving Employment and Earnings in Twenty-First Century Labor Market," edited by E. Groshen and H. Holzer. *RSF: The Russell Sage Foundation Journal of the Social Sciences* 5, no. 5, pp. 22–42.

Bound, John, and Harry Holzer. 2000. "Demand Shifts, Population Adjustments, and Labor Market Outcomes in the 1980s." *Journal of Labor Economics*, 18, no. 1, pp. 20–54.

Brown, Sara. 2019. "The Lure of So-So Technology and How to Avoid It." *Sloan School of Management Newsletter* (Massachusetts Institute of Technology).

Burning Glass Technologies. 2019. *The New Foundation Skills of the Digital Economy*. Business Higher Education Forum (Washington, DC).

Button, Graham. 2019. *Augmentative AI and the Future of Work* (Stanford University Institute for Human-Centered Artificial Intelligence).

Card, David, and Jonathan Dinardo. 2002. "Skill-Biased Technical Change and Rising Inequality: Some Problems and Puzzles." NBER Working Paper 8769 (Cambridge, MA: National Bureau of Economic Research).

Case, Anne, and Angus Deaton. 2020. *Deaths of Despair and the Future of American Capitalism* (Princeton University Press).

Chandler, Daniel, and Michael Webb. 2020. "How Does Automation Destroy Jobs? The 'Mother Machine' in British Manufacturing, 2000–15." Unpublished manuscript (Stanford University).

Collins, Brett, Andrew Garin, Emilie Jackson, Dmitri Koustas, and Mark Payne. 2019. "Is Gig Work Replacing Traditional Employment? Evidence from Two Decades of Tax Returns." Working Paper (Washington, DC: Statistics of Income, Internal Revenue Service).

Congressional Budget Office. 2020. *The Budget and Economic Outlook: 2020–2030* (US Government Printing Office).

Deming, David. 2019. "In the Salary Race, Engineers Sprint but English Majors Endure." *New York Times*, September 20.

Eberstadt, Nicholas. 2016. *Men without Work: America's Invisible Crisis* (Washington, DC: American Enterprise Institute).

Ekins, Gavin. 2017. "France Seeks to Overhaul Taxes and Unemployment Insurance." *Global Tax Newsletter*, October 22 (Washington, DC: Tax Foundation).

Farber, Henry. 2017. "Employment, Hours and Earnings Consequences of Job Loss: US Evidence from the Displaced Worker Survey." *Journal of Labor Economics* 35, S1, pp. S235–S272.

Fitzpayne, Alistair, and Ethan Pollack. 2018. *Lifelong Learning and Training Accounts: Helping Workers Adapt and Succeed in a Changing Economy* (Washington DC: Aspen Institute).

Fortin, Nicole, Thomas Lemieux, and Neil Lloyd. 2018. "Labor Market Institutions and the Distribution of Wages: The Role of Spillover Effects." NBER Working Paper 28375 (Cambridge MA, National Bureau of Economic Research).

Frey, Carl Benedikt, and Michael Osborne. 2013. "The Future of Employment." Working Paper (University of Oxford).

Frey, William. 2019. "US-Born Gains Are Smallest in a Decade, Except in Trump States." Policy Brief (Brookings Institution).

Groshen, Erica, and Harry Holzer. 2019. "Improving Employment and Earnings in Twenty-First Century Labor Markets: An Introduction," in "Improving Employment and Earnings in Twenty-First Century Labor Market," edited by E. Groshen and H. Holzer. Special issue, *RSF: The Russell Sage Foundation Journal of the Social Sciences* 5, no. 5, pp. 1–19.

Hanson, Gordon. 2017. "Along the Watchtower: The Rise and Fall of Low-Skill Immigration." Policy Brief (Brookings Institution).

Helper, Susan, Raphael Martins, and Robert Seamans. 2019. "Who Profits from Industry 4.0? Theory and Evidence from the Automotive Industry." Working Paper (Stern School of Business, New York University).

Hollenbeck, Kevin. 2008. "Is There a Role for Public Support of Incumbent Worker On-the-Job Training?" Working Paper (Kalamazoo, MI: W. E. Upjohn Institute for Employment Research).

Holzer, Harry. 2015. "Job Market Polarization and Worker Skills in the US: A Tale of Two Middles." Policy Brief (Brookings Institution).

Holzer, Harry. 2019a. *Immigration and the US Labor Market: A Look Ahead.* Migration Policy Institute, Washington DC.

Holzer, Harry. 2019b. "The US Labor Market in 2050: Supply, Demand and Policies to Improve Outcomes." Policy Brief (Brookings Institution).

Holzer, Harry. 2019c. "Yes, Corporate Tax Cuts Can Raise Wages. Here's How." *Washington Post*, May 8.

Holzer, Harry. 2020. "Improving Workforce Success among America's College Students." Policy Brief (Brookings Institution).

Holzer, Harry, Richard Block, Marcus Cheatham, and Jack Knott. 1993. "Are Training Subsidies for Firms Effective? The Michigan Experience." *Industrial and Labor Relations Review* 46, no. 4, pp. 241–60.

Hughes, Joanna. 2018. "France Shifts Focus to Lifelong Learning." *Academic Courses.* https://www.academiccourses.com/news/france-shifts-focus-to-lifelong-learning-3105/.

Jacobson, Louis, Robert J. Lalonde, and Daniel Sullivan. 2005. "The Impacts of Community College Retraining on Older Displaced Workers: Should We

Teach Old Dogs New Tricks?" *Industrial and Labor Relations Review* 58, no. 3, pp. 398–415.

Jovanovic, Boyan. 1979. "Firm-Specific Capital and Turnover." *Journal of Political Economy* 87, no. 6, pp. 1246–60.

Katz, Lawrence, and Alan Krueger. 2019. "Understanding Trends in Alternative Work Arrangements in the United States," in "Improving Employment and Earnings in Twenty-First Century Labor Markets," edited by E. Groshen and H. Holzer. *RSF: The Russell Sage Foundation Journal of the Social Sciences* 5, no. 5, pp. 132–46.

Katz, Lawrence, Ai-Jen Poo, and Elaine Waxman. 2018. *Imagining a Future of Work That Fosters Mobility for All* (US Partnership on Mobility from Poverty). https://scholar.harvard.edu/files/lkatz/files/future_of_work_paper.pdf.

Kochan, Thomas, and William Kimball. 2019. "Unions, Worker Voice, and Management Practices: Implications for a High-Productivity, High-Wage Economy," in "Improving Employment and Earnings in Twenty-First Century Labor Markets," edited by E. Groshen and H. Holzer. *RSF: The Russell Sage Foundation Journal of the Social Sciences* 5, no 5, pp. 88–108.

Lerman, Robert. 2018. "The Virtue of Apprenticeship." *American Interest*, October 17.

Lerman, Robert, Signe-Mary McKernan, and Stephanie Riegg. 2004. "The Scope of Employer-Provided Training in the United States: Who, What, Where and How Much?" Working Paper (Kalamazoo, MI: W. E. Upjohn Institute for Employment Research).

Levy, Frank. 2018. "Computers and Populism: Artificial Intelligence, Jobs and Populism in the Near Term." *Oxford Review of Economic Policy* 34, no. 3, pp. 393–417.

Lowery, Annie. 2018. *Give People Money: How a Universal Basic Income Would End Poverty, Revolutionize Work and Remake the World* (New York: Crown).

Maguire, Sheila, Joshua Freely, Carol Clymer, Maureen Conway, and Deena Schwartz. 2010. *Tuning In to Local Labor Markets* (Philadelphia: PPV).

Massachusetts Institute of Technology. 2019. *The Work of the Future: Shaping Technology and Institutions* (MIT Future of Work Commission).

McClelland, Robert, and Shannon Mok. 2012. *A Review of Recent Research on Labor Supply Elasticities* (Washington, DC: Congressional Budget Office).

Mincer, Jacob. 1974. *Schooling, Experience and Earnings* (University of Chicago Press).

Molloy, Raven, Christopher L. Smith, Riccardo Trezzi, and Abigail Wozniak. 2016. "Understanding Declining Fluidity in the US Labor Market." Policy Brief (Brookings Institution).

Munnell, Alicia. 2007. "Policies to Promote Labor Force Participation of Older People," in *Reshaping the American Workforce in a Changing Economy*, edited by H. Holzer and D. Nightingale (Washington, DC: Urban Institute Press).

National Academy of Sciences. 2014. *Education for Life and Work: Developing Transferable Knowledge and Skills in the 21st Century* (Washington, DC: National Academies Press).

Nedelkoska, Ljubica, and Glenda Quintini. 2018. *Automation, Skills Use and Training.* OECD Social, Employment and Migration Working Paper (Paris: OECD Publishing).

Nichols, Austin, and Jesse Rothstein. 2015. "The Earned Income Tax Credit (EITC)." NBER Working Paper 21211 (Cambridge, MA: National Bureau of Economic Research).

Osterman, Paul. 2018. "In Search of the High Road: Meaning and Evidence." *Industrial and Labor Relations Review* 71, no. 1, pp. 3–34.

Parolin, Zachary. 2020. "Organized Labor and Employment Trajectories of Workers in Routine Jobs: Evidence from US Panel Data." Policy Brief (Brookings Institution).

Phelps, Edmund. 1997. *Rewarding Work* (Harvard University Press).

Roder, Anne, and Mark Elliott. 2019. *Nine Year Gains: Project Quest's Continuing Impact* (New York: Economic Mobility Corporation).

Stansbury, Anna, and Lawrence Summers. 2017. "Productivity and Pay: Is the Link Broken?" NBER Working Paper 24165 (Cambridge, MA: National Bureau of Economic Research).

Sundarajan, Arun. 2016. *The Sharing Economy: The End of Employment and the Rise of Crowd-Based Capitalism* (MIT Press).

Ton, Zeynep. 2014. *The Good Jobs Strategy* (MIT Press).

Wandner, Stephen, ed. 2018. *Unemployment Insurance Reform: Fixing a Broken System* (Kalamazoo, MI: W. E. Upjohn Institute for Employment Research).

Webb, Michael. 2020. "The Impact of Artificial Intelligence on the Labor Market." Unpublished manuscript (Stanford University).

Weil, David. 2014. *The Fissured Workplace* (Harvard University Press).

Weil, David. 2019. "Understanding the Present and Future of Work in the Fissured Workplace Context," in "Improving Employment and Earnings in Twenty-First Century Labor Market," edited by E. Groshen and H. Holzer, *RSF: The Russell Sage Foundation Journal of the Social Sciences* 5, no. 5, pp. 147–65.

West, Darrell. 2018. *The Future of Work: Robots, AI and Automation* (Brookings Institution Press).

SIX

Organizing for Digitalization at the Firm Level

SUNGHOON CHUNG AND SANGMIN AUM

Digitalization (or digital transformation) is widely considered a key new source of competitive advantage among firms. However, actual progress on digitalization varies greatly across firms.[1] The process involves investment in newly developed digital technologies such as mobile technology, big-data analytics, cloud computing, robotics, artificial intelligence (AI), and the internet of things (IoT). But we do not observe concurrent adoption of these technologies even among firms of similar size and engaged in similar production activity. Why do some firms become early adopters of new digital technologies while others wait and see? In particular, what organizational characteristics at the firm level, among other internal and external determinants, facilitate or hinder technology adoption?

This chapter aims to provide some answers to the above questions. Addressing them is important for firm managers, policymakers, and academic researchers. Managers in firms considering digitalization can learn about what organizational changes are necessary to prepare the company. In designing policies to promote digitalization, policymakers can benefit from a better understanding of stumbling blocks within firms in achieving successful digital transformation. Researchers have the task of coming up with findings that can inform both managers and policymakers.

It is well documented in both economic and management literature that a firm's technology adoption and its organizational characteristics are linked. The two have a mutually causal relationship often referred to as complementarity.[2] For example, greater use of information technology (IT) makes firms invest more in worker training; demand higher-level skills in their workforce; practice more team-based work; and allow greater autonomy for workers.[3] These changes jointly improve firm performance in complementary ways. Milgrom and Roberts (1990, 1995) provide theoretical foundations of the relationship between technology and organizational features.

Unfortunately, research has not yet had enough time and collected enough data to fully investigate whether firm organizational mechanisms related to IT can also be applied to the more recently commercialized digital technologies such as big-data analytics, AI, or IoT (hereinafter we refer to these collectively as *digital technology*, or DT). One may view that DT is in large part just an upgraded version of the existing IT hardware and software, and that the main function of these technologies remains information processing. In that case, firm organizational characteristics suitable for DT would mostly be the same as for IT. As Kane and others (2019) state, however, "Cheaper processors, more robust storage, and faster networking don't threaten organizations. The threat comes when someone realizes that this faster, cheaper, better computing environment presents new ways of solving business problems." For example, cloud computing can process a large amount of data much faster than a stand-alone computer, but the faster execution of the same task does not necessarily require organizational redesign. A redesign is needed when cloud computing is connected with, say, sensors embedded in physical machines for real-time monitoring and controlling of a production process. More generally, DT departs from IT when it performs new tasks in an environment where people and things are more connected with each other and it thereby provides new solutions to business problems. The more interconnected environment and the new solutions made possible by it may require some distinct organizational properties that have not been as important in the IT-centric organization.

To understand the relationship between DT and organizational characteristics, we empirically investigate this relationship in the case of Korea. Specifically, we consider five organizational characteristics potentially related to a firm's adoption of DT and subsequent digital transformation: (1) length of the firm's decision process, (2) use of profit-based worker payment schemes, (3) utilization of task analysis, (4) practice of and approach toward worker training within firms, and (5) formal education level of workers. The selection of these characteristics is based on the literature, which we will review in the next section. Among the five characteristics, we pay particular attention to those associated with human resources—numbers four and five—as we believe that it is fundamentally people who make the new ways of problem-solving using DT happen. Our hypothesis is as follows: Firms that want to utilize DT need employees with problem-solving capability. Therefore, firms would tend to hire more-educated workers, expecting that they are the ones with the capability. Also, firms would train their workers or at least encourage them to learn new skills by themselves, expecting that continuous learning enhances capabilities, particularly in the face of rapidly changing technology.

To test the hypothesis, we employ two different datasets. The first is the Human Capital Corporate Panel by the Korea Research Institute for Vocational Education and Training (KRIVET). This biyearly panel survey records how a firm organizes and incentivizes its human resources and how worker skills are accumulated in the firm. The second dataset is the annual Survey of Business Activities by Statistics Korea, which records whether a firm has adopted DT and what type. Merging the two datasets allows us to investigate which organizational structures and practices are conducive to DT adoption and subsequent digitalization.

The empirical analysis reveals two main findings. First, consistent with our hypothesis, the most robust and significant factor related to the adoption of DT is workers' human capital. Interestingly, however, it is only continuous learning supported by firms that shows a strong, positive relationship with technology adoption. Hiring workers with more formal education, on the other hand, does not show a significant relation with DT adoption. This result contrasts with the case of IT adoption, such as in customer relationship management (CRM) or learning management systems (LMS), which shows a significantly positive relation only with formal education. These results suggest that improvement of worker capabilities through continuous learning within firms would be a key factor in DT adoption, which may call for strategic coordination between government and firms in promoting continuous learning.

Second, although firms equipped with DT generally have higher total factor productivity (TFP), we do not find evidence supporting faster productivity growth of those firms. The result is consistent with the recent slowdown in aggregate productivity growth despite rising investment in DT. The first finding, the importance of on-the-job training within firms to complement DT adoption, could be one of the reasons behind this result. Since DT adoption requires intensive support for worker learning, firms have to incur significant worker training costs before the new technology starts to show positive effects on productivity.[4]

Section 1 of the chapter discusses the organizational features that promote or hinder technology adoption in general, and then examines how DT differs from older technologies. The dataset used in our analysis is introduced with some essential descriptive statistics in section 2. Section 3 presents the empirical framework and main findings. Section 4 discusses the policy implications of the findings, and section 5 concludes.

Background and Related Literature

Much effort has been made to understand the relationship between firm organization and technology adoption. More recently, research has focused on how DT may present different organizational challenges for a firm from those associated with IT.

Organizational Fitness for Technology

When a firm considers adopting a new technology, it necessarily compares the costs and expected benefits of doing so. The technology would be adopted only if returns are greater than costs. Organizational fitness is closely related to these costs: the better fit an organization has for the new technology, the lower the costs to adopt and utilize it. As the literature stresses,[5] the costs include not only the price of new technology but also all auxiliary expenses for its appropriate implementation, such as installing it into the existing system, consulting, redesigning production processes, hiring and training skilled workers who can handle the technology, and conducting experimentation and discovery.[6] These additional, complementary activities can cost much more than the acquisition of the technology itself. For example, Brynjolfsson, Hitt, and Yang (2002) find that the auxiliary expenses are about ten times greater than the price of information technology.

Nonpecuniary, organizational changes are equally important costs. We can easily observe real examples of technology adoption failure due to poor organizational adjustment. Davenport (1998) examines a few cases that failed to implement the enterprise resource planning (ERP) system because it "imposes its own logic on a company's strategy, organization, and culture." The ERP system, for instance, requires a firm to move toward a fully integrated organization even when some degree of segregation is a source of its competitive advantage. Atkin and others (2017) found in their field experiment that a more cost efficient and simpler technology was not used because firms' pay schemes and incentives were not aligned with the higher productivity offered by the technology. Thus, organizational fitness is one of the main reasons for the widely heterogenous adoption of new technologies across firms.

A branch of the literature investigates larger samples of industries and firms to examine synergies between organizational characteristics and new technology, especially information technology.[7] We find from the literature at least three broadly categorized organizational characteristics that are related to the adoption of new technology: (1) skill composition of workers, (2) worker payment schemes and related incentives, and (3) organizational hierarchy and worker autonomy.[8]

A skilled workforce and new technology adoption are shown to have strong positive synergy. Early studies that rely on industry-level data find complementarity between high-tech equipment and high-skilled workers—also known as skill-biased technological change.[9] The relationship is confirmed by later firm- or plant-level studies.[10] Note that the skill composition in an organization can be enhanced by either hiring high-skilled workers (and/or laying off low-skilled workers) or training existing workers. In fact, both organizational practices are consistently found in the firm- or plant-level studies.[11]

The second characteristic, the worker pay schemes, is also closely associated with technology adoption. The literature finds that incentive-based payment schemes are complementary to the adoption and use of information technology to achieve higher productivity.[12]

The fitness of organizational features such as hierarchy and worker autonomy appears to depend on the type of technology adopted. Studies that focus only on information technology find that the adoption of IT tends to be associated with a more delayered organization and decentralized worker authority. This is because IT allows frontline workers to access relevant information more easily, empowering them to handle problems. An interesting study by Bloom and others (2014) finds, however, that advanced communication technology can have the opposite effect because improved communication (such as through intranets) allows managers at headquarters to better know the situation at the frontline, enabling them to do more of the decision making.

What's New about Digital Technology?

The literature reviewed above suggests some key organizational factors that are important for the adoption and use of new technologies. However, the question remains whether the same factors matter equally in the case of *newly* commercialized digital technologies, or DT. The question arises because DT may have characteristics that differ from older technologies, notably traditional IT, that typically use computers to process information or digitized data. So what is new about DT?

First of all, it should be made clear that there is no official or single definition or classification of what we call DT in this chapter. One can broadly define digital technology as "the representation of information in bits."[13] The mechanical definition by itself, however, does not distinguish DT from IT so long as information is processed in a digital format.[14] From this perspective, the newly commercialized digital technology is nothing but an upgrade of existing IT that further reduces the cost of storage, transmission, and computation of data at the intensive margin. A classic example is Moore's law, according to which computing power doubles roughly every twenty-four months while its cost is halved.

Our main interest is in digitalization at the firm level, and we consider that DT is the fundamental enabler of a firm's digital transformation. In this sense, DT also needs to be considered within the framework of a firm's business strategy in the digital era. Bharadwaj and others (2013) clarify the difference between DT and traditional IT in this context. They note that IT strategy is "a functional-level strategy that must be aligned with the firm's chosen business strategy." Although IT strategy does affect the formation of business strategy, its main function is to facilitate existing business processes. Hence, it is subordinate to and directed by the business strategy. On the other hand, DT, equipped with interconnectivity and real-time information exchange across all production entities, allows firms to fundamentally reshape their business strategy through more "cross-functional" business processes. The DT strategy is not directed by a chosen business strategy. It is a business strategy.

There have been further developments in DT since the work of Bharadwaj and others (2013). More recently, Adner, Puranam, and Zhu (2019) identify three core processes related to digitalization—representation, connectivity, and aggregation—and highlight the increasing role of DT in these processes. Digitalization begins with the digitization of information (representation), just as in Goldfarb and Tucker (2019). But its focus is at the extensive margin—the real-time information that had not been considered as data previously, such as the location of parts during manufacturing, and idle time of automobile engines that have recently been digitized for value creation. Next, digitized information becomes much more valuable when it is linked with information from other sources through a digital network (connectivity) and when all linked information is jointly analyzed to provide new insights (aggregation)—again in real time. These three core processes and their interactions define much of digitalization.

Consider the case of Google Maps. It started with digitizing paper maps into desktop software, a representation of maps in bits. Soon after, it transformed into a web-based application, integrated the GPS connection to provide real-time traffic information, and added the mobile version to serve as a navigation device. The digital map has also merged other information such as local business addresses and points of interest, coupled with a user-rating function. More recent services include traffic predictions—which utilize deep learning and big-data analysis—and live view, which shows you your surroundings on a smartphone screen with the directions overlaid via augmented reality (AR) and digital camera.

The digitalization of Google Maps is well explained by the three processes and their interaction. Moreover, we can easily see that the recent services would have been impossible without newly developed digital technologies such as AI, big-data analytics, AR, and mobile technologies. Rather than individually, a variety of new digital technologies collectively broaden their applicability to tasks that have not been solvable before. This in turn allows managers to approach problems differently and come up with new business strategies. In other words, the firm's digitalization necessarily involves new business strategies relying on DT.

A key property of DT that differentiates it from previous IT is that it has built-in, real-time connectivity among all production entities—including workers, materials, machines, and equipment—and to a central "data lake" where digitized information is collected, exchanged, and aggregated.[15] Because of this interconnectivity or interoperability, DT collectively, rather than individually, creates a new realm of business strategy that is qualitatively different from a typical IT strategy. This, in turn, is likely to require different organizational structures and practices.

Data Description

We combine two different datasets in our analysis.

Data Sources

The first one is the Human Capital Corporate Panel (HCCP) by KRIVET.[16] This panel survey, conducted every other year from 2005 to 2017, is officially approved by Statistics Korea. The main purpose of the survey is to understand how firms organize and incentivize their workforces, and how worker skills are accumulated within firms. The HCCP is surveyed at both the enterprise level and the worker level within the enterprise. This unique survey structure allows a cross-check of survey results on firms' organization and human resource policies. The HCCP surveys typically cover around 700 firms from all sectors in each wave.

The second dataset is the annual Survey of Business Activities (SBA) by Statistics Korea.[17] The SBA is an annual survey of all enterprises with more than fifty employees and service companies with more than 1 billion Korean won of paid-in capital. The number of firms covered by the survey has been more than 12,000 in recent years. Conducted since 2006, the survey covers a wide range of firm activities, such as employment, investment in tangible and intangible capital, all active businesses (at the three-digit level of industry classification), and financial information. Of particular interest to us is the information provided since 2017 on the firm's adoption of newly commercialized digital technologies by nine types.

Combining the two datasets provides a unique opportunity to investigate what organizational structures or practices are favorable to DT adoption and subsequent digitalization. However, a major limitation of the combined data is the period and size of the sample. Although each dataset contains a range of information that can potentially be utilized, it is only for the year 2017 that relevant information is concurrently available from both datasets. In addition, since not all firms have more than fifty employees in the HCCP, the final sample includes only a subset of firms from both datasets.

Given the limitation, we assume that the firm's organizational characteristics, which are drawn from the last wave of the HCCP in 2017, are constant in a short period. The characteristics are then matched with the 2017 and 2018 status of DT adoption, taken from the SBA, to examine the relationship between the two. Consequently, the final sample has 1,022 observations at the firm level over the two years, with slightly more than 500 firms each year.

Construction of Variables

For the analysis of firms' organizational characteristics, we construct five variables capturing important aspects of a firm's organization: (1) length of the decision process, (2) use of profit-based worker payment scheme, (3) utilization of task analysis, (4) firm-specific worker training, and (5) formal education.

First, we attempt to measure the length of a firm's decision process. In most cases, for a project to be implemented, a manager must approve it. How many decision processes a project has to go through differs across firms, and the average number of approvals needed is recorded in the HCCP. A firm with a lengthier decision process is likely to have a greater number of hierarchical positions among its workers, which is also recorded in the HCCP. We normalize these two variables (average number of approvals and the number of positions among workers), and take an average of them to construct a decision-layer index.

Second, how firms pay their workers can also influence the utilization of digital technology. For example, Kim (2020) finds that the adoption of digital technology is more likely to boost a firm's total factor productivity when the firm links workers' compensation to its profit. To see whether worker payment schemes are related to firms' adoption of new technology in Korea, we utilize information on the use of stock options and profit-sharing schemes, available in the SBA dataset. Specifically, the SBA reports the extent to which a firm is using stock options or profit sharing in a range from 1 to 5. We convert these two variables into two dummy variables (either uses it or not), and take an average of the two dummy variables after normalization. We then use the resulting variable to represent a firm's utilization of profit-based payment schemes.

Third, we construct an index showing how much a firm utilizes task-based analysis, which we label a task-utilization index. This index consists of four variables provided in the HCCP: whether a firm does task analysis, whether it uses task analysis when assigning workers to tasks, whether it uses task analysis when hiring new employees, and the extent to which new employees' experience of specific tasks is recognized at the firm. The first three variables are dummy variables, and the last variable (the extent of recognition of new employees' task experience) is a categorical variable ranging from 0 to 100. Again, we normalize these four variables, and take an average of them to construct an index of task utilization.

Fourth, regarding workers' human capital, we consider two different types of human capital. The first type is related to continuous learning after joining the firm, or firm-specific human capital accumulated through workers' job experiences. To measure this firm-specific human capital, we consider two types of efforts made by firms. One is the observable investment in workers' human capital by firms, which we measure from two variables: the share of worker training cost in the firm's total labor costs, and average training hours of workers at the firm. The other is managers' attitudes toward worker training, something not easily observable. Fortunately, the HCCP tries to capture managers' attitudes toward worker training through nine different questions: (1) how much a manager cares about workers' training within a firm, (2) how much a manager tries to persuade workers to get training, (3) how tight a manager thinks the budget is for firm-specific training, (4) how strongly a manager feels about the necessity of firm-specific training, (5) how strongly a manager feels about the necessity of having human resource development specialists in the firm, (6) how difficult a manager feels it is to make time for training workers, (7) how good a manager feels about the firm's training program, (8) how good a manager feels about workers' progress in firm-provided training, and (9) how difficult a manager feels it is to prepare for a training program. All these variables are modified to represent more positive attitudes with larger values. We normalize all the variables and take an average of them to construct a firm-specific training index.

Last, the second type of human capital is general human capital accumulated through formal education before entering the job market. We measure this as the share of a firm's workers with an advanced (master's or doctoral) degree. Again, we normalize the variable.

Summary Statistics

Table 6-1 shows the status of DT adoption in our sample of firms over 2017 and 2018 together. The variable in the first row labeled "digital" is a dummy variable equal to one, if at least one out of nine specific newly available digital technologies has been adopted by the firm, and zero otherwise. The adoption status of the nine technologies individually is shown similarly in the rows that follow. The nine technologies are: IoT, cloud computing, big-data analytics, mobile technology, AI, blockchain (BC), 3D printing (3DP), industrial robots, and augmented or virtual reality (AR/VR). The table indicates that about 18 percent of the sample firms have adopted at least one digital technology during the two years. We view this adoption rate as quite remarkable given the short sample periods. The adoption of each individual technology is much lower, though. IoT and big-data analytics have been adopted by 7.3 percent and 6.9 percent of the sample firms, respectively. Adoption rates of the other technologies are in most cases below 5 percent.

Aside from DT, information technology traditionally has been applied by Korean firms as stand-alone software programs for enterprise management, often called e-business systems. The adoption status of several kinds of e-business systems had been recorded in the SBA until its survey questionnaire shifted to DT adoption in 2017. Table 6-1 shows the cumulative adoption rates of four different e-business systems prior to 2017: customer relationship management (CRM), learning management system (LMS), knowledge management system (KMS), and human resource management system (HRMS). We will use this information to see whether DT requires an organizational fit different from that of traditional e-business systems.

Table 6-2 summarizes key organizational characteristics of firms that we discussed in the preceding section and that we will use as explanatory variables in our empirical analysis below.

Empirical Analysis

We start our empirical analysis by asking what organizational characteristics are well suited to newly commercialized digital technologies.

Table 6-1. *Summary Statistics: Technology Adoption*

	Count	Mean	SD	Min	Max
Digital	1,022	0.178	0.383	0	1
IoT	1,022	0.073	0.261	0	1
Cloud	1,022	0.059	0.235	0	1
Big data	1,022	0.069	0.254	0	1
Mobile	1,022	0.059	0.235	0	1
AI	1,022	0.044	0.205	0	1
BC	1,022	0.016	0.124	0	1
3DP	1,022	0.036	0.187	0	1
Robots	1,022	0.029	0.169	0	1
AR/VR	1,022	0.026	0.160	0	1
CRM	1,022	0.137	0.344	0	1
LMS	1,022	0.129	0.336	0	1
KMS	1,022	0.096	0.295	0	1
HRMS	1,022	0.185	0.388	0	1

Source: Authors' calculations based on data from KRIVET (n.d.) and Statistics Korea (n.d.).

Note: "Count" is total number of firms in the sample. "SD," "Min," and "Max" are standard deviation and minimum and maximum, respectively.

Table 6-2. *Summary Statistics: Explanatory Variables*

	Count	Mean	SD	Min	Max
Decision layer	1,022	0.036	0.941	−5.017	4.581
Profit-based payment	1,022	0.002	0.917	−0.482	2.233
Task utilization	580	0.370	0.797	−0.906	2.097
Firm training	362	−0.082	0.598	−2.156	1.671
Formal education	362	−0.024	0.925	−0.756	5.472

Source: Authors' calculations based on data from KRIVET (n.d.) and Statistics Korea (n.d.).

Note: "Count" is total number of firms in the sample. "SD," "Min," and "Max" are standard deviation and minimum and maximum, respectively. The variables are constructed as normalized indices.

Empirical Framework

To see the relationship between DT adoption and organizational characteristics, we estimate the following equation:

$$\log\left(\frac{\mathrm{p}_{i,t}}{1-\mathrm{p}_{i,t}}\right) = F(X'_{i,t}\beta), \text{ and } p_{i,t} = \Pr(y_{i,t} = 1), \tag{6-1}$$

where $y_{i,t}$ is an indicator variable of DT adoption for firm i in year t, $X_{i,t}$ is a vector of variables related to the firm's organization, and $F(\cdot)$ is the logistic function. The dependent variable is whether firms have adopted DT. The variable $y_{i,t}$ is 1 if a firm uses any one of the above-mentioned nine digital technologies, and 0 otherwise. Since $y_{i,t}$ is an indicator variable, we estimate the logistic model assuming a logistic function $F(\cdot)$.

For the explanatory variables, we consider the five categories of variables discussed earlier: (1) length of the decision process (as measured by the decision-layer index), (2) use of profit-based worker payment scheme, (3) utilization of task analysis, (4) firm-specific training, and (5) formal education.

Note that we use the HCCP for the construction of the five variables comprising $X_{i,t}$. Since the most recent wave of the HCCP was in 2017, and the questionnaires on DT start only in 2017 in the SBA, equation 6-1 has to be estimated using data for the year 2017 only. Also, $y_{i,t}$ is an indicator variable of 1 or 0, so the benchmark estimation does not give any information on the timing or the degree of technology adoption. In order to alleviate this shortcoming, we consider variations of equation 6-1. First, we consider how firms' precondition in 2017 was related to technology adoption the next year, in 2018 (i.e., $y_{i,t+1}$), which is equation 6-2. In addition, we restrict the sample to firms that had not adopted DT in 2017, which is equation 6-3. Last, in equation 6-4, we estimate the ordered-logit model using the number of digital technologies (out of nine) for the dependent variable to reflect the degree of technology usage:

$$\log\left(\frac{\mathrm{p}_{i,t+1}}{1-\mathrm{p}_{i,t+1}}\right) = F(X'_{i,t}\beta), \text{ and } p_{i,t+1} = \Pr(y_{i,t+1}=1). \tag{6-2}$$

$$\log\left(\frac{\mathrm{p}_{i,t+1}}{1-\mathrm{p}_{i,t+1}}\right) = F(X'_{i,t}\beta), \tag{6-3}$$

and restrict the sample to those with $y_{i,t}=0$.

$$\Pr(z_{i,t}=n) = \Pr(\kappa_{n-1} < X'_{i,t}\beta + u_{i,t} \leq \kappa_n), \tag{6-4}$$

where $z_{i,t}$ is the number of adopted technologies by firm i.

Finally, we ask whether the newly commercialized digital technologies present a different relationship with organizational characteristics from traditional information technology. To see this, we run a regression similar to equation 6-1 but with the adoption of e-business systems (i.e., CRM, LMS, KMS, and HRMS) as the dependent variable.

Table 6-3. *Estimation Results*

	Equation 6-1 Tech(t)	Equation 6-2 Tech(t+1)	Equation 6-3 Tech(t+1|t=0)	Equation 6-4 # Tech(t)
Decision layer	−0.268**	−0.107	0.019	−0.296***
	(0.121)	(0.129)	(0.176)	(0.114)
Profit-based payment	0.575***	0.283	0.030	0.650***
	(0.207)	(0.191)	(0.268)	(0.226)
Task utilization	0.724**	0.648**	0.524	0.728**
	(0.329)	(0.267)	(0.355)	(0.328)
Firm training	0.521**	0.830***	0.703**	0.563**
	(0.256)	(0.230)	(0.313)	(0.270)
Formal education	0.134	0.090	0.118	0.121
	(0.153)	(0.135)	(0.163)	(0.151)
Observations	362	363	318	362
pseudo R-sq	0.150	0.106	0.055	0.121

Note: Robust standard errors in parentheses. $* = p < .1$, $** = p < .05$, $*** = p < .01$. Constant term and size dummy included in the regressions.

Results

Table 6-3 shows the estimation results. For the benchmark estimation (the first column), we see that all variables except formal education show statistical significance. The decision-layer index has a negative coefficient, meaning that firms with a more compact organization are more likely to adopt DT. Previous literature, such as Bloom and others (2014), argues that information technology makes an organization more centralized, and communication technology leads to a more decentralized organization. The result here implies that digitalization could be closer to communication technology than information technology in terms of its effect on organizational structure.

The results also suggest that the more workers' compensation is linked to the firm's performance, the more likely it is that the firm adopts DT. Also, a firm's utilization of task analysis is positively related to DT adoption. These results are consistent with previous literature. For example, Kim (2020) finds that firms use their intangible capital more effectively when they link workers' compensation to the firm's performance. Acemoglu and Restrepo (2019) and Agrawal, Gans, and Goldfarb (2019) argue that a detailed understanding of workers' tasks is important in assessing the consequences of new technologies, and of AI in particular.

Table 6-4. *Estimation Results*

	CRM	LMS	KMS	HRMS
Decision layer	−0.014	−0.043	−0.019	0.002
	(0.051)	(0.057)	(0.053)	(0.043)
Profit-based payment	−0.002	0.127	−0.051	−0.015
	(0.073)	(0.079)	(0.079)	(0.069)
Task utilization	0.320**	0.336**	0.194	0.144
	(0.127)	(0.131)	(0.130)	(0.107)
Firm training	−0.114	−0.176	0.376***	0.079
	(0.126)	(0.124)	(0.128)	(0.104)
Formal education	0.126**	0.268***	0.321***	0.213***
	(0.054)	(0.055)	(0.051)	(0.051)
Observations	2,590	2,590	2,590	2,590
pseudo R-sq	0.092	0.136	0.109	0.097

Note: Robust standard errors in parentheses. $^* = p < .1$, $^{**} = p < .05$, $^{***} = p < .01$. Constant, size, and year dummy included in the regressions.

What is particularly interesting is that we have two types of education in the estimation, but only one of them shows significance: continuous learning in the firm. Continuous learning by workers that firms support is the most robust and significant variable related to the adoption of DT. This variable remains significant across all specifications from equation 6-1 to equation 6-4. Formal education, on the other hand, presents a striking contrast. It does not have a statistically significant relation with DT adoption in any of the four specifications. What's more, this is not the case if we focus on the adoption of IT-based e-business systems, such as LMS or KMS. From table 6-4, we can see that formal education has a robust and significant relationship with the adoption of these systems, unlike the results for the adoption of newer digital technologies.

Note that our dependent variable is 1 if a firm has adopted one or more of the nine new digital technologies: IoT, cloud, big data, mobile, AI, BC, 3DP, robots, or AR/VR. To check exactly which type of technology drives the results, we estimate equation 6-1 by replacing the dependent variable with the adoption of a specific technology. Table 6-5 shows the estimation results. For example, the decision-layer index has a significant negative relationship with the adoption of IoT, cloud, big data, and AI, among the nine types of DT. Profit-based worker payment schemes are positively and significantly related to the adoption of cloud, mobile technology, AI, and BC. The utilization of task analysis prevails more in firms using IoT, cloud, BC,

Table 6-5. *Estimation Results*

	IoT	Cloud	Big data	Mobile	AI	BC	3DP	Robot	AR/VR
Decision layer	-0.32*	-0.30*	-0.47**	-0.05	-0.50**	-0.33	-0.29	-0.24	-0.18
	(0.19)	(0.17)	(0.20)	(0.13)	(0.21)	(0.50)	(0.23)	(0.17)	(0.19)
Profit-based payment	0.32	0.86**	0.52	0.73***	1.27**	2.83**	0.29	0.12	0.78
	(0.33)	(0.38)	(0.33)	(0.25)	(0.54)	(1.26)	(0.41)	(0.48)	(0.56)
Task utilization	1.17***	1.24***	0.64	0.15	0.01	1.80**	0.67	1.63**	-0.28
	(0.39)	(0.47)	(0.49)	(0.48)	(0.79)	(0.74)	(0.51)	(0.77)	(0.82)
Firm training	0.30	0.76**	0.82*	0.81**	2.26***	-0.20	0.19	0.50	0.90
	(0.35)	(0.37)	(0.47)	(0.32)	(0.82)	(0.38)	(0.42)	(0.48)	(1.00)
Formal education	0.32	-0.02	0.28	-0.01	-0.64	-2.89	-0.35	-0.18	-0.30
	(0.20)	(0.17)	(0.27)	(0.23)	(0.47)	(1.98)	(0.29)	(0.22)	(0.31)
Observations	362	362	362	362	362	164	362	362	216
pseudo R-sq	0.194	0.342	0.336	0.162	0.533	0.511	0.084	0.216	0.212

Note: Robust standard errors in parentheses. * = $p < .1$, ** = $p < .05$, *** = $p < .01$. Size dummy included in the regressions.

Table 6-6. *Estimation Results*

	Tech(t)	Tech(t+1)	Tech(t+1|t=0)	# Tech(t)
Ln TFP(t)	0.367***	0.378***	0.348**	0.407***
	(0.069)	(0.103)	(0.146)	(0.073)
Observations	989	487	415	989
pseudo R-sq	0.057	0.065	0.054	0.045

Note: Robust standard errors in parentheses. $*=p<.1$, $**=p<.05$, $***=p<.01$. Size dummy included in the regressions.

and robots. The firm-training index shows significance with respect to the adoption of cloud, big data, mobile technology, and AI. Interestingly, again, formal education shows no significant relation to any of the nine types of technology.

The next question we ask is whether and how DT adoption is related to firms' productivity. Specifically, we compute total factor productivity (TFP) of firms by applying the methods suggested by Ackerberg, Caves, and Frazer (2015), and implemented in Manjón and Mañez (2016), using the SBA dataset. In other words, we estimate production function parameters using intermediate cost and the capital stock as proxy variables for unobserved firm productivity. We then estimate the logit or ordered-logit model (i.e., similar to equation 6-1 or 6-4) using technology adoption as a dependent variable, but now with the log of TFP as an explanatory variable instead of variables related to the firm's organization. The estimation results are shown in table 6-6, which indicate that a higher level of TFP is positively associated with the adoption of DT.

But is DT adoption also related to faster growth of TFP? To answer this, we regress the adoption of technology on the growth of TFP. As can be seen in the first column of table 6-7, we could not find any statistically significant relationship between DT adoption and the growth of TFP. When we additionally consider interaction terms of technology adoption and the five explanatory variables relating to firm organizational characteristics used in our benchmark analysis, we see weakly significant relations with variables related to education: both firm training and formal education. Note, however, that we have the variable recording the adoption of technology only since 2017, and the sample periods end in 2018. This means that the estimation compares only one-year TFP growth of firms adopting or not adopting DT in 2017, which is too short to establish a medium-to longer-run association with TFP.

Table 6-7. *Estimation Results*

	$\Delta ln\ TFP(t+1)$	$\Delta ln\ TFP(t+1)$
Tech(t)	0.038	
	(0.069)	
Decision layer*Tech(t)		0.032
		(0.037)
Profit-based payment*Tech(t)		−0.064
		(0.080)
Task utilization*Tech(t)		−0.020
		(0.110)
Firm training*Tech(t)		0.246*
		(0.142)
Formal education*Tech(t)		0.089*
		(0.049)
Observations	476	329
R-sq	0.001	0.011

Note: Robust standard errors in parentheses. *=p<.1, **=p<.05, ***=p<.01.

Interpretation

Our main estimation results can be summarized as follows. Digitalization is well fitted for firms that provide learning opportunities directly and/or indirectly to their employees to update their skills. Formal higher education of employees is conducive to traditional IT adoption (and its utilization) but not necessarily to DT adoption.

The strategic fitness of DT adoption with continuous learning within firms, but not formal education, is rooted in the fundamental characteristics of DT and IT. When technology is used functionally and independently, as the traditional IT is, the preferred worker skill is the ability to understand and utilize the technology well. Such skill can be acquired from formal education, which explains why workers with higher education levels raise the return to IT adoption. However, DT becomes significantly different from IT when, and only when, it is used cross-functionally, collaboratively, and extensively. Good use of DT necessitates worker creativity, communication skills, and adaptiveness.[18] These soft skills cannot simply be obtained by taking classes at a university. Moreover, the cross-functional, extensive application of DT produces an ever-changing work environment requiring new skill sets. It is difficult to train workers with new skills in short order. Also, firms cannot easily hire new employees whenever they need new skills. Hence the synergy between DT and continuous learning within the firm.

Continuous learning practices within firms not only facilitate DT adoption and utilization but may also be enhanced by DT. The following case illustrates the mutually causal relationship. In the mid-2010s, Ericsson created a peer-based e-learning platform, Ericsson Play, in which anyone could upload videos, share their experiences or ideas, and ask colleagues for help. For more formal content, another online training program called Ericsson Academy Virtual Campus was available to all employees, which also included a mobile version so workers could learn on the go.[19] Cases are not limited to Ericsson, of course. Many frontier firms have been developing their own educational and training systems by actively embracing DT, which is likely reflected in our main findings.

Policy Implications

A clear implication of our findings is that firms need to keep promoting their employees' learning for successful digital transformation.

Promoting Continuous Learning within Firms

There is considerable heterogeneity across firms in adopting DT, and there is a risk that the new technologies may leave many firms behind. Government can promote digital transformation through policies such as provision of incentives and information to improve firms' management of employee learning, which may also be packaged with other support for DT adoption.

In Korea, there is such a government-supported program called Main-Biz (Management, Innovation, Business) for the promotion of technology innovation among small and medium enterprises. The program evaluates how innovative a firm is in its business management. Providing workers with a better learning environment is an important element of this evaluation. Once a firm is certified under the program as innovative, it becomes eligible for several benefits such as a lower interest rate on financing, extra points in competition for government procurement, and different kinds of export subsidies.

Broader Implications for Lifelong Learning

The complementarity between DT adoption and continuous worker learning is also relevant to current policy discussions that more broadly emphasize the role of education and (re)training in the digital era. Our main findings underscore an important point that is often missed in these discussions: the increasing role of the firm in providing the necessary education and training in the context of digital transformation.

To elaborate on why that point is important, let us first review briefly the policy discussions mentioned above. Brynjolfsson and McAfee (2011, 2014) argue in their influential books that the nature of work in the digital era will change a lot because of the substantially improved versatility of machines in the "second machine age." Significant job destruction and creation will follow. Fortunately, human beings are still superior to the machine in "ideation"—coming up with new ideas or concepts. Individuals need to take advantage of the skill to think outside the box. Government should aim to help individuals improve the soft skills of ideation by providing them with better education from childhood onward. To do so, teachers need to be paid better.[20] Schools need to develop well-designed curricula that can meet the changing demand from business, and they need to actively utilize digital technologies for better content delivery.

Recent reports from international organizations conclude with similar policy suggestions, calling upon governments to increase support for life-long learning.[21] Lifelong learning is regarded as a core strategy in preparing for the future of work. The International Labour Organization (ILO) (2019b) specifically called for "the formal recognition of a universal entitlement to lifelong learning and the establishment of an effective lifelong learning system."

Two comments on these discussions follow. First, despite the role of school emphasized by Brynjolfsson and McAfee (2011, 2014), there is a growing concern in the business world that formal education—especially tertiary education—falls short of equipping students with the skills that firms need in the digital era. As Frankiewicz and Chamorro-Premuzic (2020) note, current formal education is doomed to lag behind the changing demand of firms, because it takes at least several years for universities to perceive the change in demand, develop a proper curriculum, and teach students until their graduation. Given the fast pace of technological change, the time lag may become a more serious issue in the future. Furthermore, firms engaged in digital transformation need soft skills and the ability to think outside the box, but current formal education is more geared toward producing specialists with hard skills. Remember that in our empirical analysis, a higher share of more formally educated employees in a firm is not necessarily associated with a higher probability of DT adoption.

Second, while the need for lifelong learning amid today's rapid technological change is clear, the question is how to implement "an effective lifelong learning system." The current learning system does not work well interactively between schools and firms. Although the former gets some input from the latter, it is far from the strategic interaction needed to better match skill supply and demand. Meanwhile, firms' approach to training their workers is changing with digital transformation. Firms realizing the skill deficiencies have been developing their own training systems, including by actively embracing DT, as illustrated by the example of Ericsson. New business models of corporate e-learning are becoming available.[22] Start-ups like Coorpacademy, Skillsoft, and SmartUp are offering programs targeting specific worker groups within firms.[23] These online programs can be much more flexible, practical, and responsive to different needs than those offered by formal educational institutions. Such corporate e-learning programs can be attractive to firms, especially small to medium-sized firms that do not have their own programs.

The strategic fitness of DT adoption with continuous learning within firms, but not with formal education, implies a misalignment between the two suppliers of learning: traditional educational institutions and firms. Promoting these two suppliers independently, leaving the learning system disconnected, can make current problems worse. For example, policies may merely support more students in acquiring hard skills at school, when in fact those skills may not be so helpful to digitalized firms. Firms will then only reinforce the provision of learning to their workers through both their own digital platforms and the e-learning programs offered by commercial suppliers.

What the current policy discussions miss is how to align the learning provided by the two educational suppliers. An effective lifelong learning system in the digital era can only be built on active collaboration between schools and firms, with more engagement of the latter. Policymakers can play their part in encouraging such cooperation. The ILO (2019b) understands the need in principle, as it states that "governments, workers and employers, as well as educational institutions, have complementary responsibilities in building an effective and appropriately financed lifelong learning ecosystem." This vision needs to be translated into more detailed strategies and programs.

Conclusion

In this chapter, we have investigated which organizational characteristics of firms are complementary to digital transformation involving the adoption of recently developed digital technologies. We highlight the role of continuous learning within firms in the adoption and utilization of these technologies, in contrast to the hiring of more workers with higher formal education. Given the rapidly changing work environment due to the cross-functional, dynamic, and extensive applications of the new technologies, workers need to keep upgrading their skills and apply them to the new environment in a collaborative manner. Digitalized firms also have incentive to provide their employees continuous learning opportunities, and not just to rely on new hiring. Therefore, improving the management of worker learning within firms can be a key policy strategy to spur overall digital transformation.

More generally, the new digital technologies provide firms that seek new sources of competitive advantage a huge potential to realize them, but it is ultimately the people who come up with new ideas for using these technologies, who redesign business processes, and who make technology function smoothly with other production resources. Although formal educational institutions will continue to play a central role in accumulating human capital even in the digital era, a rising role of the firm as another teacher should be seriously taken into account by policymakers. We hope to see government, educational institutions, and firms get together for deeper cooperation in promoting lifelong learning.

NOTES

1. Throughout the chapter, we use the terms *digitalization* and *digital transformation* interchangeably.

2. Brynjolfsson and Hitt (2000) and Brynjolfsson and Milgrom (2013).

3. Black and Lynch (2001), Bartel, Ichniowski, and Shaw (2007), Bresnahan, Brynjolfsson, and Hitt (2002), and Bloom and others (2014).

4. We have to be cautious about this result though. The sample periods in our dataset end in the year 2018, and we have data on technology adoption only since 2017. Hence, we do not have enough sample periods to test the medium- to longer-term consequences of technology adoption on firm productivity.

5. See Hall (2005) for an overview of the literature on the cost and benefit of technology adoption.

6. Bresnahan and Greenstein (1996) call these activities coinvention.

7. See Brynjolfsson and Hitt (2000) for a comprehensive review of the literature on the relationship between IT and organization.

8. These three characteristics may also be complementary to one another. For example, Caroli and Van Reenen (2001) find that organizational change toward more decentralization and autonomy favors more skilled workers (i.e., skill-biased organizational change). Brynjolfsson and Milgrom (2013) provide a more detailed discussion.

9. Berman, Bound, and Griliches (1994), Berman, Bound, and Machin (1998), and Autor, Katz, and Krueger (1998).

10. Bresnahan, Brynjolfsson, and Hitt (2002) and Bartel, Ichniowski, and Shaw (2007).

11. The skill level is generally measured by educational degrees in these studies.

12. Black and Lynch (2001, 2004), Aral, Brynjolfsson, and Wu (2012), and Bloom, Sadun, and Van Reenen (2012).

13. Goldfarb and Tucker (2019).

14. A straightforward example of digital technology, according to this definition, is a scanner that converts paper documents into a digital format—a technology that is already well classified as information technology.

15. Porter and Heppelmann (2014, 2015).

16. KRIVET (n.d.).

17. Statistics Korea (n.d).

18. This relationship is also underscored by Brynjolfsson and McAfee (2011, 2014).

19. *McKinsey Quarterly* (2016).

20. See also Chetty, Friedman, and Rockoff (2014a, 2014b).

21. For example, International Labour Organization (2019a, 2019b) and Organization for Economic Cooperation and Development (2019).

22. The massive open online courses (MOOCs), such as those offered by the Khan Academy and Coursera, have been around for more than a decade, but their contents are mostly limited to academic courses.

23. Moules (2018).

REFERENCES

Acemoglu, D., and Restrepo, P. 2019. "Automation and New Tasks: How Technology Displaces and Reinstates Labor." *Journal of Economic Perspectives* 33, no. 2, pp. 3–30.

Ackerberg, D. A., K. Caves, and G. Frazer. 2015. "Identification Properties of Recent Production Function Estimators." *Econometrica* 83, no. 6, pp. 2411–51.

Adner, R., P. Puranam, and F. Zhu. 2019. "What Is Different about Digital Strategy? From Quantitative to Qualitative Change." *Strategy Science* 4, no. 4, pp. 253–61.

Agrawal, A., J. S. Gans, and A. Goldfarb. 2019. "Artificial Intelligence: The Ambiguous Labor Market Impact of Automating Prediction." *Journal of Economic Perspectives* 33, no. 2, pp. 31–50.

Aral, S., E. Brynjolfsson, and L. Wu. 2012. "Three-Way Complementarities: Performance Pay, Human Resource Analytics, and Information Technology." *Management Science* 58, no. 5, pp. 913–31.

Atkin, D., A. Chaudhry, S. Chaudry, A. K. Khandelwal, and E. Verhoogen. 2017. "Organizational Barriers to Technology Adoption: Evidence from Soccer-Ball Producers in Pakistan." *Quarterly Journal of Economics* 132, no. 3, pp. 1101–64.

Autor, D. H., L. F. Katz, and A. B. Krueger. 1998. "Computing Inequality: Have Computers Changed the Labor Market?" *Quarterly Journal of Economics* 113, no. 4, pp. 1169–1213.

Bartel, A., C. Ichniowski, and K. Shaw. 2007. "How Does Information Technology Affect Productivity? Plant-Level Comparisons of Product Innovation, Process Improvement, and Worker Skills." *Quarterly Journal of Economics* 122, no. 4, pp. 1721–58.

Berman, E., J. Bound, and Z. Griliches. 1994. "Changes in the Demand for Skilled Labor within U.S. Manufacturing: Evidence from the Annual Survey of Manufactures." *Quarterly Journal of Economics* 109, no. 2, pp. 367–97.

Berman, E., J. Bound, and S. Machin. 1998. "Implications of Skill-Biased Technological Change: International Evidence." *Quarterly Journal of Economics* 113, no. 4, pp. 1245–79.

Bharadwaj, A., O. A. El Sawy, P. A. Pavlou, and N. Venkatraman. 2013. "Digital Business Strategy: Toward a Next Generation of Insights." *MIS Quarterly* 37, no. 2, pp. 471–82.

Black, S. E., and L. M. Lynch. 2001. "How to Compete: The Impact of Workplace Practices and Information Technology on Productivity." *Review of Economics and Statistics* 83, no. 3, pp. 434–45.

Black, S. E., and L. M. Lynch. 2004. "What's Driving the New Economy?: The Benefits of Workplace Innovation." *Economic Journal* 114, no. 493, pp. F97–F116.

Bloom, N., L. Garicano, R. Sadun, and J. Van Reenen. 2014. "The Distinct Effects of Information Technology and Communication Technology on Firm Organization." *Management Science* 60, no. 12, pp. 2859–85.

Bloom, N., R. Sadun, and J. Van Reenen. 2012. "Americans Do IT Better: US Multinationals and the Productivity Miracle." *American Economic Review* 102, no. 1, pp. 167–201.

Bresnahan, T. F., E. Brynjolfsson, and L. M. Hitt. 2002. "Information Technology, Workplace Organization, and the Demand for Skilled Labor: Firm-Level Evidence." *Quarterly Journal of Economics* 117, no. 1, pp. 339–76.

Bresnahan, T. F., and S. Greenstein. 1996. "Technical Progress and Co-invention in Computing and in the Uses of Computers." *Brookings Papers on Economic Activity* 27 (1996 Microeconomics), pp. 1–83.

Brynjolfsson, E., and L. M. Hitt. 2000. "Beyond Computation: Information Technology, Organizational Transformation and Business Performance." *Journal of Economic Perspectives* 14, no. 4, pp. 23–48.

Brynjolfsson, E., L. M. Hitt, and S. Yang. 2002. "Intangible Assets: Computers and Organizational Capital." *Brookings Papers on Economic Activity* 2002, no. 1, pp. 137–81.

Brynjolfsson, E., and A. McAfee. 2011. *Race against the Machine: How the Digital Revolution Is Accelerating Innovation, Driving Productivity, and Irreversibly Transforming Employment and the Economy* (Lexington, MA: Digital Frontier Press).

Brynjolfsson, E., and A. McAfee. 2014. *The Second Machine Age: Work, Progress, and Prosperity in a Time of Brilliant Technologies* (New York: Norton).

Brynjolfsson, E., and P. Milgrom. 2013. "Complementarity in Organizations." In *The Handbook of Organizational Economics*, edited by R. Gibbons and J. Roberts (Princeton University Press).

Caroli, E., and J. Van Reenen. 2001. "Skill-Biased Organizational Change: Evidence from a Panel of British and French Establishments." *Quarterly Journal of Economics* 116, no. 4, pp. 1449–92.

Chetty, R., J. N. Friedman, and J. E. Rockoff. 2014a. "Measuring the Impacts of Teachers I: Evaluating Bias in Teacher Value-Added Estimates." *American Economic Review* 104, no. 9, pp. 2593–632.

Chetty, R., J. N. Friedman, and J. E. Rockoff. 2014b. "Measuring the Impacts of Teachers II: Teacher Value-Added and Student Outcomes in Adulthood." *American Economic Review* 104, no. 9, pp. 2633–79.

Davenport, T. H. 1998. "Putting the Enterprise into the Enterprise System." *Harvard Business Review* 76, no. 4, pp. 121–31.

Frankiewicz, B., and T. Chamorro-Premuzic. 2020. "Digital Transformation Is about Talent, Not Technology." *Harvard Business Review* (online). https://hbr.org/2020/05/digital-transformation-is-about-talent-not-technology.

Goldfarb, A., and C. Tucker. 2019. "Digital Economics." *Journal of Economic Literature* 57, no. 1, pp. 3–43.

Hall, B. H. 2005. "Innovation and Diffusion." In *The Oxford Handbook of Innovation*, edited by J. Fagerberg, D. C. Mowery, and R. R. Nelson (Oxford University Press).

International Labour Organization. 2019a. *Lifelong Learning: Concepts, Issues and Actions* (Geneva).

International Labour Organization. 2019b. *Work for a Brighter Future* (Geneva).

Kane, G. C., A. N. Phillips, J. R. Copulsky, and G. R. Andrus. 2019. *The Technology Fallacy: How People Are the Real Key to Digital Transformation* (MIT Press).

Kim, M. 2020. "Knowledge Capital and Firm Productivity." Research Monograph (Korea Development Institute). [In Korean.]

KRIVET. n.d. The Human Capital Corporate Panel. https://www.krivet.re.kr /eng/eu/eh/euDAADs.jsp.

Manjón, M., and J. Mañez. 2016. "Production Function Estimation in Stata Using the Ackerberg-Caves-Frazer Method." *Stata Journal* 16, no. 4, pp. 900–916.

McKinsey Quarterly. 2016. "How Ericsson Aligned Its People with Its Transformation Strategy: An Interview with Chief HR Officer Bina Chaurasia." January.

Milgrom, P., and J. Roberts. 1990. "The Economics of Modern Manufacturing: Technology, Strategy, and Organization." *American Economic Review* 80, no. 3, pp. 511–28.

Milgrom, P., and J. Roberts. 1995. "Complementarities and Fit: Strategy, Structure, and Organizational Change in Manufacturing." *Journal of Accounting and Economics* 19, no. 2, pp. 179–208.

Moules, J. 2018. "Employers Buy into 'Netflixisation' of Executive Education." *Financial Times*, August 2. www.ft.com/content/4fcd2360-8e91-11e8-bb8f -a6a2f7bca546.

Organization for Economic Cooperation and Development. 2019. *Preparing for the Changing Nature of Work in the Digital Era*. OECD Going Digital Policy Note (Paris: OECD Publishing).

Porter, M. E., and J. E. Heppelmann. 2014. "How Smart, Connected Products Are Transforming Competition." *Harvard Business Review* 92, no. 11, pp. 64–88.

Porter, M. E., and J. E. Heppelmann. 2015. "How Smart, Connected Products Are Transforming Companies." *Harvard Business Review* 93, no. 10, pp. 96–114.

Statistics Korea. n.d. Survey of Business Activities. http://kostat.go.kr/portal /eng/surveyOutline/3/8/index.static.

SEVEN

Digitalization and Inequality

FRANÇOIS BOURGUIGNON

The technological change induced by the digital revolution raises fears in most advanced countries of countless jobs replaced by robots or artificial intelligence, an increasing proportion of the labor force forced into inactivity, and a surge in income inequality. Futurologists compete in predicting ever-increasing numbers of tasks and jobs to be automated in the coming one or two decades. McKinsey recently estimated that as much as 50 percent of occupations would be affected in one way or another by technological change.[1] Optimists expect that new jobs will replace those displaced by automation, as in previous industrial revolutions. Pessimists predict a major crisis. Still others see in the present digitalization-led technological change the seeds of a new society where work will have become unnecessary.[2]

Digitalization-based technological change has already proceeded for quite some time now in advanced countries. If no major drop has taken place in the volume of employment, noticeable changes can be observed in its composition. The proportion of routine manual or nonmanual jobs has fallen, whereas that of nonroutine jobs has increased. On the inequality front, on the other hand, major increases have taken place in several countries.

Market income inequality has increased since the mid-1980s, but the trend appears to have stabilized now in many countries except the United States. Disposable income inequality has shown more heterogeneity across countries and time periods. At the aggregate level, a notable feature is that the share of capital, or nonlabor, income in GDP has risen in a way roughly parallel to market income inequality.

Such an evolution in employment and income distribution is apparently consistent with an automation bias in technological change. Robots and artificial intelligence displaced routine jobs whose earnings rate went down, possibly contributing to more labor income inequality. The increase in the nonlabor income share of value added also fits well the view that automation is first meant to transfer income from labor to firms' owners. Yet many other factors may explain the same facts and the heterogeneity of distributional changes across countries. Modifications in the skill structure of labor supply or in labor legislation may also have caused changes in the distribution of earnings. Market power concentration or the diminishing power of labor unions may be behind the drop in the labor income share. Such factors may well have moderated or even hidden the true effects of digitalization, or, on the contrary, they may have accentuated them so that it is now difficult to identify what is specifically due to technology in observed changes in inequality.

These sources of change in the distribution of market incomes combine with major indirect effects of technological change that tend to attenuate its direct distributional impact. These are the creation of jobs made necessary by new technologies and, most important, the new jobs generated by the increase in aggregate demand resulting from the productivity gains permitted by technological innovation. Over the long run, these effects are held to have made past industrial revolutions benefit the whole population in a relatively egalitarian way and avoid employment collapses.

This chapter reviews the relationship between the current wave of digitalization-based technological change and income inequality, based on analysis of past and present trends in advanced economies and the abundant recent academic literature on this topic. It reflects on likely consequences of the acceleration of the digital revolution predicted by futurologists, and on policies to address potential adverse effects.

The chapter's first section sets the scene by reviewing the evolution of market income inequality in selected advanced economies since the late 1970s. The next three sections then review different strands of recent literature on digitalization and inequality. The potential effect of digitalization in the labor market is reviewed first, with a focus on the structure of employment and the distribution of earnings. Of special importance is the examination of the hypotheses of skill-biased technical change and job polarization, according to which digitalization displaces routine jobs at the middle of the earnings scale and feeds earnings inequality. A second set of questions is concerned with the observed fall of the GDP share of labor and the corresponding increase in the share of capital or property income, which in turn raises inequality at the top of the distribution of market incomes. The key question there is whether such an evolution is consistent with the expected effects of digitalization on employment, wages, and profits. Attention then turns to a third set of questions on whether the drop in the labor income share and the increase in inequality are related to rising corporate rents associated with the observed increase in market concentration, and whether the latter has some relationship with digitalization.

A review of the literature in these three areas shows that digitalization contributes to more inequality both through job displacement that leads to changes in the distribution of earnings in favor of higher skills, and through a drop in the labor income share in sectors most exposed to automation as well as in the whole economy. In turn, these effects entail an increase in the market income share of households at the top of the income scale. There is less evidence that technological change may also be responsible for more market concentration and rising rents outside the high-tech sectors, even though this hypothesis cannot be discarded.

The final two sections of the chapter are more forward looking and policy oriented. Given the inegalitarian impact of automation and digitalization observed over the recent past, an impact likely to be magnified in coming decades if futurologists are right, what can be done to minimize the adverse effects while keeping the benefits of innovation? Some considerations are offered on the role of labor market policies and taxation.

Evolution of Income Inequality in Advanced Economies and Its Link with Digitalization

There are many dimensions of economic inequality, income being one of them and the most widely referred to. Even when focusing on income, however, different options are available depending on the kind of inequality one is interested in. The most frequently used concept is the distribution of equivalized household disposable incomes (EHDIs), in which everyone in the population is imputed the total income, after taxes and transfers, accruing to the household he/she belongs to, divided by the number of "adult equivalents" in the household. Yet this is not the concept that this section will focus upon.

There are two sources of variation in the EHDI distribution. One is income before redistribution by taxes and transfers, that is, the distribution of market income, or income that results from household or individual economic endowments and market operations. The other is redistribution by the tax system and transfers from private or public sources. Because of redistribution, the distribution of disposable and market income need not evolve in a parallel way over time, especially in the presence of changes in the structure of the redistribution system.

Concerning the impact of technology on income inequality, it is reasonable to consider that it bears primarily on market income and then affects disposable income through the filter of redistribution. Indeed, redistribution is presumably less affected by technological change than market incomes.

Figure 7-1 shows the evolution of inequality of market income per adult measured by the share of the top decile in total household market income over the last forty to fifty years. It is based on data from tax returns, which are a better source to capture market incomes than household surveys, particularly at the top of the income scale. Countries appearing in that figure are the Group of Seven (G7) countries plus Sweden (to see whether inequality trends are different in a country with a Nordic egalitarian culture).

The parallelism of inequality trends among the eight countries during a middle period extending from the early 1980s to the mid-2000s is striking. Trends are flat, downward sloping, or upward sloping in the 1970s. They are heterogeneous also in the last ten years. In between, the share of the top decile substantially increased in all countries, even though at different speeds: close to 10 percentage points overall in the United States and Japan, and between 5 and 7 percentage points in the other countries. Inequality fell with the 2008 crisis in all countries. Then the previous trend restarted, although at a slower pace, in the United States and Germany. In other countries, however, the share of the top decile stabilized at a level comparable to what was observed in the early 2000s, at the beginning of the cycle that led to the Great Recession. Thus, if one were to look only at the last eighteen years or so, one

FIGURE 7-1. **Inequality of Market Income per Adult in Selected Advanced Economies, 1970–2017 (Tax Data, Share of Top 10 Percent)**

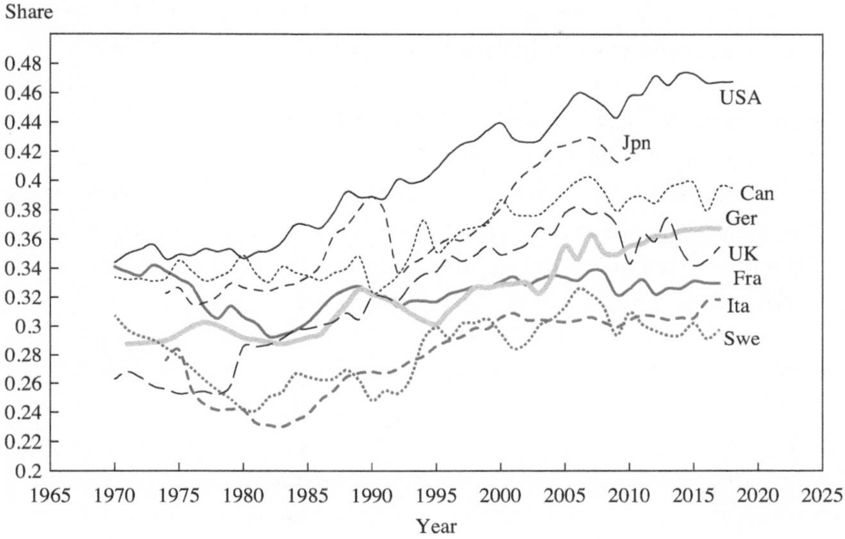

Share

Source: Based on data from World Inequality Database (n.d.).

would detect no ascending, or descending, trend in Canada, France, Italy, Sweden, or the United Kingdom—the same being probably true of Japan, judging from disposable income inequality data since market income inequality data are unavailable there after 2010.

Although not shown here, the evolution of disposable income inequality does not follow the same pattern as that of market income. Disposable income inequality in recent years is higher than what it was thirty or thirty-five years ago, but the time profiles are much more heterogeneous across countries.[3] Among the eight countries, only the United States and Sweden show an ascending inequality trend over the whole period. Other countries exhibit a one-off rise at some stage during the period, with flat trends before and after, even at times when market income inequality rises. This shows the power of redistribution systems in dampening changes in market income inequality.

The most obvious interpretation of the common ascending trend in market income inequality among advanced countries from the early 1980s to the mid-2000s is that common factors were at work among these countries. They may still be present in the recent decade, as suggested by the case of the United States and Germany, and possibly hidden by other, country-specific factors in other countries.

What could be these common factors? Globalization and technological change are most frequently mentioned. But one could also think of a succession of more limited events. For instance, it is likely that the global disinflation of 1982–1985 benefited high incomes by raising returns on financial assets. A little later, the acceleration of merchandise trade and capital movements associated with globalization benefited capital owners more than workers, until the sudden stop of 2008. These are events or trends that can be dated, even though in an imprecise way. Things are different for technological change.

As can be seen in figure 7-2, it would indeed seem that, in some respects, the digitalization process has been continuous throughout the last forty years. If the share of information-processing equipment and software in private investment seems to have stabilized after 2000, this is not true at constant prices. Because the price of information technology (IT) equipment went systematically down relative to other equipment, it turns out that IT investment has progressed twice as rapidly as other types of investment since 2000, and even faster before then. The same continuous trend is observed for personal computer ownership, another indicator of the digitalization process.

The growth of industrial robots relative to private investment is more concentrated over time. As shown by available statistics from the International Federation of Robotics, the use of robots really surged over the last few years, with the number of new robots installed annually in the world growing twice as fast as private investment in Organization for Economic Cooperation and Development (OECD) countries between 2012 and 2018.[4] Yet this discontinuity does not seem to have any counterpart in the evolution of market income inequality as shown in figure 7-1.

Without any knowledge a priori of what might be the impact of common factors on income inequality, it is difficult to distinguish which ones have contributed most to the marked increase in market income inequality among advanced economies. Digitalization-based technological change almost certainly is one of them, but it is hard to clearly identify its role in a general framework where so many phenomena may influence the evolution of inequality. The rest of the chapter examines whether technology's role may be better assessed by considering constituent parts of overall inequality, starting with the distribution of earnings.

FIGURE 7-2. Selected Indicators of Digitalization, 1980–2018

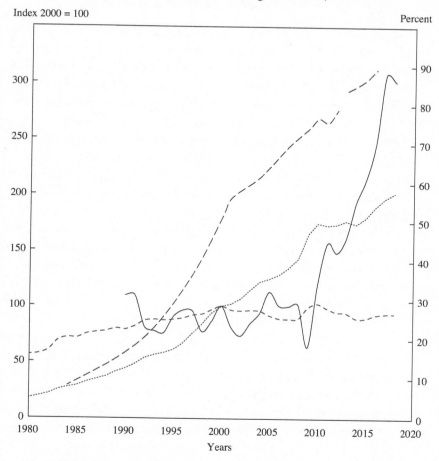

Index 2000 = 100   Percent

——— Estimated worldwide shipments of industrial robots per 2010 dollar of gross fixed
      capital formation in OECD countries (LHA)

- - - - Share of information processing equipment and software in non-residential private
       investment at current prices in United States (LHA)

·········· Share of information processing equipment and software in non-residential private
       investment at constant 2012 prices in United States (LHA)

– – – – Households with computers in United States (RHA)

Source: Author calculations based on data from International Federation of Robotics (n.d.),
World Development Indicators (n.d.), Bureau of Economic Analysis (n.d.), and Ryan (2018).

Note: LHA and RHA stand for left-hand axis and right-hand axis, respectively.

Digitalization, the Labor Market, and Earnings Inequality

Figures 7-3a, 7-3b, and 7-3c show the evolution of the inequality of earnings since the mid-1970s for the same advanced countries as before. Inequality is measured, respectively, by the ratio of the 90th to the 10th percentile (P90/P10), the ratio of the 90th percentile to the median (P90/P50, upper inequality), and the ratio of the median to the 10th percentile (P50/P10, lower inequality). Data were compiled by the OECD based on administrative registers or standard labor force or household surveys. Unfortunately, they are available only for the last two or three decades for some countries. They are complemented by data from Atkinson and Morelli (2014) in figure 7-3b, additional sources for France and Italy in figure 7-3a, and additional sources for France in figure 7-3c.

Much emphasis has been put lately on rising inequality at the very top of the earnings scale. Indeed, the share of total wage income accruing to the top 1 percent has substantially increased in the United States and in other countries. However, the very top earners are scarcely representative of what may be happening in the labor market more broadly—and considering quantiles above P90 would be of limited interest.[5]

The dominant feature in the evolution of the overall dispersion of earnings—figure 7-3a—is the difference between the United States, where the dispersion has increased almost continuously and at roughly the same pace over the last forty years, and the other countries, where the dispersion is more stable or has risen overall but at a much slower pace than in the United States. Germany is somewhat exceptional because the dispersion of earnings did increase overall but in an abrupt way and only toward the end of the period.

The evolution is more homogeneous when considering the dispersion in the upper part of the distribution (figure 7-3b). In most countries, the upper inequality of earnings rose significantly until the late 1990s or early 2000s, a bit like market income inequality. Then it stabilized, except in the United States, where it kept rising, and in Germany, where it started to increase after years of stability.

The lower earnings inequality (figure 7-3c) shows more heterogeneity both across countries and over time. The dispersion increased in the United Kingdom and in the United States until the mid-1990s but thereafter declined in the former and stabilized in the latter. It fell continuously in Canada, France, and Japan, fluctuated around a flat trend in Italy, and rose continuously in Sweden from the early 1990s on.

Skill-Biased Technological Change and Earnings Inequality

The surge of earnings inequality in the 1980s in the United States quickly triggered an intense reflection on its causes. Skill heterogeneity being the main source of earnings inequality, the debate focused on the supply and demand of skilled labor and on the return to skill, proxied by the "skill premium" or the ratio of the mean wage of workers with college education or more over that of other workers. Within a simple competitive aggregate model of the labor market, the increase in earnings inequality, which coincided with a surge in the skill premium, was imputed to the relative demand for college-educated workers growing faster than the supply.

A first explanation for the acceleration of the relative demand for skilled labor was globalization and the change that it implied in the structure of economic activity. Imports from emerging economies in a more open global economy reduced the weight of tradable sectors that were relatively intensive in unskilled labor and increased the relative demand for skilled labor overall. However, it turned out that this restructuring of the economy was not enough to explain the observed rise in the skill premium. The remainder was imputed to an autonomous change in technology that was making production relatively more intensive in skilled labor, an effect soon termed skill-biased technological change or SBTC.[6]

Except for a relatively small part explained by globalization, the rise in earnings inequality in the United States was thus another illustration of Tinbergen's famous education-technology race. Technological change was increasing the relative demand for skilled labor faster than the expansion of college education in the population.[7] Table 7-1, based on Goldin and Katz (2009) and extended to the last two decades, shows estimates of the rate of SBTC over the last seventy years in the United States. Estimates of the growth of the relative demand for skilled labor (third column) are obtained by assuming that the growth of the skill premium is proportional to the difference between the growth of the relative demand and relative supply of college-educated workers.[8] Except in the 1970s, when the supply of college-educated workers accelerated because of the postwar surge of college education, the skill premium has systematically moved upward, revealing a demand for skilled labor growing faster than the supply. The skill

FIGURE 7-3. **Inequality of Earnings in Selected Advanced Economies, 1975–2018**

(A)

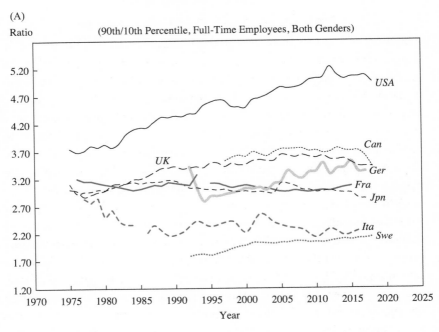

(B)

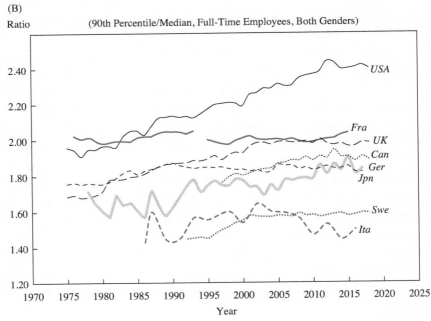

(C)

Ratio   (Median/10th Percentile, Full-Time Employees, Both Genders)

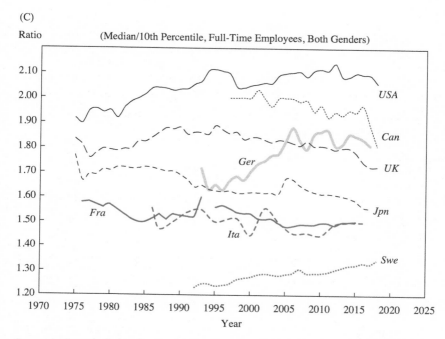

Source: Author calculations based on OECD (n.d.a), Atkinson and Morelli (2014), INSEE (2020) for France prior to 1994, and Brandolini, Cipollone, and Sestito (2001) for Italy prior to 1996.

premium surged in the 1980s and has continued to rise since then, although at a slower pace. Such deceleration at a time when technological change is thought to have accelerated is somewhat paradoxical.

A similar evolution has been observed in the 1980s and 1990s in other advanced economies. This is clear in figure 7-3b, which shows the trend in upper earnings inequality that is more relevant in this context than the overall dispersion of earnings because of labor market institutions, particularly in European countries, that limit wage flexibility at the bottom of the wage scale. As the speed of SBTC is likely to be similar in these countries to that in the United States, the stabilization of earnings inequality observed after the turn of the millennium could be imputed to the supply of skilled labor growing faster. In the United Kingdom, for instance, the relative supply of skilled workers increased at an annual rate of 4.2 percent between 2006 and 2014, almost twice as rapidly as in the United States, whereas the skill premium fell at an annual rate of 1 percent. This is consistent with SBTC leading to a growth rate of relative demand for

Table 7-1. *Annual Growth Rate of the Skill Premium, Relative Supply of Skilled Workers, and Estimated SBTC, United States 1950–2019*

Period	Observed annual growth rate of skilled/ unskilled wage ratio	Observed annual growth rate of relative supply of skilled workers	SBTC: estimated annual growth rate of relative demand for skilled workers
(Goldin and Katz, 2009)			
1950–60	0.83	2.91	4.08
1960–70	0.69	2.55	3.52
1970–80	−0.74	4.99	3.95
1980–90	1.51	2.53	4.65
1990–00	0.58	2.03	2.84
(BLS data)			
2000–10	0.30	2.18	2.60
2010–19	0.09	2.34	2.47

Source: Goldin and Katz (2009), updated by the author based on data from Bureau of Labor Statistics (BLS) (n.d.).

skilled workers slightly below 3 percent, a figure comparable to the available estimates in the United States.[9]

A host of labor market–related factors other than technological change, globalization, and college education or the equivalent may have affected the dispersion of earnings independently from the skill premium. For instance, changes in the composition of the labor force by gender, age, and geographical location, or changes in labor market institutions such as employment protection, minimum wage legislation, and the degree of unionization, are known to have a substantial impact on earnings inequality, and possibly on the skill premium itself. Changes in the distribution of unobserved personal determinants of earnings may matter too.[10]

More generally, it must be stressed that, as in the empirical analysis of economic growth, the estimation of the effect of technological change on earnings inequality essentially is a residual of what cannot be explained by standard supply and demand–related factors like the distribution of observed skills—including educational attainment and job experience—in the population, participation behavior conditional on skills, or the sectoral structure of the economy. Such an indirect estimation necessarily involves some ambiguity.

It also prevents going deeper into the nature of technological change so as, for instance, to distinguish the effect of digitalization or automation, my focus in this chapter, from engineering innovation. Doing so requires a more detailed description of labor inputs in the production process than a dichotomous distinction by educational attainment. Specifically, one needs to focus on the very nature of occupations and tasks, precisely as futurologists do when trying to forecast how digitalization and artificial intelligence may affect jobs.

Job Polarization

Following the same line as futurologists, the job polarization hypothesis consists of recognizing that automation displaces routine manual and non-manual jobs whose tasks are easily replaced by digital devices and artificial intelligence. Reciprocally, digitalization causes a rise in the relative demand for cognitive and interpersonal skills on the one hand and for nonroutine manual skills, typically in services, on the other hand. Given the relative earnings of these three groups of jobs, digitalization thus tends to polarize the earnings distribution, displacing jobs at the middle of the earnings scale and increasing the share of jobs in the upper and lower parts of the scale.

Evidence of such polarization is obtained through the following procedure. For each occupation in the recorded set of occupations, the median earnings in some base year of all workers employed in that occupation are determined. A distribution of occupational skills is thus obtained, where the skill level of an occupation is its median earnings in some base year. It is then possible to represent in a simple way the changes that take place in the skill structure of occupations over time and their impact on earnings inequality. It suffices to observe how the proportion of jobs with a given occupational skill, proxied by their relative median earnings in year t_0, changed between years t_0 and t_1, independently of the level of earnings the jobs command in t_1.

When applied to the 1990s, this occupation approach to the impact of technological change shows a clear polarization of jobs in the United States, with the shares of high- and low-skill jobs (that is, high- and low-median-wage jobs) going up at the expense of middle-skill jobs. Following Autor and Dorn (2013), this was interpreted as confirmation of computerization and automation replacing routine jobs. Goos and Manning (2007) and Goos, Manning, and Salomons (2009) found evidence of job polarization in the UK and in several European Union (EU) economies.[11] Goos, Manning, and Salomons (2014) went one step further by checking that those occupations in the middle part of the median earnings scale with declining employment in the EU were indeed "routine task intensive" according to an index built by Autor and Dorn (2013).

The interpretation of the widely observed job polarization phenomenon raises an issue. If the increasing share of upper-end jobs in the occupational skill scale is another illustration of the SBTC, the issue is whether the rising share at the lower end results from an increase in the demand for occupations with that kind of skill—that is, nonroutine manual work or interpersonal relationships—or from a relocation of workers from displaced routine occupations. In the former case, job polarization should come with wage polarization, with wages increasing faster at both ends of the scale. In the latter case, wages at the bottom of the scale should be negatively affected by the labor supply increment in those occupational categories. Evidence of wage polarization was found for the United States in the 1990s[12] but not in other periods. On the other hand, wage polarization seems to be absent in European countries—see Goos and Manning (2007) for the United Kingdom and Dustmann, Ludsteck, and Schönberg (2009) for Germany.

What are the implications of job polarization and the implicit antiroutine bias of technological change behind it for earnings inequality? In the upper part of the earnings distribution, they are presumably the same as for SBTC, with the same balancing role as before played by the supply of more-educated workers who are more fit for nonroutine cognitive tasks. In the lower part, wage polarization should correspond to a drop or at least a stabilization of the P50/P10 ratio, as indeed observed in the 1990s in the United States (see figure 7-3c). However, even without wage polarization, that is, with only some downgrading of jobs initially in the middle part of occupational skills, the same changes could be observed, as the relative downward pressure on wages would be stronger on those middle-range occupations that are displaced, especially in countries where low-wage jobs are protected by minimum wage legislation.

It must be kept in mind, however, that relying on median earnings of occupations to define an occupational skill index to represent the impact of technological change on the distribution of earnings is rather restrictive. It amounts to ignoring differences in the within-occupation distribution of earnings across occupations and, more importantly, changes in those distributions. On the one hand, changing the structure of occupations modifies the earnings distribution beyond what can be gauged from median earnings. On the other hand, exits from some occupations and entries into others necessarily modify the distribution of earnings in each of them, whereas the nature of tasks within a given occupation and therefore the skills it requires may vary over time, precisely because of automation and computerization. In a study of the evolution of job characteristics in Germany, it was found that most of the changes in several job skill requirements aggregated into a single index were taking place within occupations rather than between them.[13] A systematic educational upgrading of occupations was also found, as in other countries, meaning that apparently the same job was held today by more educated people who could still claim higher earnings than others in the same occupation.

Digitalization and Earnings Distribution

What conclusions can be drawn from the huge literature on the role of technological change in modifying the distribution of labor earnings? The simplest story consistent with earnings distribution data seems to be as follows. Digitalization has increased the demand for workers with higher education, particularly for nonroutine analytic and interpersonal tasks. It has also reduced the demand for less-educated people involved in routine tasks, whether cognitive or manual; that is, workers in the middle and lower parts of the distribution of educational attainments. There seems to be a broad consensus on these effects. The changes observed in the distribution of earnings result from a combination of these demand-side effects and changes in the volume and composition of labor supply.

This story fits the United States rather well. Demand increased continuously faster than supply of higher-educated workers after 1980, due partly to globalization and, more importantly, to technological change. This resulted in a sustained upward trend in upper income and overall inequality. Signs exist, however, of a slowing of the relative demand of high-skill workers over the last two decades or so.[14] In the lower part of the earnings distribution, the early displacement of routine manual jobs first affected relatively more the earnings at the low end, resulting in an increase of lower earnings inequality. Later, the displacement of routine nonmanual jobs hit relative earnings in the middle range of the scale, causing first a drop and then a stabilization of lower earnings inequality.

In Europe, and possibly Canada and Japan, the story would be the same except that the relative supply of more-educated workers may have grown faster than the relative demand caused by technological change, especially in the last two decades, thus reversing the ascending P90/P50 trend observed until the mid- or late 1990s. In the lower part of the distribution, the evolution could have been similar to that in the United States, except for the presence of a binding minimum wage in several countries (Canada, France, Japan, and the United Kingdom since 1998), which prevented lower wages from falling as they did in the United States and explains the falling P50/P10 trend from the late 1990s on.

Germany seems atypical as P90/P50 increased in the recent past, possibly showing supply growing short of demand. The relatively recent shortage of engineers and technicians has motivated new legislation encouraging high-skill immigration, especially in the IT field, including from outside the EU.[15] The increase in P50/P10 in the 2000s in Germany is also atypical in comparison with other countries. Biewen, Fitzenberger, and de Lazzer (2017) relate it to high unemployment in the early 2000s and the wave of labor market reforms undertaken then—the Hartz reforms—which reduced unemployment but negatively affected workers' wage potential, especially for women.

Technological Change and the Property Income Share

Decomposing changes in market income inequality would in principle require analyzing changes in the distribution of property income in the same way as was done above for labor earnings. Unlike labor earnings, there are few data sources that exclusively focus on individual or household distribution of property income, are comparable across countries, and extend over long enough periods. Because of the high concentration of property in the population, however, the share of property income in market income is a good indicator of the contribution to changes in inequality that originate in property income.

This section focuses on the evolution of the share of property income in total value added, that is, GDP, data on which are more readily available, rather than household market income. Although this measure incorporates undistributed profits and capital consumption expenditures, which do not accrue to households, its correlation with inequality is still expected to be high. Being closer to the production side of the economy, it may also be more directly sensitive to technological change.

Evolution of Labor/Property Income Shares in Advanced Economies

There is a strong similarity between the evolution of the GDP share of property income, as shown in figure 7-4, and the top market income share for the same countries, as shown in figure 7-1. Both figures exhibit a rising trend for almost all countries from around the mid-1980s to the years preceding the Great Recession, and a plateauing afterward, except in the United States, where the trend keeps rising. There are exceptions, however, so that the correlation is far from perfect. A clear case is the United Kingdom, where the ascending trend is much weaker in figure 7-4 and flattens much earlier than in figure 7-1. Differences are also notable before the mid-1980s.

Given the rough consistency of the evolution of property or nonlabor income shares of GDP with that of market income inequality, the question is whether digitalization has played a significant role in the former. To approach this question more effectively, it might have been better to restrict the analysis to those sectors where technological change is likely to have played a major role. Doing so would weaken the link with the household distribution of income, however. Moreover, it turns out that the overall evolution of the nonlabor income share in the business or industrial sectors compares well with that in the whole economy, although the magnitudes may be different. In the United States, for instance, the increase in the nonlabor income share is more pronounced in the business sector, particularly in manufacturing, than in GDP.[16]

Technological Change and Nonlabor Income Share
in a Neoclassical Framework

Within the restrictive but simple two-factor aggregate competitive representation of an economy, the evolution of factor shares depends on two factors: the increase of the capital-labor ratio—capital deepening—and technological change. With constant technology, the nonlabor (labor) share increases (decreases) with capital deepening, depending on whether the elasticity of substitution between capital and labor is greater (smaller) than unity. Several authors, including Karabarbounis and Neiman (2014) and Piketty (2014), indeed interpreted the rise in the nonlabor income share in advanced economies as the result of an elasticity of substitution substantially above unity, that is, labor easily replaced by machines or digital devices. Yet that interpretation goes against most econometric estimates of

FIGURE 7-4. **Nonlabor (Property) Income Share in GDP in Selected Advanced Economies, 1975–2015 (Five-Year Moving Average)**

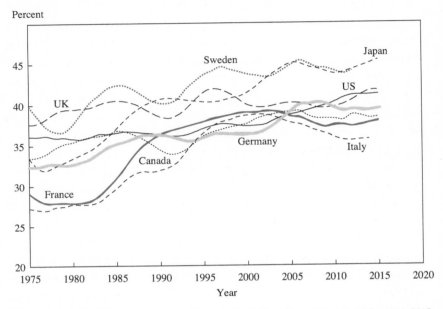

Source: OECD (n.d.b) for 1975–2003 and International Labor Organization (n.d.) for 2004–2015. The two series are made consistent by scaling the former to coincide with the latter at the point of juncture.

that elasticity, which point to an elasticity below unity, as well summarized by Lawrence (2015).

These estimates are based on a model where factor shares depend on the capital-labor ratio and a time trend, the former standing for the substitution effect and the latter for technological change. In the case of US industry, for instance, Lawrence (2015) finds an elasticity of substitution of 0.19 and a labor-saving annual rate of technical progress of 2.4 percent. Accordingly, it would be technological change rather than a high elasticity of substitution between capital and labor that would be responsible for the observed increase in the nonlabor income share.

It is not clear whether this distinction between capital-deepening and labor-augmenting technical change is relevant. After all, labor-saving technical progress results either from labor with higher skill, in which case a model with homogeneous labor is ill adapted to the problem, or from changing equipment, in which case a distinction should be made among vintages in the stock of capital. More fundamentally, an aggregate two-factor neo-classical model seems to be too simple a framework for analyzing the causes of change in the functional distribution of income, as noted by Elsby, Hobijn, and Sahin (2013). Also, interpreting a time trend as the effect of technological change is arguably putting an arbitrary name on what is essentially an unexplained residual. Even abstracting from the many factors that may influence the labor share and are not causally related to technology or capital accumulation, a more structural model is needed to identify the role of technology, and especially its digitalization component.

Tasks, Automation, and Nonlabor Income Share

Several such structural models have been recently proposed in economic literature with an explicit focus on automation.[17] These models are mostly theoretical, but some of them also include a numerical calibration to evaluate the order of magnitude of the effects of automation.

This family of models is based on a threefold decomposition of the effects of automation, mostly considered in what follows as the consequence of digitalization. First, it displaces jobs or tasks. Second, innovation reinstates jobs by creating new and more productive tasks to be filled by human labor in combination with capital equipment. Third, additional income is generated by the resulting gain in productivity, which generates more final demand and more jobs. The displacement effect clearly benefits the nonlabor income share, whereas the task creation and the productivity effects possibly favor labor. The resulting overall effect thus depends on the strength of these three forces. Some authors add labor skills to the model. As skilled labor is generally a complement of automation equipment, an increase in the nonlabor share goes hand in hand with an increase in the skill premium, thus reinforcing the impact on inequality.[18]

If the theoretical mechanisms by which automation and artificial intelligence affect labor and nonlabor income shares and wage inequality through the skill premium are well understood, evidence on these mechanisms and their outcomes is limited.

A decomposition of the evolution of US factor income shares aimed at isolating the effect of automation has been undertaken by Acemoglu and Restrepo (2019). The overall change in the aggregate wage bill is decomposed into (1) an overall productivity effect, (2) a composition effect, that is, the change in the sectoral structure of the economy, with factor shares differing across sectors, and (3) a substitution effect arising from capital deepening at the sectoral level with a constant structure of tasks and a constant elasticity of substitution. What is left, then, is the net effect on the labor share of task displacements and reinstatements at the sectoral level. Interestingly, this net effect proved to be very limited in the forty-year period prior to 1987 but was then clearly negative in the next thirty years. Even though this conclusion fits the intuition that the recent digitalization drive has accelerated automation and task displacement, it is still problematic that it is reached only as a residual explanation, once the effects of sectoral composition, capital deepening, and productivity change have been accounted for within a (possibly questionable) competitive economy framework.

Direct Evidence on the Impact of Robot Densification

The availability of data on the use of industrial robots has allowed researchers to provide more direct evidence on the effect of automation not only on factor shares but also on employment and wages—and to put more empirical flesh on the theoretical model sketched above. This research generally finds that robotization has increased the nonlabor income share and, possibly, also income inequality.

Two studies are particularly noteworthy because of their methodology and results. The first one, by Acemoglu and Restrepo (2020a), examines the US case. It relies on regressions of various key indicators on robot exposure across local labor markets.[19] The study covers the 1990–2007 period, during which robot density increased by roughly one robot per 1,000 workers. Direct estimates suggest that local employment shrank on average by 0.4 percent—one robot replacing four workers—and wages by 0.8 percent. These estimates are then used to calibrate key parameters in a theoretical model close to that outlined in Acemoglu and Restrepo (2018), which accounts for spillover effects across local markets and thus provides an estimate of the aggregate effect of robotization. It turns out that the preceding negative employment and wage effects are approximately halved, implying that the productivity gain and employment spillovers reduce but fail to fully offset the job displacement effect. Overall, with a higher productivity and lower wages, the nonlabor income share was positively affected by the densification of robots.

The second study, by Dauth and others (2017), is based on the same methodology and refers to the period 1994–2014 in Germany, a country that, together with Japan, has the highest industrial robot density in the world. It also finds that the densification of robots raised productivity, but, unlike in the United States, had no significant effect on average local wages and employment rates. Together, these effects increased the nonlabor income share by 2 percent. Concerning the absence of a significant effect on employment, the analysis shows that it results from a combination of displacement of two workers per additional robot in the manufacturing sector and the net creation of two jobs in the services sector. The job displacement effect is less pronounced than that found in the US study, and the spillover in services fully compensates the employment loss.

Three additional results are worth stressing in this study of Germany. First, wage inequality tends to increase as medium-skill wages lose and high-skill wages gain from robotization.[20] Second, a parallel analysis of the effect of the densification of information and communication technology (ICT) equipment shows no significant impact on employment or wages, but possibly a positive effect on the nonlabor share through productivity gain. Third, when the period of estimation is split into two ten-year periods, the overall employment effect becomes significantly negative in the later subperiod, suggesting some recent intensification of the displacement effect.

A more recent study of the effects of robotization at the firm level in France confirms the preceding results on local labor markets. In a sample of more than 50,000 firms observed between 2010 and 2015, Acemoglu, Lelarge, and Restrepo (2020) find the same negative effects on employment and wages and positive effects on productivity and the nonlabor income share—and they find that these effects hold at the four-digit industry level.[21]

Graetz and Michaels (2018) is another study that makes use of differences in robotization speed, but on a cross-country and industry basis.[22] Based on seventeen countries between 1993 and 2007, they find evidence of productivity gain, no significant effect on employment, a tiny increase in average wage, and no significant effect on factor shares as productivity gains are absorbed by a drop in prices. Averaging across countries and industries may hide important national disparities, so the findings do not necessarily contradict the results of the preceding studies. Several other recent cross-country studies find a significant positive impact of automation, or technological change in general, on the nonlabor share. However, they only use indirect proxies rather than robots or ICT equipment to describe automation. Autor and Salomons (2018) proxy automation at the industry level by total factor productivity gain in a sample of nineteen countries over the last four decades. Dao and others (2017) work on a sample of forty-nine advanced and emerging economies and use the relative price of investment times the initial level of routinization of tasks as an indicator of the incentive to automate.

Although the strength of the evidence varies across studies, they together confirm that, in agreement with intuition, automation contributes to increasing the nonlabor income share of value added both at the industry level and in local labor markets and, through that channel, likely contributes to raising market income inequality. There thus seems to be some consistency between direct evidence based on studies of robotization and indirect evidence based on more macro approaches where the effect of technological change is treated as a kind of residual once other determinants of factor income shares have been accounted for.

There also is a consensus that, at the level of local labor markets or individual firms, robot investments tend to lower employment. The same agreement seems to be present among studies that also focus on the productivity gain derived from automation. As wage effects are generally found to be moderate, this evidence on employment and productivity corroborates findings that automation has contributed to increasing the nonlabor share and income inequality.

Some studies also show that, in terms of both employment and wages, skilled workers are less negatively affected or even positively affected by automation, unlike less-skilled workers, thus adding to the inegalitarian impact of automation.

Several of the preceding results rely on the assumption that economies are fully competitive. This is problematic since such an assumption may influence the estimated effect of technological change, especially when defined as a residual after accounting for observable sources of change in factor shares. The residual may well include the effect of the actual behavior of the economy departing from a competitive framework. A shift away from competitive markets, its impact on nonlabor income shares, and its possible link with digitalization are analyzed in the next section.

Factor Shares, Rising Market Power, and Technological Change

In their decomposition of the drop in the labor income share since the turn of the millennium in the United States, Mischke, Kotz, and Bughin (2019) impute only 12 percent to capital substitution and technology but 18 percent to the increasing market power of superstar firms.[23] Much interest has arisen lately in the apparently increasing concentration of market power in several sectors of advanced economies, especially in the United States. In the present framework, this raises two sets of issues: whether market power and associated rents have indeed increased in recent decades, thus feeding the increase in the nonlabor income share and inequality; and to what extent this is the consequence of technological change, particularly digitalization. It is rather obvious that intuition in this area is very much influenced by the spectacular success of the FAANGs,[24] those big firms that have come to represent the digital economy. The issue is much more general, however, as it concerns a broader range of activities.

In an influential paper, Autor and others (2020) investigate the relationship between the fall of the labor income share and increasing market concentration by industrial sector in the United States over the period 1982–2012. The implicit model they use is simple. In a monopolistic competition framework, a positive shock to the productivity of a single firm lowers the price it charges and increases its volume of production as well as its markup rate over costs and, consequently, the nonlabor share in its value added. In other words, its market power rises thanks to its productivity gain, and its profits rise with the corresponding increase in its monopolistic rent. If positive productivity shocks tend to be more frequent or larger in bigger companies, then market concentration rises over time, superstar firms appear, and the average markup rate and the nonlabor income share of the industry move up.

The evidence for the joint evolution of market concentration and factor shares by four-digit sectors of activity in the United States is rather strong, with most of the increase in sectoral nonlabor share being due to the reallocation of employment from small or medium firms to large ones. That the underlying cause is an increase in market power in large firms is confirmed by the evolution of the distribution of firms' markup rates, which show practically no change in the median and a sizable increase of the mean.

This increase in the concentration of market power, the widening divergence in productivity growth between large firms at the global technology frontier and lagging small and medium firms, and the simultaneous rise in the nonlabor income share over the last three or four decades are confirmed by several firm-level studies in the United States and at the global level. See, for instance, De Loecker, Eeckhout, and Unger (2020), De

Loecker and Eeckhout (2018), and Andrews, Criscuolo, and Gal (2016). The key issue, however, is the cause of this evolution.

In a competitive framework, globalization and technological change are obvious explanatory factors. Both can make product markets tougher and can reallocate production toward larger and more productive firms. Technological change may also generate economies of scale or may itself be the result of more investment in research and development (R&D) in large firms. Finally, competition may be weakening—as suggested, for example, by the drop in firm entry and increase in big mergers in the United States.[25]

What can be the role of digital technology in the increasing concentration of market power? Somewhat paradoxically, it may both contribute to enhancing market competition and, like other innovations, reinforce the competitive advantage of major players within some kind of a winner-takes-all game.

A key aspect of the digital economy is the broader and quicker diffusion of information. The new information and communication facilities increase market competition, making it easier for buyers to compare products and to opt for the most advantageous in terms of quality and price. They thus help concentrate demand on the most advantageous products. At the same time, they permit small producers to enter the market more easily, even though only those few who offer the most competitive products will survive, as illustrated by the churning of start-ups.[26]

On the other side of the spectrum, digitalization is opening innovation possibilities that are best exploited, at least in the first stage, by large firms able to invest sufficient resources in R&D with the aim of enhancing their competitive advantage. For instance, Walmart's innovative inventory-management system, based on digital technology and developed at high in-house cost in the 1980s, helped it achieve a dominant position in retail trade. Although essentially a retailer, Walmart has become a digital company, competing in this area with Amazon, an archetype of the digital economy. In other areas, it is the nature of digital innovation to create dominant positions through economies of scale and scope and network effects, as in the platform or networking business model where more clients attract more clients, or through enabling acquisition of information on clients or users that is of great value to optimize advertising and marketing strategies. Still, in other activities digital technology has simply replaced old technology without necessarily modifying the structure of the market. Phone companies are indeed highly digitalized, but the market remains oligopolistic due to the high fixed cost of installing fixed lines being replaced by the high fixed cost of installing networks of cell phone towers.

To be sure, superstar firms do not all reside in the digital economy, far from it, and the observed increase in the concentration of market power that leads to a higher nonlabor income share and more individual income inequality is certainly not due exclusively to the digital economy and tech giants such as the FAANGs.

Only a few studies have tried to empirically relate market power and digitalization. Bessen (2017) found a positive correlation among US four-, five-, and six-digit industries between sectoral concentration and IT proprietary systems—for example, the Walmart model mentioned above—proxied by the share of the workforce employed in occupations such as systems analyst and software developer. Yet the estimated model is static and essentially shows that large firms can invest more in IT. It does not necessarily follow that there is a relationship between a rise in firms' IT capacity and a change in their market power, which is the question of interest.

The study by Calligaris, Criscuolo, and Marcolin (2018), which looks at the correlation between market power and digitalization in a sample of roughly 30,000 firms in twenty-six OECD countries over the period 2001–2014, is half convincing too. Market power is proxied by markup rates estimated at the firm level, whereas digitalization is measured at the sectoral level by an index that summarizes the exposure of industrial sectors to various aspects of digitalization. It is found that markup rates are correlated with digital intensity, which would seem to provide a link between digitalization and market power, although not much can be said about causality. Moreover, the correlation is rather weak except when comparing the few firms in the most digital-intensive sectors and others, a relationship strongly influenced by the high-tech giants.

At this stage, it is fair to say that the contribution of digitalization-based technological change to the concentration of market power in advanced economies and, through that channel, to an increase in nonlabor income shares and personal income inequality can only be rather speculative. If there is ample evidence about rising concentration and rising market power in most sectors of the economy, in the United States and elsewhere,[27] one may conjecture about what is causing that evolution. It may be enhanced (monopolistic) competition due to technological change, including digitalization, as advocated by Autor and others (2020), but it may also be other factors that favor the most productive and already large firms. It may be less competition, as argued by Philippon (2019) and long advocated by several noted observers of the US economy, such as Stiglitz (2017) and Krugman (2016). It may also be a combination of these factors, which are impossible to disentangle, preventing observers from clearly seeing the direction in which the causality runs, as suggested by Qureshi (2019). Increased market power may well be caused by some aspects of technological change, especially digitalization, but market power may also generate technological innovations, the problem apparently being that they do not diffuse well from the powerful to smaller firms.

A last point linking market power and inequality needs to be emphasized. It is that large firms with strong market power are indeed more productive than others, but they also pay higher wages. There thus is a link between increasing market power and increasing earnings inequality within a given occupation and a given sector.[28] But, again, the role of digitalization in this evolution is still rather uncertain.

Where from Here?

For some time now, futurologists have been sending alarming messages about the consequences of accelerating digital-based technological change, some of them already imagining the disappearance of jobs. Others are confident that this new technological revolution will be like the preceding ones and lead to an age of enhanced affluence with full employment, although they do not say much about how unequal society would be. What can we expect based on what we've learned from the preceding sections about the effects of digitalization? This question becomes even more important as the pace of digitalization is likely to accelerate.

What We Know about Digitalization and Inequality from Recent Experience

Theory provides a meaningful three-step decomposition of the effects of digitalization and automation on employment and inequality: the displacement of some tasks or jobs; the creation of new tasks or jobs to provide the inputs needed by automation but also new goods and services made possible by the digital technology; and the creation of jobs to meet the increase in aggregate demand due to higher overall productivity. The first effect contributes to more inequality by unambiguously reducing the relative earnings of workers in the middle or bottom of the earnings scale and increasing the nonlabor income share. The second effect may contribute to more upper earnings inequality by increasing the demand for high skills. The third effect may work in either way, depending on the increase in aggregate demand and in the structure of goods and services demanded. The effect of digitalization thus is ambiguous a priori. However, without a sufficiently fast expansion of the supply of high-skill workers, inequality would most likely increase.

On top of these effects comes the hypothesis that digitalization has contributed to higher market concentration, as superstar firms are more able than others to take advantage of digital advances. To what extent digitalization or a weakening of competition regulation is behind the rising concentration is difficult to say, however. Both factors seem to have been at play.

Theoretical ambiguity should be resolved through empirical evidence. Yet direct evidence about automation, employment, and inequality is scarce. This is why most studies rely on indirect evidence derived from theoretical assumptions. Evidence of a skill bias in technological change and its potential impact on earnings inequality is obtained from a supply-demand framework applied to the labor market. The same applies to evidence on job polarization, with the (reasonable) a priori assumption that the observed relative loss of importance of routine jobs first at the bottom and then at the middle of the earnings scale results from automation and digitalization. Likewise, indirect evidence on the effects of changes in the "task content" of employment on the nonlabor income share of value added is obtained as the residual of what cannot be explained by composition effects or capital deepening, again in a competitive model of the economy. Although the arguments and conclusions in all these cases are intuitively convincing, they nevertheless are somewhat speculative.

Measured exposure to robotization and the densification of ICT equipment provide more direct evidence of the potential effects of automation and digitalization. There is little doubt that industrial robots have a negative direct and indirect impact on low- and medium-skill employment and a positive impact on high-skill employment, productivity, and the nonlabor share of value added. Overall, robotization thus appears as inegalitarian, since it tends to favor high-skill earnings and capital income. Interestingly, this does not seem to have been the case with the increasing use of ICT equipment, which appears more as a complement to than as a substitute for labor.

Evidence also shows that these effects may have accelerated in recent decades. In Germany, the negative impact of robotization on employment is recent. It dates back farther in the United States, but Acemoglu and Restrepo (2019) find that the task-displacement effect of technological change became sizable only in the last three decades.

This apparent acceleration of the digitalization drive in advanced countries sits somewhat paradoxically against observed changes in market income and earnings inequality, as well as factor shares. Considering digitalization and technological change as a common trend in advanced countries, one may understand why a common increase in inequality was observed among them. But why did it stop in the mid-2000s in most countries except the United States, and perhaps Germany, precisely at a time when digitalization is thought to have accelerated? This heterogeneity is consistent with the view that other forces also act on the evolution of inequality and may counteract the effect of technological change.

Furman (2018) suggests that "we should be reassured if automation in the future looks like automation in the past." This may be an optimistic view. Automation in the past has most likely contributed to surging inequality in the United States, and it is difficult to imagine that this process could continue without some political or social disruption taking place. The same forces are undoubtedly present in other countries, even though they have been less inegalitarian and seem to be temporarily checked by other factors or policies. Arguably, the worst may still be to come.

An Incoming Technological Innovation Tsunami?

A few years ago, Frey and Osborne (2013) hit the headlines when they estimated the proportion of automatable jobs in the United States to be 47 percent over one to two decades. Other estimates were less drastic. Arntz, Gregory, and Zierahn (2016) even suggested that the proportion of automatable jobs would be only 9 percent in a sample of twenty-one OECD countries. Yet McKinsey Global Institute (2017b) still estimates that up to one-third of the 2030 workforce in the United States and Germany may need to learn new skills and to find work in new occupations.

Of course, there is much uncertainty about these predictions. Experience shows that major technological innovations always take more time to be fully implemented than anticipated. To offer an idea of the potential

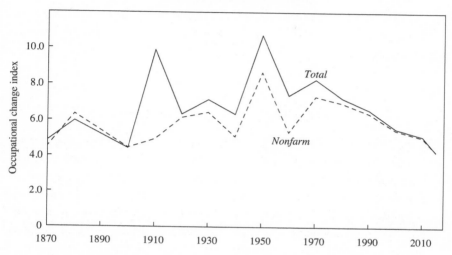

FIGURE 7-5. **A Metric of Ten-Year Change in the Occupational Mix:**
United States 1860–2015

Source: Elvery (2019). The occupational change index is the percentage of employed workers who would need to change occupational group for the distribution across occupational groups to be the same as it was ten years earlier.

challenge of technology-driven occupational changes, figure 7-5 shows the historical evolution of change in the occupational mix of employment in the United States since 1860, based on decennial censuses and the American Community Survey. The metric used here is the percentage of jobs that need to be transferred across occupational groups for the occupational distribution in a year to be the same as the one observed ten years earlier. Focusing on the nonfarm sectors and excluding the war periods, when occupational changes were exceptionally strong, the peak change took place between 1960 and 1970, when it reached a little more than 7 percent of employment. It has slowed down since then, despite accelerating technological change and digitalization in recent decades. This suggests that the full impact of current technological change is yet to be felt.

Taking at face value the above predictions about job displacement due to digitalization, the process seems about to accelerate seriously. Using only half of McKinsey's prediction about changes in skill needs and moves to new occupations and spreading it over two decades rather than a little more than one still leads to a decadal job displacement rate of around 8 percent, almost double that observed in the recent past. The effects of digitalization-based technological change on employment, factor shares, and inequality may thus be expected to be much stronger in the coming one or two decades than what was observed in the preceding ones, as digital technologies work their way through economies and are reinforced by new innovations, notably in artificial intelligence.

Policy Implications and Conclusions

I conclude this review of the relationship between digitalization and inequality with a few considerations on policies that could attenuate potential inegalitarian consequences of digitalization-based technological change. The first point to stress goes back to a remark in the first section of the chapter on the difference between the evolution of market income and disposable income inequality in advanced countries. It turns out that the latter proves more stable than the former, which suggests that redistribution was able to offset some inequality shock on market incomes. For these countries, the issue is thus whether redistribution may be as effective in the future if inequality shocks on market incomes amplify under the pressure of automation.

Taxation is likely to play a leading stabilizing role with at least four objectives: to influence the pace and direction of innovation; to finance safety nets for occupational transitions in the labor market; to prevent an excessive increase in disposable income inequality; and to make sure that mechanisms that compensate for job displacement, in particular the aggregate demand effect, can fully play their role. But, of course, other policies must also be envisaged, most importantly those relating to education, training, and retraining.

Time is needed for mechanisms and policies that may counteract the adverse effects of automation-caused job displacements to be effective—that is, for new jobs to appear, for workers to retrain, and for new entrants into the labor market to prepare for jobs of the future. A danger in what futurologists predict is that technology changes too fast for these adjustments to take place in time. The current speed at which industrial robots are installed, as shown in figure 7-2, is impressive, and the spread of artificial intelligence may go still faster.

A way to slow robotization would be to tax robots, as suggested by some.[29] It is not clear whether such an idea is realistic, however. Practically, it seems difficult to design a tax that would exclusively apply to automation machinery or devices without affecting capital equipment in general. How should a robot be defined, and how can it be distinguished from another piece of equipment or an algorithm that saves labor? Taxing automation may thus inevitably have to go through increased taxation of capital.

Under these conditions, one may ask whether existing tax systems provide excessive incentives to automation investment, or to labor-saving equipment in general. Re-establishing some balance between the taxation of capital and the taxation of labor against a history of tax changes in most advanced countries that have favored capital might be an efficient and fair way to moderate the pace of labor-displacing automation, incentivize more employment-friendly innovation, and facilitate economic and social adjustments to new technology. Also, providing safety nets to temporarily protect displaced workers and retrain them requires additional public resources and, therefore, an increase in taxation. Having the burden of additional taxation be borne by labor rather than capital would either make labor more expensive to producers and incentivize still more automation, or would redistribute income from labor to capital and add to inequality.

An additional argument in favor of preventing a worsening of inequality is that it can bolster the income effect on demand that is expected to compensate for technological job displacement. This effect depends on how the income generated by technological change is distributed in the population. If it goes to the very top of the income distribution, where the share of capital (or robot) income is the highest, then the marginal propensity to consume out of that income will be low, and the compensation for labor displacement from additional aggregate demand will be limited. Inequality may thus increase further because of automation, dragging the economy into a rising inequality spiral. Redistribution could avoid falling into that trap.

The increase in inequality may also come from the skill premium entailed by a change in the skill structure of labor demand and displacement of routine jobs. The policy response to that risk consists of adjusting the skill structure of labor supply through retraining and educational policies. But it may also involve adjusting the progressivity of the overall redistribution system to dampen the rise in the inequality of disposable incomes.

It is thus the case that an important part of the response to an acceleration of automation-biased technological change lies in the reform of the taxation system that would combine a higher tax rate on tangible and intangible capital—or less taxation on labor—with more progressivity in household income taxation. Such tax reform should also come with responsive policies in matters of training and retraining of the labor force affected by automation, as well as a broader reorientation of education systems.

If the reform of education and training policies would not pose major difficulty other than raising the necessary public resources and adjusting the national educational, training, and retraining capacity, the same cannot be said of capital taxation. Unilateral increases in capital taxation are bound to be strongly opposed because of their presumed deleterious long-run effects on countries' international competitiveness and growth. That argument has been used again and again to lower capital taxation in a kind of race to the bottom among advanced countries. Given the high mobility of capital, some international coordination would be essential if meaningful reform of capital taxation is to proceed.

Other ways of addressing the consequences of the automation bias of technological advances might be to support, through subsidies or otherwise, automation in some activities but not in others. Acemoglu and Restrepo (2020b) draw attention to the "wrong kind of AI"—artificial intelligence innovations that displace labor and increase inequality but with little gain in productivity. A key proposal made by the late Anthony Atkinson to tame inequality stated, "The direction of technological change should be an explicit concern of policy-makers, encouraging innovation in a form that increases the employability of workers."[30] While this may be desirable, the difficulty of implementing such policies in a market environment cannot be ignored, as they would be subject to strong political pressures and run the risk of affecting the long-run innovation capacity of a country.

Overall, redistribution through adequate taxation tools and safety nets, as well as labor market and educational policies that facilitate adjustment to shifts in the structure of occupations, are the main instruments to counteract the inegalitarian impact of digitalization. This agenda demands more attention, especially if digital transformation accelerates and its effects amplify.

NOTES

I would like to thank Jason Furman and Zia Qureshi for their helpful comments.

1. McKinsey Global Institute (2017a, p. 6). Strong warnings on the employment effect of digital technology had been made earlier by Brynjolfsson and McAfee (2014) and Frey and Osborne (2013).

2. See Rifkin (1999).

3. See Bourguignon (2018, 2019).

4. This statistic, which implicitly assumes that robots are mainly bought by OECD countries, may overestimate the speed of diffusion of robots in these countries, because China's possession of robots may have grown increasingly over the recent past.

5. To illustrate, the average wage of the 99th percentile of wages was above $738,000 in the United States in 2018, whereas the limit of the 90th percentile was around $100,000.

6. For a more complete review of the SBTC literature, see Acemoglu and Autor (2011).

7. Goldin and Katz (2008) explicitly referred to this view of the relationship between technology and inequality when they titled their book on the US labor market and earnings inequality *The Race between Education and Technology*.

8. Assuming a constant elasticity of substitution aggregate production function, the coefficient of proportionality is the elasticity of substitution between college-educated and other workers, taken to be 1.4.

9. See "Qualifications in the Population" (last updated 2016), a statistical dataset based on the UK Labor Force Survey. A study of Germany by Dustmann, Ludsteck, and Schönberg (2009), along the lines of Autor, Katz, and Kearney (2008) for the United States, leads to similar conclusions about the dominant role of SBTC in explaining the rise of earnings inequality.

10. In an influential paper, Juhn, Murphy, and Pierce (1993) found that the residual variance of a standard Mincer equation of log earnings on education and job experience increased during the 1980s; they interpreted this finding as an increase in the return to unobserved skills. Lemieux (2006) found that composition effects and institutional changes were responsible for much of that effect, a conclusion later somewhat attenuated by Autor, Katz, and Kearney (2008).

11. Oesh and Piccitto (2019) express doubts about the job polarization hypothesis when considering a period longer than the 1990s. The significance of this point is weakened by the fact that they define *occupational skills* by the median education rather than earnings level of an occupation.

12. Autor (2014), figures 6 and 7.

13. Spitz-Oener (2006), table 5.

14. See table 7-1 and Beaudry, Green, and Sand (2016).

15. Notably, the Fachkräftezuwanderungsgesetz (Skilled Immigration Act), which came into force in 2020.

16. According to Berger and Wolff (2017), the labor income share lost 3 percentage points between 1970 and 2010 when related to GDP, 7 points when

related to value added of the business sector, and 16 points when related to value added in manufacturing.

17. See, for instance, Acemoglu and Restrepo (2018, 2019), Aghion, Jones, and Jones (2017), Hemous and Olsen (2018), Prettner (2019), and Zeira (1998)—probably the pioneer theoretical paper in this area.

18. Models that explicitly include skill differentiation and thus combine labor market and capital income inequality include Berg, Buffie, and Zanna (2018), Cords and Prettner (2018), Hemous and Olsen (2018), and Prettner and Strulik (2019).

19. Local robot exposure is measured by a weighted average of sectoral robot density at the national level, using weights that correspond to the local industrial structure.

20. This effect is also present in Acemoglu and Restrepo (2020a).

21. Aghion and others (2020) also use a sample of French firms to show that, paradoxically, automation entails an increment of jobs, even at the industry level. Their definition of automation—consumption of motive power—is rather debatable, however.

22. This study was the first to make use of data provided by the International Federation of Robots. There are also other studies based on these data, which confirm the negative local impact of robotization on employment, but without consideration of wages and factor shares. See, for instance, Chiacchio, Petropoulos, and Pichler (2018) for five EU countries, and Aghion, Antonin, and Bunel (2019) for France.

23. They also impute 33 percent to the "super-cycle" in extractive industries and real estate due to booming prices in the first fifteen years of the millennium, 26 percent to increasing capital consumption and the shift to intellectual-property products, and 11 percent to the effect of globalization and loss of labor bargaining power. Guttierez and Piton (2019) and Cette, Koehl, and Philippon (2019) also emphasize the role of real estate rent in the evolution of the nonlabor share in several countries.

24. An acronym for Facebook, Apple, Amazon, Netflix, and Google.

25. Philippon (2019).

26. Yet the dynamism of the US business sector has been declining, with the share of young firms—less than five years old—falling over the last four decades. See Philippon (2019), p. 83.

27. See Autor and others (2020), Bessen (2017), De Loecker and others (2020), Guttierez and Philippon (2017), and Philippon (2019).

28. See, for instance, Barth and others (2014) and Berlingieri, Blanchenay, and Criscuolo (2017).

29. See, among others, Costinot and Werning (2018), Guerreiro and others (2020), and Thuemmel (2018).

30. Atkinson (2015).

REFERENCES

Acemoglu, D., and D. Autor. 2011. "Skills, Tasks and Technologies: Implications for Employment and Earnings," in *Handbook of Labor Economics*, vol. 4B, edited by O. Ashenfelter and D. Card (Amsterdam: Elsevier B.V.).

Acemoglu, D., C. Lelarge, and P. Restrepo. 2020. "Competing with Robots: Firm-Level Evidence from France." *AEA Papers and Proceedings* 110, pp. 383–88.

Acemoglu, D., and P. Restrepo. 2018. "The Race between Man and Machine: Implications of Technology for Growth, Factor Shares, and Employment." *American Economic Review* 108, no. 6, pp. 1488–1542.

Acemoglu, D., and P. Restrepo. 2019. "Automation and New Tasks: Technology Displaces and Reinstates Labor." *Journal of Economic Perspectives* 33, no. 2, pp. 3–30.

Acemoglu, D., and P. Restrepo. 2020a. "Robots and Jobs: Evidence from US Labor Markets." *Journal of Political Economy* 128, no. 6, pp. 2188–2244.

Acemoglu, D., and P. Restrepo. 2020b. "The Wrong Kind of AI? Artificial Intelligence and the Future of Labour Demand?" *Cambridge Journal of Regions, Economy and Society* 13, pp. 25–35.

Aghion, P., C. Antonin, and S. Bunel. 2019. "Artificial Intelligence, Growth and Employment: The Role of Policy." *Economie et Statistique* 510–512, pp. 149–64.

Aghion, P., C. Antonin, S. Bunel, and X. Jaravel. 2020. "What Are the Labor and Product Market Effects of Automation? New Evidence from France." CEPR Discussion Paper DP14443 (Washington, DC: Center for Economic and Policy Research).

Aghion, P., B. Jones, and C. Jones. 2017. "Artificial Intelligence and Economic Growth." NBER Working Paper 23928 (Cambridge, MA: National Bureau of Economic Research).

Andrews, D., C. Criscuolo, and P. Gal. 2016. *The Global Productivity Slowdown, Technology Divergence and Public Policy: A Firm Level Perspective* (Paris: OECD Publishing).

Arntz, M., T. Gregory, and U. Zierahn. 2016. "The Risk of Automation for Jobs in OECD Countries: A Comparative Analysis." Working Paper on Social, Employment and Migration Issues 189 (Paris: OECD Publishing).

Atkinson, A. B. 2015. *Inequality: What Can Be Done?* (Harvard University Press).

Atkinson, A. B., and S. Morelli. 2014. "Chartbook of Economic Inequality." Working Paper 324 (Palma, Sp.: Society for the Study of Economic Inequality [ECINEQ]).

Autor, D. 2014. "Polanyi's Paradox and the Shape of Employment Growth." NBER Working Paper 20485 (Cambridge, MA: National Bureau of Economic Research).

Autor, D., and D. Dorn. 2013. "The Growth of Low-Skill Service Jobs and the Polarization of the US Labor Market." *American Economic Review* 103, no. 5, pp. 1553–97.

Autor, D., D. Dorn, L. Katz, C. Patterson, and J. Van Reenen. 2020. "The Fall of the Labor Share and the Rise of Superstar Firms." *Quarterly Journal of Economics* 135, no. 2, pp. 645–709.

Autor, D., L. Katz, and M. Kearney. 2008. "Trends in US Wage Inequality: Revising the Revisionists." *Review of Economics and Statistics* 90, no. 2, pp. 300–23.

Autor, D., and A. Salomons. 2018. "Is Automation Labor-Displacing? Productivity, Growth, Employment and the Labor Share." Brookings Papers on Economic Activity (Brookings Institution).

Barth, E., A. Bryson, J. C. Davis, and R. Freeman. 2014. "It's Where You Work: Increases in Earnings Dispersion across Establishments and Individuals in the U.S." NBER Working Paper 20447 (Cambridge, MA: National Bureau of Economic Research).

Beaudry, P., D. Green, and B. Sand. 2016. "The Great Reversal in the Demand for Skill and Cognitive Tasks." *Journal of Labor Economics* 34, no. 5, pp. S199–S247.

Berg, A., E. Buffie, and L.-F. Zanna. 2018. "Should We Fear the Robot Revolution? (The Correct Answer Is Yes)." Working Paper 18/116 (Washington, DC: International Monetary Fund).

Berger, B., and G. Wolff. 2017. "The Global Decline in the Labour Income Share: Is Capital the Answer to Germany's Current Account Surplus?" Bruegel Policy Contribution 12 (Brussels: Bruegel).

Berlingieri, G., P. Blanchenay, and C. Criscuolo. 2017. "The Great Divergence(s)." OECD Science, Technology and Industry Policy Paper 39 (Paris: OECD Publishing).

Bessen, J. 2017. "Information Technology and Industry Concentration." Boston University School of Law, Law and Economics Paper 17–41.

Biewen, M, B. Fitzenberger, and J. de Lazzer. 2017. "Rising Wage Inequality in Germany: Increasing Heterogeneity and Changing Selection into Full-Time Work." Discussion Paper 11072 (Bonn: Institute of the Study of Labor [IZA]).

Bourguignon, F. 2018. "World Changes in Inequality: An Overview of Facts, Causes, Consequences, and Policies." *CESifo Economic Studies* 64, no. 3, pp. 345–70.

Bourguignon, F. 2019. "Inequality, Globalization, and Technical Change in Advanced Countries: A Brief Synopsis," in *Meeting Globalization's Challenges: Policies to Make Trade Work for All*, edited by L. Catão and M. Obstfeld (Princeton University Press).

Brandolini, A., P. Cipollone, and P. Sestito. 2001. "Earnings Dispersion, Low Pay and Household Poverty in Italy, 1977–1998." Economic Working Paper 427, Bank of Italy, Economic Research and International Relations Area (Rome: Bank of Italy).

Brynjolfsson, E., and A. McAfee. 2014. *The Second Machine Age: Work, Progress, and Prosperity in a Time of Brilliant Technologies* (New York: Norton).

Bureau of Economic Analysis. n.d. https://apps.bea.gov/histdata/Releases/FA /2019/AnnualUpdate_September-2-2020/Section2all_xls.xlsx.

Bureau of Labor Statistics. n.d. https://beta.bls.gov/dataQuery/search.

Calligaris, S., C. Criscuolo, and L. Marcolin. 2018. "Mark-Ups in the Digital Era." OECD Science, Technology and Industry Working Paper 2018/10 (Paris: OECD Publishing).

Cette, G., L. Koehl, and T. Philippon. 2019. "Labor Shares in Advanced Economies." NBER Working Paper 26136 (Cambridge, MA: National Bureau of Economic Research).

Chiacchio, F., G. Petropoulos, and D. Pichler. 2018. "The Impact of Industrial Robots on EU Employment and Wages: A Local Labor Market Approach." Bruegel Working Paper 2 (Brussels: Bruegel).

Cords, D., and K. Prettner. 2018. "Technological Unemployment Revisited: Automation in a Search and Matching Framework." Hohenheim Discussion Papers in Business, Economics and Social Sciences 19-2018 (Stuttgart).

Costinot, A., and I. Werning. 2018. "Robots, Trade and Luddism: A Sufficient Statistics Approach to Optimal Technology Regulation." NBER Working Paper 25103 (Cambridge, MA: National Bureau of Economic Research).

Dao, M., M. Das, Z. Koczan, and W. Lian. 2017. "Why Is Labor Receiving a Smaller Share of Global Income? Theory and Evidence." IMF Working Paper WP/A7/A9 (Washington, DC: International Monetary Fund).

Dauth, W., S. Findeisen, J. Südekum, and N. Wössner. 2017. "German Robots: The Impact of Industrial Robots on Workers." IAB Discussion Paper 30/2017 (Nuremberg: Institute for Employment Research).

De Loecker, J., and J. Eeckhout. 2018. "Global Market Power." NBER Working Paper 24768 (Cambridge, MA: National Bureau of Economic Research).

De Loecker, J., J. Eeckhout, and G. Unger. 2020. "The Rise of Market Power and the Macroeconomic Implications." *Quarterly Journal of Economics* 135, no. 2, pp. 561–644.

Dustmann, C., J. Ludsteck, and U. Schönberg. 2009. "Revisiting the German Wage Structure." *Quarterly Journal of Economics* 124, no. 2, pp. 843–81.

Elsby, M., B. Hobijn, and A. Sahin. 2013. "The Decline of the US Labor Share." Brookings Papers on Economic Activity (Brookings Institution).

Elvery, J. 2019. "Changes in the Occupational Structure of the United States: 1860 to 2015." Economic Commentary 2019-09 (Cleveland: Federal Reserve Bank of Cleveland). https://doi.org/10.26509/frbc-ec-201909.

Frey, C. B., and M. Osborne. 2013. "The Future of Employment: How Susceptible Are Jobs to Computerization?" Unpublished manuscript (Oxford Martin School, Oxford University).

Furman, J. 2018. "Should We Be Reassured if Automation in the Future Looks Like Automation in the Past?" In *The Economics of Artificial Intelligence: An Agenda* (Cambridge, MA: National Bureau of Economic Research).

Goldin, C., and L. Katz. 2008. *The Race between Education and Technology* (Harvard University Press).

Goldin, C., and L. Katz. 2009. "The Race between Education and Technology: The Evolution of U.S. Educational Wage Differentials, 1890 to 2005." NBER Working Paper 12984 (Cambridge, MA: National Bureau of Economic Research).

Goos, M., and A. Manning. 2007. "Lousy and Lovely Jobs: The Rising Polarization of Work in Britain." *Review of Economics and Statistics* 89, no. 1, pp. 118–33.

Goos, M., A. Manning, and A. Salomons. 2009. "Job Polarization in Europe." *American Economic Review* 99, no. 2, pp. 58–63.

Goos, M., A. Manning, and A. Salomons. 2014. "Explaining Job Polarization: Routine-Biased Technological Change and Offshoring." *American Economic Review* 104, no. 8, p. 2509–26.

Graetz, G., and G. Michaels. 2018. "Robots at Work." *Review of Economics and Statistics* 100, no. 5, pp. 753–68.

Guerreiro, J., S. Rebelo, and P. Teles. 2020. "Should Robots Be Taxed?" NBER Working Paper 23583 (Cambridge, MA: National Bureau of Economic Research).

Guttierez, G., and T. Philippon. 2017. "Declining Competition and Investment in the US." NBER Working Paper 23583 (Cambridge, MA: National Bureau of Economic Research).

Guttierez, G., and S. Piton. 2019. "Revisiting the Global Decline of the (Non-Housing) Labor Share." Staff Working Paper 811 (London: Bank of England).

Hemous, D., and M. Olsen. 2018. "The Rise of the Machines: Automation, Horizontal Innovation and Income Inequality." CEPR Discussion Paper 10244 (Washington, DC: Center for Economic and Policy Research).)

INSEE. 2020. Inégalités salariales, INSEE référence, https://www.insee.fr/fr/statistiques/fichier/4503070/ECRT2020_F5-8.xlsx.

International Federation of Robotics. n.d. Annual report, executive summary, various years.

International Labor Organization. n.d. ILOSTAT, https://www.ilo.org/ilostat
-files/Documents/Excel/INDICATOR/SDG_1041_NOC_RT_A_EN.xlsx.

Juhn, C., K. Murphy, and B. Pierce. 1993. "Wage Inequality and the Rise in
Returns to Skill." *Journal of Political Economy* 101, no. 3, pp. 410–42.

Karabarbounis, L., and B. Neiman. 2014. "The Global Decline of the Labor
Share." *Quarterly Journal of Economics* 129, no. 1, pp. 61–103.

Krugman, P. 2016. "Monopoly Capitalism Is Killing US Economy." *Irish Times*,
April 19.

Lawrence, R. Z. 2015. "Recent Declines in Labor's Share in US Income: A Pre-
liminary Neoclassical Account." NBER Working Paper 21296 (Cambridge,
MA: National Bureau of Economic Research).

Lemieux, T. 2006. "Increasing Residual Wage Inequality: Composition Effects, Noisy Data, or Rising Demand for Skill?" *American Economic Review*
96, no. 3, pp. 461–98.

McKinsey Global Institute. 2017a. *A Future That Works: Automation, Employment and Productivity.*

McKinsey Global Institute. 2017b. *Jobs Lost, Jobs Gained: Workforce Transition
in Times of Automation.*

Mischke, J., H.-H. Kotz, and J. Bughin. 2019. "The Declining Labour Share
of Income: Accounting for the Main Factors from a Meso Perspective."
VoxEU, July 26. https://voxeu.org/article/declining-labour-share-income
-accounting-main-factors.

OECD. n.d.a. Employment data base: earnings and wages, OECD.Stat. https://
stats.oecd.org/Index.aspx?DatasetCode=DEC_I.

OECD. n.d.b. Productivity Archives, OECD.Stat. https://stats.oecd.org/Index
.aspx?DataSetCode=IDD#.

Oesh, D., and G. Piccitto. 2019. "The Polarization Myth: Occupational Upgrading in Germany, Spain, Sweden, and the UK, 1992–2015." *Work and
Occupations* 46, no. 4, pp. 441–69.

Philippon, T. 2019. *The Great Reversal: How America Gave Up on Free Markets*
(Harvard University Press).

Piketty, T. 2014. *Capital in the Twenty-First Century* (Harvard University Press).

Prettner, K. 2019. "A Note on the Implications of Automation for Economic
Growth and the Labor Share." *Macroeconomic Dynamics* 23, pp. 1294–1301.

Prettner, K., and H. Strulik. 2019. "Innovation, Automation, and Inequality:
Policy Challenges in the Race against the Machine." *Journal of Monetary Economics* 116, pp. 249–65.

"Qualifications in the Population." Last updated 2016. Gov.UK. www.gov
.uk/government/statistical-data-sets/fe-data-library-qualifications-in
-the-population-based-on-the-labour-force-survey.

Qureshi, Z. 2019. "The Rise of Corporate Market Power" (Brookings
Institution).

Rifkin, J. 1999. *The End of Work: The Decline of the Global Labor Force and the Dawn of the Post-Market Era* (New York: G. P. Putnam's Sons).

Ryan, C. 2018. "Computer and Internet Use in the United States: 2016, American Community Survey Reports" (Washington, DC: US Census Bureau).

Spitz-Oener, A. 2006. "Technical Change, Job Tasks, and Rising Educational Demands: Looking Outside the Wage Structure." *Journal of Labor Economics* 24, no. 2, pp. 235–70.

Stiglitz, J. 2017. "Inequality, Stagnation and Market Power: The Need for a New Progressive Era." Talk delivered at Market Power Rising: Do We Have a Monopoly Problem?, Roosevelt Institute, Washington, DC September 25.

Thuemmel, U. 2018. "Optimal Taxation of Robots." CESifo Working Paper 7317 (Munich: Center for Economic Studies).

World Development Indicators. n.d. https://databank.worldbank.org/source/world-development-indicators.

World Inequality Database. n.d. https://wid.world/data.

Zeira, J. 1998. "Workers, Machines and Economic Growth." *Quarterly Journal of Economics* 113, no. 4, pp. 1091–1117.

EIGHT

Technological Change and Inequality in Korea

JUNGSOO PARK

Over the past several decades, many countries have witnessed a gradual rise in income inequality. In searching for an explanation for the worsening income distribution, economists are giving attention to technological change. Technological innovation can lead to changes in market demand and abrupt transformation of industrial production modes. This, in turn, may have important implications for the functional income distribution between factors of production. If capital-biased technological change becomes a dominant form of innovation, it may cause a decline in the share of labor income.[1] Changes in functional income distribution, in turn, may influence household income distribution.

Technological change may also influence income distribution through widening wage gaps. In the case of skill-biased technological change, wage disparity among workers may increase. Adoption of new technologies raises the relative demand for workers with complementary skills. This benefits workers with higher human capital, but at the same time hurts the unskilled. In reality, the adoption of new technology generally occurs at the firm level. Firms with successful implementation of new technology experience higher productivity gains that enable them to compensate their workers with higher wages. These firms are able to attract high-skilled workers. On the other hand, firms that are unable to adjust to the new technological environment fail to raise the productivity and wages of their workers. These differences in outcomes among firms may result in widening wage gaps and in turn have important implications for income distribution.

This chapter scrutinizes Korean economic data to gauge the extent to which the hypothesized relationships between technological change, functional income distribution, wage disparity, and income inequality have been significant for Korea, an economy considered to have been heavily influenced by recent technological changes. One challenge in this task is that technological change is a broad and abstract concept that is difficult to quantify satisfactorily in observable variables. Furthermore, income inequality is a macroeconomic condition that is slow to change and can be identified only at low frequency.

Instead of attempting to identify a direct causal relationship between technological change and income inequality, I take an indirect approach in this chapter. Although the approach I used in the chapter may not unveil conclusive causal relationships, my hope is to provide useful empirical evidence that may support or negate the hypothesized relationships. First, to gauge the long-run effect of capital-biased technology on functional income distribution, the long-run trend of labor income share is examined. The purpose of this examination is to determine whether there has been a long-run trend of declining labor income share in Korea.

Second, to measure the impact of skill-biased technological change on wage disparity, I focus on firm-level data. I pay attention to the fact that there are distinct groups of firms (large versus small and medium-sized firms) with heterogeneous performance. Evidence suggests that firms with higher performance are strongly associated with higher innovative capacity. These "high-capacity firms" are likely to successfully adopt new technology and adjust to take advantage of the new technological environment. I cautiously ascribe widening performance gaps between firms to differences in technological adoption and innovative capacity. I then examine the link between performance gaps and wage disparity. Finally, I investigate the influence of wage disparity on household income distribution.

How to define *firm capacity* and how to group firms are important issues in this analysis. The firm capacity of interest here pertains to a firm's ability to adapt effectively to a changing environment. An ideal grouping strategy should reflect features such as human capital of personnel, innovative capacity, management practices, financial constraints, business networks, and the like. Unfortunately, such a grouping strategy cannot be implemented using the available large survey datasets of firms in Korea as they don't provide information on all such features.

As a second-best approach, I use firm size for the grouping strategy. One well-known feature of Korean firms is that their size may serve as a key characteristic in identifying their potential. Firm size acts to attract and secure many valuable resources (e.g., human capital, research and development personnel, financing) that aid in efficiently adopting new technologies and reaping economies of scale. Firm size can also reflect successful past performance. Performance gaps between large firms and small and medium-sized enterprises (SMEs) are well documented in Kim (2017) and Park (2019a).[2] Furthermore, wage gaps between large firms and SMEs have long been considered a distinct feature of a dual economy in Korea. In examining the link between widening wage gaps and heterogeneous performance outcomes of firms, I use firm size as a practical distinguishing characteristic to group Korean firms.

The aim of this chapter is to identify and evaluate channels through which technological change may influence household income distribution. Figure 8-1 presents a flow diagram sketching how technology can affect household income inequality. First, it can change the distribution of national income between labor and capital (panel A), which in turn can affect household income inequality. Second, technological change can affect high-capacity and low-capacity firms differently and lead to differential performance (panel A). This will affect individual workers' wage gap (panel B). The wage gap will affect household income distribution, as wage income is a major source of household income (panel C). Household income distribution may also be affected by income from other sources, such as business income or property income, or changes in the number of working household members (multiple incomes).

FIGURE 8-1. **Relation between Technological Change and Household Income Inequality**

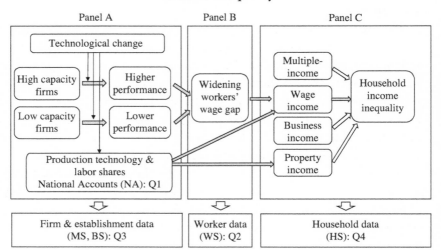

Source: Author's illustration.

Note: Q1, Q2, Q3, and Q4 refer to the four main questions posed in the chapter. NA=National Accounts from Bank of Korea; MS=Mining and Manufacturing Survey; BS=Survey of Business Activities; WS=Survey on Labor Conditions by Employment Type; HS=Household Surveys.

This chapter poses four questions related to the linkages depicted in figure 8-1:

(Q1) Does the labor income share show a long-run downward trend?

(Q2) Is wage disparity increasing? If so, what is the main reason?

(Q3) Do we see heterogeneous performance of firms and changes in the composition of industries, and how have they influenced wage disparity?

(Q4) Is greater wage disparity causing significant changes in income distribution?

The main datasets used in the chapter are the National Accounts (NA) from the Bank of Korea, the Survey on Labor Conditions by Employment Type (WS) from the Ministry of Employment and Labor, and the following surveys from Statistics Korea: Mining and Manufacturing Survey (MS), Survey of Business Activities (BS), Household Income and Expenditure Survey (HS1), and Survey of Household Finances and Living Conditions

(HS2).[3] These are the most comprehensive datasets available in Korea to address these questions.

Related to the first question (Q1), there is a controversy at the global level regarding the long-run trend of labor income shares. Studies such as Karabarbounis and Neiman (2014) and Autor and Salomons (2018) report that labor shares of the corporate sector in most major advanced economies show a long-run declining trend.[4] Technological change is suggested as one of the key reasons behind this phenomenon. However, these findings have been recently challenged by Gutiérrez and Piton (2020) and Cette, Koehl, and Philippon (2019). Gutiérrez and Piton (2020) find that labor shares of the corporate sector are stable or increasing for most major advanced countries (except for the United States and Canada) when corporate sector value added is correctly adjusted based on the system of national accounts.[5]

The labor share trend for the Korean economy has also been a subject of controversy. Several existing studies, such as Lee (2015) and Joo and Cheon (2014), suggest that the Korean labor share shows a long-run downward trend. However, Park (2020) points out that the labor share calculations in these studies are subject to biases. The biases arise because the existing studies do not correctly account for the existence of paid employees in the self-employment sector. The self-employment sector in the Korean National Accounts includes both self-operated businesses with and without employees. Labor income share calculations are subject to bias if they neglect the existence of self-operated businesses with employees. In section 1 of this chapter, I draw on the work of Park (2020) to adjust for the bias. The revised calculations show that the labor income share has not fallen over the long run but rather has been relatively stable.

Wage income disparity has become more conspicuous in Korea in recent decades. Section 2 of the chapter addresses the second question (Q2) and performs decomposition analyses on wage income disparity using a worker-level wage dataset based on establishment surveys. I examine worker characteristics that can contribute to the widening wage gaps and find that the size of the firm that workers belong to is a key feature in explaining the rise in wage disparity.

Focusing on differences in firm performance across different-sized firms, section 3 addresses the third question (Q3) and provides estimates of wage and labor productivity across different establishments based on Korean manufacturing-sector data. I examine changes in wage and labor productivity disparities across different-sized establishments and firms over time.

Lastly, section 4 addresses the fourth question (Q4) and examines the relationship between worker wage disparity and household income inequality. Given that household income is composed of different sources of income, we investigate the extent to which changes in wage disparity explain changes in household income inequality. Section 5 concludes with policy implications.

Long-Run Trend of Labor Income Share

Labor income share is calculated as a proportion of total national income originating from labor. Most early studies of Korean labor income shares find a declining long-run trend.[6]

Controversies in Labor Income Calculation

However, recent studies are challenging these findings. Oh (2020) uses a comprehensive firm-level dataset to show that the labor income share for listed and externally audited firms has been increasing. Park (2019b) uses a Financial Statement Analysis from Bank of Korea, which covers all corporate firms, to show that the labor income share for the corporate sector has a slight rising trend for the post-2000 period. Park (2020) shows that the labor income share for the aggregate economy has not declined in the past three decades when biases due to miscalculations are corrected.

The main difficulty in calculating the labor income share at the aggregate economy level arises from the existence of the self-employed sector, where the distinction between labor and capital incomes is not so clear.[7] Korea has a large proportion of the self-employed, which has been declining over time. The self-employed comprised 34 percent of total employment in 1980 but 21 percent in 2018.[8] Since the self-employed invest their own capital to run their businesses, the resulting income can be viewed as mixed income arising from both labor and capital. Thus, to derive a correct labor income share, labor income from these mixed incomes needs to be imputed and added to total wage income.[9] For this purpose, imputation methods suggested by Gollin (2002) have been widely used. However, Park (2020) shows that these methods create biases in labor income share calculation when the self-employed sector is large and its proportion is changing over time.

Worker Composition by Types of Employment

Labor income imputation of workers in the self-employment (SE) sector may not be a significant problem if their proportion is relatively small and unchanging, as in most advanced economies. However, it becomes a major issue if the SE sector represents a large portion of the economy. Table 8-1 shows the distribution of workers by types of employment in Korea over the last few decades. Broadly, there are two types of workers: wage workers (W) and nonwage workers (NW). The latter is the sum of SE workers and unpaid family workers (U), who constituted 21 percent and 4.1 percent of all employment, respectively, in 2018.

Within the SE sector, there are two types of businesses: self-employed without employees (SE1) and self-employed with employees (SE2). SE1 businesses are operated without paid employees, but unpaid family members (U) may work for them. In SE2 businesses, the self-employed owners hire paid employees, just like corporate firms. Business owners in the SE2 sector are classified as self-employed for tax purposes and their operating surpluses are added to those of SE1 in the National Accounts statistics. Given a conservative estimate of 2.55 employees per SE2 business, Park (2020) estimates wage income employees in the SE2 sector (W2) to constitute 15.7 percent of total employment in 2018. Thus, the share of all workers in the SE sector, including owners, unpaid family members, and employees (SE+U+W2), is considerable; although it fell from an estimated 64.8 percent in 1980, it still amounted to 40.8 percent in 2018.

Biases in Labor Income Share Calculations of Existing Studies

Gollin's approach to estimating adjusted labor income shares does not appropriately take into account the aforementioned structure and composition of the SE sector. Thus, Gollin's methods may lead to biased imputation of the SE sector's labor income and, in turn, biased estimation of the trend in overall labor income share.

National income, as aggregate net value added of an economy, is composed of compensation of employees, operating surplus of the corporate sector, operating surplus of the household sector (i.e., SE), and operating

Table 8-1. *Distribution of Workers by Employment Types, 1980–2018 (Percent)*

	Nonwage workers (NW)				Wage income workers (W)			All workers in SE sector (SE+U+W2)*
	Self-employed (SE)			Unpaid family workers (U)		Corporate & gov't sectors (W1)*	SE sector (W2)*	
		SE without employees (SE1)	SE with employees (SE2)					
1980	34.0	29.3	4.7	18.8	47.2	35.2	12.0	64.8
1990	28.0	21.6	6.5	11.4	60.5	44.1	16.5	55.9
2000	27.8	20.9	6.9	9.2	63.1	45.5	17.5	54.5
2010	23.5	17.2	6.3	5.3	71.2	55.1	16.1	44.9
2018	21.0	14.9	6.2	4.1	74.9	59.2	15.7	40.8

Source: Park (2020). Original data are from the Economically Active Population Survey, Statistics Korea.

Note: *These are estimated values from Park (2020) as actual values are unavailable.

FIGURE 8-2. **Functional Distribution of National Income, 1980–2017**

Percent

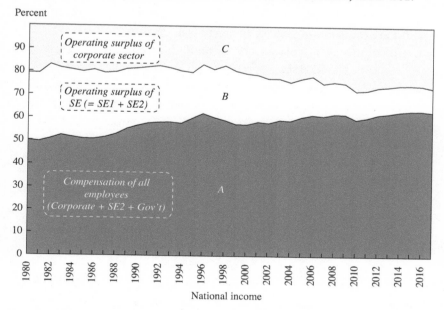

National income

Source: Author calculations based on National Accounts, Bank of Korea.

surplus of government.[10] Figure 8-2 shows how national income is distributed among each component for the period 1980–2017 based on National Accounts from Bank of Korea (the operating surplus of government is not shown as it is minimal). The key issue in correctly calculating the labor income share is determining how to separate imputed labor income from the operating surplus of SEs (area B in the figure) and add it to the compensation of all employees (area A).

The share of employees' compensation (area A) has a long-run rising trend. However, it is easy to see that the labor share adjusted to include imputed labor income from the SE sector can be very different, as the operating surplus of SEs (area B) is large and changing.[11] There are two common approaches used in the labor share accounting literature. The first approach suggested by Gollin (labeled M1 here) assumes that average imputed wages for the SE sector are the same as those of workers in the rest of the sectors. This approach is used in several databases, such as the European Union's KLEMS (capital, labor, energy, materials, and services) database and the productivity database of the Organization for Economic

Cooperation and Development (OECD). The second approach suggested by Gollin (labeled M2 here) assumes that imputed labor shares of the SE sector are the same as those of the rest of the sectors.

Unfortunately, calculations based on both approaches reveal problems and result in biased estimates in Korea's case. When approach M1 is applied to Korean data, it turns out that the adjusted labor share estimates rise above one for some years. This is obviously due to overestimation of imputed labor income as the majority of the self-employed are self-run businesses with no employees (SE1) and their average operating surpluses are even below the wage of an average wage worker in other sectors. Moreover, the proportion of SE1 is considerable and changing.

The key problem with approach M2 is that it relies on an accurate calculation of the labor share of the rest of the sectors. However, this calculation is difficult.[12] Existing studies simply exclude the operating surplus of SE (area B in figure 8-2) and assume that the remaining value added (areas A+C) arises from the rest of the sectors: corporate and government. Then, the labor share of the rest of the sectors is produced by taking the ratio of compensation of employees (area A) to the remaining value added (areas A+C). However, this calculation is incorrect. As shown in figure 8-2, both the compensation of employees (area A) and the remaining value added (areas A+C) do not completely exclude value added arising from the SE sector, as they include wages paid to workers in the SE2 sector. Wages paid to workers in the SE2 sector need to be excluded from area A.

Correcting the Biases

Park (2020) suggests three alternative methods to approach M2: methods P0, P1, and P2. First, the method P0 excludes employees' compensation originating from SE2 when calculating the labor share of the rest of the sectors to correctly obtain the labor shares of corporate and government sectors. This method requires detailed statistics decomposing employees' compensation into three sectors: corporate, self-employed, and government. As Bank of Korea only began to publish this decomposition from 2010 onward, this method can be applied only for the subsequent period. So we cannot observe the long-run trend of labor share.

Second, the method P1 estimates the labor share of all sectors except for SE1. Here, SE2 businesses are considered to be similar to corporations in terms of operations and functions, as they hire employees and use capital for production. This share is derived and assumed to be the imputed labor share of SE1. This method does not count the imputed wages of owners of SE2 businesses. To implement this, we need to separate the operating surplus of SE2 from that of SE and add it to the remaining value added (areas A + C in figure 8-2). However, statistics on the division of the operating surplus between SE1 and SE2 are usually unavailable in Korea, just as in most other countries.

To estimate the respective shares of the operating surplus, we take the following approach. The Survey of Household Finances and Living Conditions (HS2) from Statistics Korea provides information on business incomes for individual SE1 and SE2 from 2010 onward.[13] The average ratios of business incomes of individual SE2 to those of individual SE1 are relatively stable from 2011 to 2017, and the period average ratio is 2.32.[14] Assuming that this ratio is constant for all periods, we can calculate and separate out the operating surpluses of the two sectors: SE1 and SE2.[15] The estimated operating surplus for SE2 is then added to A + C to derive the labor share of all sectors except SE1.

Third, the method P2 is the same as the method P1 but adds the imputed wages of the SE2 business owners to the compensation of employees, assuming that the owners of SE2 businesses have human capital similar to average wage workers in other sectors. The average imputed wage of the SE2 business owners is calculated as the ratio of employees' compensation to the number of wage income workers.[16]

The simple labor income share (A), the adjusted labor share based on Gollin's method (M2), and the adjusted labor shares (P0, P1, and P2) from Park (2020) are presented in figure 8-3. Although the adjusted labor share P0 can be calculated only for the post-2010 period, it should be considered the benchmark as it is based on actual data. It is the actual labor share of the corporate and government sectors. It is notable that the adjusted labor share P1 closely matches the adjusted labor share P0.

We see upward movement of labor shares P1 and P2 from the mid-1980s to the late 1990s. Downward movement is observed from the late 1990s to 2008, but the trend reverses to upward movement after 2010. Overall, we do not see a clear long-run trend for the labor shares P1 and P2. This contrasts with the labor share M2 from earlier studies, which shows a downward long-run trend.

For the period 1980–2017, the labor shares P1 and P2 rose 3.2 percentage points and 1.8 percentage points, respectively, whereas the labor share M2 fell by 0.3 percentage point. For the period 1990–2017, the labor shares

FIGURE 8-3. **Labor Shares and Alternative Adjusted Labor Shares of National Income, 1980–2017**

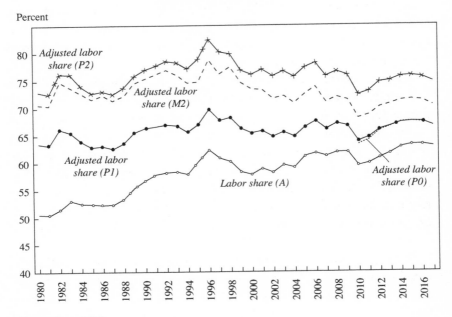

Source: Park (2020).

P1 and P2 changed by 0.3 percentage point and –2.2 percentage points, respectively, while the labor share M2 changed by –5.0 percentage points. The greater drop in M2 can be explained by a downward trend bias associated with its calculation, as discussed above.

No Evidence of Long-Run Decline in Labor Income Share

Park (2020) does not find a long-run declining trend for the labor income share in the aggregate Korean economy when the SE sector is appropriately treated in the calculation. This finding is consistent with studies of the labor income share at the corporate level where the labor share calculation is relatively clear and without issues.[17] Evidence in Park (2020) does not support the view that recent technological change has had a long-run bias favoring capital owners in Korea. This matches similar findings for some other advanced economies in Gutiérrez and Piton (2020). On the other hand, studies such as Acemoglu and Restrepo (2018), Martinez (2018), and Autor and Salomons (2018) suggest that capital-biased technological change and automation are favoring capital. One possible explanation for these seemingly conflicting findings is that the new technologies may be labor saving but are, at the same time, strongly complementary to human capital. The former aspect may negatively affect the labor income share by reducing the demand for low-skilled labor, while the latter aspect may have an opposite, positive effect by increasing the demand for complementary higher-skilled labor. The two aspects may have offsetting effects on the long-run trend of labor share. This implies widening wage disparity, which is analyzed in the next section.

Technological change may have had differential impacts on firms with different characteristics. Some firms may be more capable than others at adopting new technology and taking advantage of associated opportunities, as depicted in figure 8-1. Successful firms are able to pay out higher returns to their capital owners and higher wages to their workers. As a result, gaps between the two groups of firms will widen, and wage disparity will increase among workers.

Wage Disparity and Firm Size

Skill-biased technological change may increase wage disparity because it offers greater benefits for workers equipped with higher human capital. Firms adopt new technology and transform their operations to stay competitive in changing market conditions. The success of this transformation crucially depends on the competency of their personnel. When the productivity of firms rises due to successful transformation, workers with complementary human capital are likely to be compensated with higher wages. As firms succeed or fail in responding to challenges in a new technological environment, we expect to observe increases in heterogeneity of productivity and wages across firms.

A Rise in Wage Disparity

Wage disparity has increased in Korea in the past two decades. Workers' wage data can be accessed from the Survey on Labor Conditions by Employment Type (WS) from the Ministry of Employment and Labor, which holds the most comprehensive worker-related information—collected from more than 33,000 establishments and covering more than a million workers in the industrial sectors.[18] Wage disparity is measured by Gini indices calculated from annual earnings for all workers in all industries (Gini1) and those

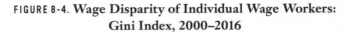

FIGURE 8-4. **Wage Disparity of Individual Wage Workers:
Gini Index, 2000–2016**

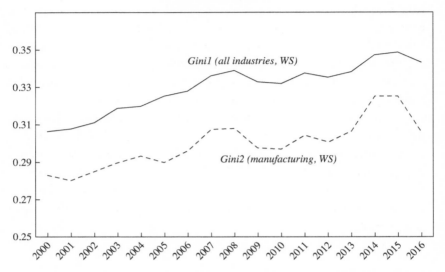

Source: Author calculations based on Survey on Labor Conditions by Employment Type, Ministry
of Employment and Labor.

in manufacturing (Gini2) over 2000–2016. Figure 8-4 shows that both indices display a strong upward trend until the global financial crisis of 2008.
They fluctuate with a slight rising trend for the postcrisis period.

Establishment Size Matters for the Rise in Wage Disparity

I examine worker characteristics to identify different factors contributing
to the observed increase in wage disparity. First, I choose among several
worker characteristics that can contribute to wage disparity, such as the
worker's age, education, workplace size, and associated industry. Second, I
categorize workers into subgroups according to the chosen characteristics.[19]
Finally, I measure how much of the total wage disparity can be explained
by wage variations between the subgroups (between effect) and within subgroups (within effect). I adopt the approach designed by Pyatt (1976) that
enables us to decompose the Gini index into "within," "between," and "overlapping" effects.[20]

Table 8-2 presents the decomposition results of wage disparity for each
of the chosen worker characteristics in the years 2000 and 2016. For each
of the worker characteristics, the between effects are significantly greater

Table 8-2. *Wage Gini Decomposition by Worker Characteristics*

Worker characteristics	Age		Education		Establishment size		Industry	
	2000	*2016*	*2000*	*2016*	*2000*	*2016*	*2000*	*2016*
Within	0.071	0.076	0.087	0.095	0.055	0.058	0.010	0.009
	(23.2%)	(22.2%)	(28.3%)	(27.8%)	(17.9%)	(17.0%)	(3.4%)	(2.6%)
Between	0.108	0.093	0.113	0.132	0.092	0.132	0.110	0.155
	(35.3%)	(27.0%)	(36.9%)	(38.6%)	(30.0%)	(38.3%)	(36.7%)	(45.3%)
Overlapping	0.127	0.174	0.107	0.115	0.160	0.153	0.180	0.179
	(41.5%)	(50.8%)	(34.8%)	(33.6%)	(52.0%)	(44.7%)	(59.9%)	(52.1%)
Total	0.307	0.343	0.307	0.343	0.307	0.343	0.307	0.343

Source: Author calculations based on Survey on Labor Conditions by Employment Type, Ministry of Employment and Labor.

Note: Calculations are based on Pyatt's inequality decomposition. Values in parentheses are relative contributions.

than the within effects for both years. This implies that wage heterogeneity between subgroups is contributing more to wage disparity than wage heterogeneity within subgroups.

The total wage Gini index rose from 0.307 to 0.343 between 2000 and 2016. It is notable that the increase in the between effects of establishment size (from 0.092 to 0.132) and that of associated industry (from 0.110 to 0.155) almost match the rise in the total Gini index. On the other hand, the between effects of age and education are relatively stable. These results suggest that the widening wage gaps between subgroups of establishment size or of industries are key candidates to explain the observed increases in wage disparity.

The analysis in table 8-2 is limited in the sense that it only allows one single characteristic for each decomposition and leaves other characteristics uncontrolled. We now examine whether establishment size was a decisive factor even when we control for the other characteristics. Table 8-3 presents wage Gini index decomposition by establishment size subgroups for subsamples of workers with similar ages: twenties, thirties, forties, fifties, and sixties and over. The index for each of the age subsamples rose from 2000 to 2016. The results show that the between effects of establishment size rose significantly for all subsamples except for that of sixties and over. Likewise, table 8-4 presents wage Gini index decomposition by establishment size subgroups for subsamples of workers with similar education levels. The Gini indices for each of the education subsamples rose from 2000 to 2016. The between effects of establishment size rose significantly for all subsamples except for high school graduates.

Table 8-5 presents wage Gini index decomposition by establishment size subgroups for subsamples of one-digit industries. Between 2000 and 2016, we observe that Gini indices rose in twelve of fifteen industries. Of those twelve, the between effects of establishment size subgroups rose in nine: agriculture, forestry, and fishery (A), mining (B), manufacturing (C), water supply, sewage, waste management, and other remediation activities (E), construction (F), transportation and storage (H), information and communication (J), educational services (P), and arts, entertainment, and recreation (R).[21]

The foregoing analysis suggests establishment size as a key factor associated with the observed rise in wage disparity—even when controlling for other worker characteristics. Our results corroborate the findings of Koh (2018) on wage inequality. Based on hourly wage data from the Survey on Labor Conditions by Employment Type (WS), he calculates the relative contribution of various worker characteristics to the wage gap. The wage

Table 8-3. *Wage Gini Decomposition by Establishment Size Subgroups for Age Group Subsamples*

Age subsamples	Ages 20 to 29 subsample		Ages 30 to 39 subsample		Ages 40 to 49 subsample		Ages 50 to 59 subsample		Ages 60 and over subsample	
	2000	2016	2000	2016	2000	2016	2000	2016	2000	2016
Within	0.041	0.038	0.044	0.043	0.057	0.057	0.070	0.072	0.082	0.096
	(17.8%)	(16.1%)	(17.5%)	(15.7%)	(18.1%)	(16.4%)	(18.8%)	(18.4%)	(21.0%)	(23.5%)
Between	0.073	0.110	0.089	0.136	0.091	0.151	0.094	0.125	0.069	0.040
	(32.0%)	(46.2%)	(35.3%)	(49.8%)	(28.6%)	(43.5%)	(25.2%)	(31.9%)	(17.8%)	(9.9%)
Overlapping	0.114	0.090	0.120	0.095	0.169	0.139	0.208	0.195	0.238	0.272
	(50.2%)	(37.8%)	(47.2%)	(34.5%)	(53.3%)	(40.1%)	(55.9%)	(49.7%)	(61.2%)	(66.7%)
Total	0.227	0.238	0.253	0.274	0.316	0.346	0.372	0.392	0.389	0.408

Source: Author calculations based on Survey on Labor Conditions by Employment Type, Ministry of Employment and Labor.

Note: Calculations are based on Pyatt's inequality decomposition. Values in parentheses are relative contributions.

Table 8-4. *Wage Gini Decomposition by Establishment Size Subgroups for Education-Level Group Subsamples*

Education subsamples	Middle school or less subsample		High school subsample		2-year college subsample		4-year university subsample		Graduate school subsample	
	2000	2016	2000	2016	2000	2016	2000	2016	2000	2016
Within	0.052	0.065	0.048	0.058	0.050	0.051	0.049	0.056	0.053	0.064
	(17.9%)	(20.1%)	(17.6%)	(18.4%)	(18.0%)	(17.4%)	(18.2%)	(17.2%)	(18.0%)	(20.3%)
Between	0.100	0.112	0.113	0.102	0.084	0.113	0.086	0.112	0.078	0.098
	(34.4%)	(34.9%)	(41.0%)	(32.4%)	(30.1%)	(38.9%)	(31.9%)	(34.5%)	(26.6%)	(30.8%)
Overlapping	0.139	0.145	0.114	0.155	0.144	0.127	0.135	0.157	0.163	0.155
	(47.7%)	(45.1%)	(41.4%)	(49.3%)	(51.9%)	(43.7%)	(49.9%)	(48.3%)	(55.3%)	(48.9%)
Total	0.291	0.322	0.275	0.316	0.278	0.291	0.270	0.325	0.294	0.316

Source: Author calculations based on Survey on Labor Conditions by Employment Type, Ministry of Employment and Labor.

Note: Calculations are based on Pyatt's inequality decomposition. Values in parentheses are relative contributions.

Table 8-5. *Wage Gini Decomposition by Establishment Size Subgroups for Industry Subsamples*

Panel A

Industry subsamples	A		B		C		D		E	
	2000	2016	2000	2016	2000	2016	2000	2016	2000	2016
Within	0.079 (27.5%)	0.082 (24.5%)	0.096 (37.6%)	0.061 (23.4%)	0.050 (17.8%)	0.049 (16.0%)	0.057 (34.1%)	0.066 (25.2%)	0.048 (19.7%)	0.076 (26.9%)
Between	0.060 (20.8%)	0.077 (23.0%)	0.048 (18.9%)	0.083 (32.0%)	0.109 (38.6%)	0.155 (50.6%)	0.087 (52.3%)	0.050 (18.9%)	0.073 (29.7%)	0.087 (30.8%)
Overlapping	0.149 (51.7%)	0.175 (52.5%)	0.111 (43.4%)	0.115 (44.6%)	0.123 (43.6%)	0.103 (33.5%)	0.023 (13.6%)	0.146 (55.9%)	0.124 (50.7%)	0.120 (42.3%)
Total	0.288	0.333	0.255	0.259	0.282	0.306	0.166	0.262	0.245	0.284

Panel B

Industry subsamples	F		G		H		I		J	
	2000	2016	2000	2016	2000	2016	2000	2016	2000	2016
Within	0.114 (50.2%)	0.058 (18.3%)	0.053 (18.5%)	0.076 (22.8%)	0.069 (22.9%)	0.073 (21.5%)	0.055 (19.7%)	0.066 (24.8%)	0.055 (21.9%)	0.054 (17.6%)
Between	0.089 (39.2%)	0.155 (49.2%)	0.124 (43.2%)	0.060 (18.2%)	0.053 (17.6%)	0.078 (23.1%)	0.129 (46.4%)	0.058 (21.7%)	0.064 (25.2%)	0.095 (31.4%)
Overlapping	0.024 (10.6%)	0.103 (32.5%)	0.110 (38.3%)	0.195 (59.0%)	0.180 (59.5%)	0.188 (55.4%)	0.094 (33.9%)	0.143 (53.6%)	0.134 (52.9%)	0.155 (51.0%)
Total	0.227	0.316	0.286	0.331	0.303	0.339	0.278	0.267	0.253	0.304

(continued)

Table 8-5. *(continued)*

Panel C

Industry subsamples	K		M		N		P		R	
	2000	2016	2000	2016	2000	2016	2000	2016	2000	2016
Within	0.067 (24.1%)	0.068 (21.8%)	0.067 (18.8%)	0.055 (16.9%)	0.061 (18.8%)	0.070 (23.0%)	0.059 (19.6%)	0.063 (17.6%)	0.073 (26.2%)	0.060 (19.9%)
Between	0.067 (23.9%)	0.052 (16.4%)	0.150 (42.3%)	0.149 (46.1%)	0.050 (15.4%)	0.025 (8.3%)	0.124 (41.3%)	0.136 (37.7%)	0.061 (22.0%)	0.084 (27.6%)
Overlapping	0.145 (52.0%)	0.194 (61.8%)	0.137 (38.8%)	0.119 (37.0%)	0.215 (65.9%)	0.208 (68.7%)	0.118 (39.2%)	0.161 (44.8%)	0.144 (51.8%)	0.159 (52.5%)
Total	0.279	0.313	0.354	0.323	0.326	0.303	0.300	0.361	0.278	0.303

Source: Author calculations based on Survey on Labor Conditions by Employment Type, Ministry of Employment and Labor.

Note: Calculations are based on Pyatt's inequality decomposition. Values in parentheses are relative contributions. The industries are agriculture, forestry, and fishery (A); mining (B); manufacturing (C); utilities—electricity and gas (D); water supply, sewage, waste management, and other remediation activities (E); construction (F); wholesale and retail trade (G); transportation and storage (H); accommodation and food services (I); information and communication (J); finance and insurance (K); professional, scientific, and technical services (M); management of companies and enterprises (N); educational services (P); and arts, entertainment, and recreation (R).

Table 8-6. *Relative Contributions to the Wage Gap (Percent)*

	1980	1990	2000	2010	2016
Sex	14.8	11.5	5.0	4.8	4.5
Age	9.7	3.9	4.4	3.4	3.6
Education	14.6	12.2	9.5	9.8	9.3
Work experience	7.3	10.1	8.0	7.9	6.6
Firm tenure	5.1	10.8	14.7	14.2	15.6
Establishment size	0.1	3.8	3.7	7.4	9.1
Occupation	14.3	12.0	14.8	9.8	10.1
Industry	7.5	8.2	7.5	4.4	4.0
Unexplained	26.6	27.5	32.4	38.3	37.2
Total	100.0	100.0	100.0	100.0	100.0

Source: Koh (2018), table 2-3.

gap is measured by the Q5 to Q1 quintile ratio. As shown in table 8-6, Koh's results indicate that the contribution of establishment size increased the most (3.7 percent to 9.1 percent) among all worker characteristics between 2000 and 2016.

Heterogeneity in Productivity and Wage Growth across Different-Sized Firms

Widening firm performance gaps can be a crucial factor in explaining the rise in wage disparity. The preceding section revealed that increasing wage disparity was strongly associated with widening wage gaps between different-sized firms. This may be the result of widening labor productivity between heterogeneous groups of firms. Larger firms have greater capacity to adopt new technology and thus may be enjoying faster growth in productivity and wages. This section examines changes in performance gaps between different-sized firms over time using establishment-level, firm-level, and worker-level data sets.[22]

Larger Firms Are Associated with Higher Human Capital, Greater Innovative Activity, and More Capital Investment

Firm size, especially in Korea, is strongly correlated with firm performance and capability in terms of production and innovative capacity. It is a well-known fact in Korea that workers with higher human capital tend to

FIGURE 8-5. **Distribution of Employees' Educational Attainment by Firm Size, 2016**

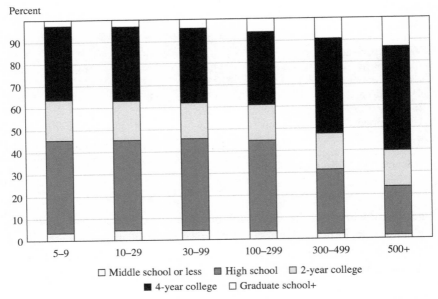

Source: Author calculations based on Survey on Labor Conditions by Employment Type, Ministry of Employment and Labor.

Note: Firms are classified by the number of their employees.

be associated with larger-sized firms. Figure 8-5 presents the distribution of employees' educational attainment by firm size in 2016 based on the worker survey data (WS). It shows that larger firms (300 employees or more) hold greater proportions of workers with higher education (four-year college and graduate degrees) than smaller firms.

Larger firms are strongly associated with greater innovative activity and higher capital intensity. Using firm-level data (BS) for manufacturing industries, table 8-7 shows that larger firms have higher ratios of research and development (R&D) to sales, and more tangible and intangible assets per employee.

Larger Firms Are Associated with Higher Productivity and Higher Wages

To examine the relationship between firm size, productivity, and wages, average labor productivity and average real wage for each establishment are

Table 8-7. *R&D, Tangible Assets, and Intangible Assets by Firm Size (2016)*

	50–99 employees	100–299 employees	300–499 employees	500 or more employees	All
R&D-to-sales ratio	1.5%	1.9%	2.2%	2.5%	1.8%
Tangible assets per employee (million KRW)	170.0	170.5	201.6	287.0	181.9
Intangible assets per employee (million KRW)	5.7	9.5	11.4	16.0	8.6

Source: Author calculations based on Survey of Business Activities, Statistics Korea.

Note: KRW = Korean won.

calculated using manufacturing establishment data (MS). As the majority of Korean firms are single-establishment firms, establishment survey data are used. Figures 8-6 and 8-7 show the distribution of average labor productivity and average real wages at the establishment level according to different establishment sizes in 1996 and 2016. Establishments of larger size show higher labor productivity and higher real wage distributions. The gap between the small and large establishment distributions widened between 1996 and 2016.

Similar findings on wage disparity across establishment sizes can also be obtained from the wage worker data set (WS). Figure 8-8 provides real wage distribution of individual workers by their workplace size for the manufacturing sector and for all industries in 2000 and 2016. It shows noticeable wage distribution gaps between different-sized establishments, and especially between establishments with fewer than 300 employees and those with more than 300 employees, as well as a widening of those gaps between 2000 and 2016.

Larger Firms Are Associated with Higher Growth
in Productivity and Wages

Figure 8-9 shows labor productivity and wages of different-sized establishments relative to those of establishments with 300 to 499 employees over 1992–2016. We can see that the labor productivity and wage growth of the larger establishments outpaced those of smaller establishments. The relative performance of the largest size class (establishments with

FIGURE 8-6. **Average Labor Productivity Distribution at Establishment Level, by Establishment Size: Manufacturing, 1996, 2016**

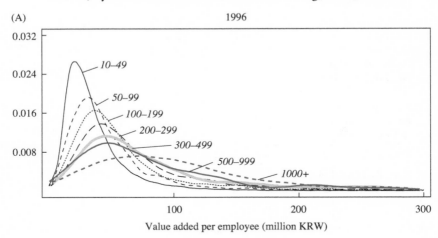

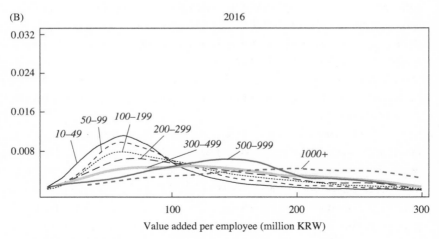

Source: Author calculations based on Mining and Manufacturing Survey, Statistics Korea.

Note: KRW = Korean won. Each distribution shows kernel density estimates of average labor productivity of establishments in subgroups classified by number of employees. Labor productivity is in 1996 constant prices, and manufacturing GDP deflators are used for the conversion.

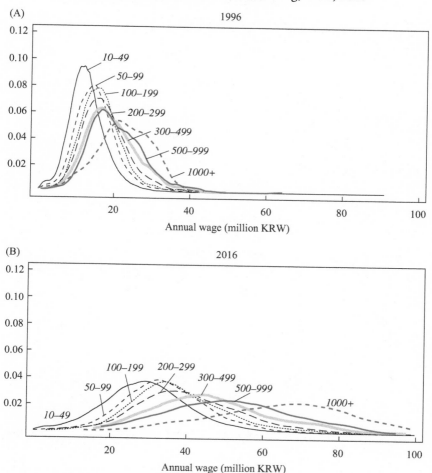

FIGURE 8-7. **Average Real Wage Distribution at Establishment Level, by Establishment Size: Manufacturing, 1996, 2016**

Source: Author calculations based on Mining and Manufacturing Survey, Statistics Korea.

Note: KRW = Korean won. Each distribution shows kernel density estimates of average annual wages paid by establishments in subgroups classified by number of employees. Real wages are in 1996 constant prices, and the consumer price index is used for the conversion.

FIGURE 8-8. Wage Distribution at Individual Worker Level, by Workplace Size: 2000, 2016

(A)

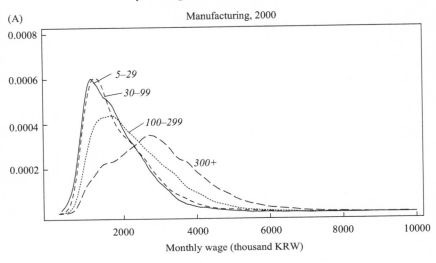

Manufacturing, 2000

(B)

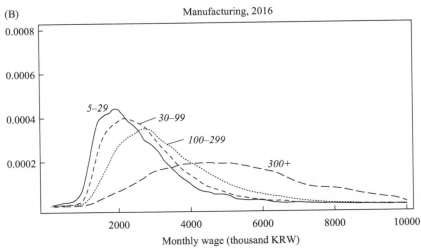

Manufacturing, 2016

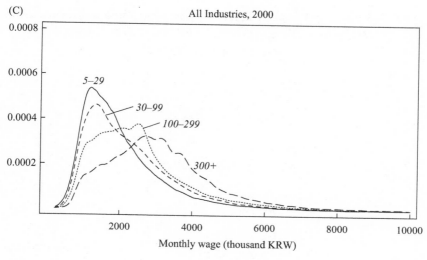

(C)   All Industries, 2000

Monthly wage (thousand KRW)

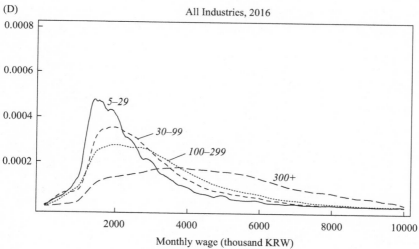

(D)   All Industries, 2016

Monthly wage (thousand KRW)

Source: Author calculations based on Survey on Labor Conditions by Employment Type, Ministry of Employment and Labor.

Note: KRW = Korean won. Each distribution shows kernel density estimates of monthly wages of individual workers according to their workplace size subgroup. Real wages are in 2015 constant prices, and the consumer price index is used for the conversion.

FIGURE 8-9. Average Labor Productivity and Wages by Establishment Size (Relative to Establishments with 300–499 Employees): Manufacturing, 1992–2016

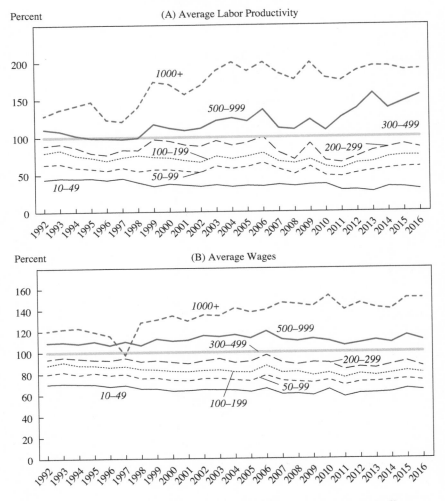

Source: Author calculations based on Mining and Manufacturing Survey, Statistics Korea.

Note: Labor productivity and wage measures shown are the same as those used in figures 8-6 and 8-7.

1,000 employees or more) has been impressive. Increases in labor productivity and wage gaps between the largest establishments and the rest are especially visible for the period leading up to the global financial crisis. The gaps seem relatively stable in the postcrisis period.

Changes in Employment Distribution by Establishment Size

Wage disparity can be affected by the transformation of industries. There are two important channels to consider: changes in the distribution of firms, and changes in firm performance heterogeneity. Changes in firm size distribution can influence wage disparity since firm size is strongly correlated with wage level. An increase in the proportion of large-sized firms may raise the proportion of highly paid individuals. While this affects wage disparity, the direction of the effect is ambiguous, as it depends on the existing distribution of wage earners. Wage disparity is also affected by changes in the labor productivity and wage gaps between different-sized firms. Given a constant firm distribution, widening productivity and wage gaps imply greater wage disparity. This subsection investigates these two channels to understand the link between the industrial landscape transformation and worker wage disparity.

I first examine how firm distribution has evolved over time. Figure 8-10 illustrates frequency histograms of manufacturing establishments by size (weighted by employees) for 1996 and 2016. As the distribution is weighted by the number of employees, it can be interpreted as employee distribution by establishment size. The sample is divided into two subsamples—establishments with fewer than 300 employees and those with 300 employees or more.

It is evident that employment increased in small-sized establishments but dropped in larger-sized establishments during the last two decades. The increase is especially prominent for establishments with fewer than fifty employees. It seems that new firm entrants resulted in a greater number of small-sized establishments that have yet to achieve internal growth. On the other hand, larger firms may have reduced their demand for low-skilled labor through the adoption of new-technology-embodied capital or process innovation. An alternative explanation is that many large-scale establishments in declining industries have closed down. Also, businesses in the new, growing industries did not open more plants domestically but relied heavily on large-scale offshoring to achieve cost efficiency.

FIGURE 8-10. **Employment Histograms by Establishment Size
in Manufacturing, 1996, 2016**

(A) Establishments with Fewer than 300 Employees

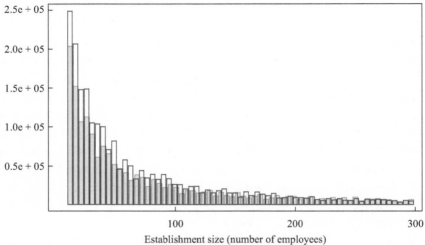

(B) Establishments with More than 300 Employees

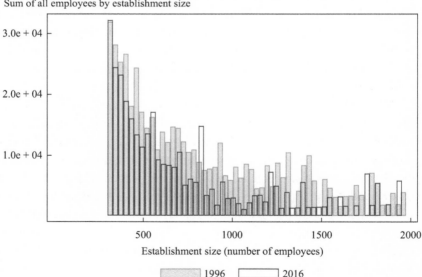

Source: Author calculations based on Mining and Manufacturing Survey, Statistics Korea.

Note: The graphs show histograms for sum of all employees at each respective establishment size.

FIGURE 8-11. **Changes in Employment between 1996 and 2016 across Industries by Establishment Size**

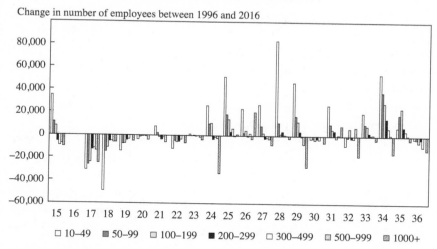

Source: Author calculations based on Mining and Manufacturing Survey, Statistics Korea.

Note: The industries covered are: food products and beverages (15), tobacco (16), textiles (17), wearing apparel and furs (18), leather, luggage, and footwear (19), wood and paper products (20), pulp, paper, and paper products (21), printing and reproduction of recorded media (22), coke and refined petroleum products (23), chemicals and chemical products (24), rubber and plastic products (25), nonmetallic mineral products (26), basic metals (27), fabricated metal products except machinery and equipment (28), other machinery and equipment (29), computers (30), electrical and optical equipment (31), electronic video and audio, communication equipment (32), medical, precision, and optical instruments (33), motor vehicles and trailers (34), other transport equipment (35), furniture (36).

Changes in Employment Distribution by Industry and by Establishment Size

Figure 8-11 shows changes in employment across manufacturing industries by establishment size between 1996 and 2016. We can observe that light and computer-manufacturing industries are shedding employment, while heavy and high-tech industries are increasing employment.[23] Many growing industries are adding workers in small-sized establishments but reducing workers in large-sized establishments.[24]

The industrial composition is moving away from light industries to heavy and high-tech industries. At the same time, the expanding industries are adding new small-sized establishments but reducing large-sized establishments. As a result, large-establishment employment has fallen in all industries except nonmetallic mineral products (26) and electrical and optical equipment (31). As for employment in small-sized establishments, reductions in contracting industries were more than offset by the increases in expanding industries. There were big increases in employment in rubber and plastic products (25), fabricated metal products except machinery and equipment (28), other machinery and equipment (29), and motor vehicles and trailers (34). In short, the share of large-establishment employment has fallen, while small-establishment employment has moved away from declining industries to expanding industries.

I now evaluate how compositional changes in industries affect overall labor productivity and wages. To address this question, I first group establishments by size-industry subgroups, which are defined by subgroups of seven different establishment sizes and by two-digit manufacturing industries. I then calculate average labor productivity and wages for each subgroup. Thus, each observation represents average labor productivity and wage of a given size-industry subgroup. Employment changes between 1996 and 2016 for each size-industry subgroup are plotted against respective average labor productivity in 2016 and presented in panel A of figure 8-12. We see that there were considerable shifts in small-sized establishment employment (10–49 and 50–99 employees) across industries. However, labor productivity of new small establishments in new industries is not much different from that of counterparts in declining industries. Panel B, on average wages, presents a qualitatively similar pattern. It is evident that employment has fallen in large establishments of high-productivity and high-wage industries.

These findings suggest that compositional change in employment may have contributed to a slowdown in the growth of overall labor productivity and wages. This is because employment in low-productivity sectors has increased while that in high-productivity sectors has declined. Since low-productivity sectors have shown slower growth in productivity than high-productivity sectors, we can deduce that overall productivity growth has declined. This in turn implies a slowdown in wage growth.

More workers are associated with low-productivity and low-wage sectors than before. Lee (2020) shows that total factor productivity growth in the manufacturing sector stayed high until 2010 but has dramatically slowed since then. Choi and Kim (2019) provide evidence that firm dynamics have deteriorated as entry and exit rates have gradually declined in the 2000s.

FIGURE 8-12. Changes in Employment, Labor Productivity, and Wages of Industries by Establishment Size, 1996–2016

(A) Labor Productivity

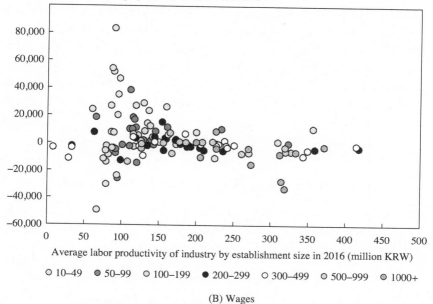

Change in number of employees between 1996 and 2016

Average labor productivity of industry by establishment size in 2016 (million KRW)

○ 10–49　◑ 50–99　○ 100–199　● 200–299　○ 300–499　◔ 500–999　◉ 1000+

(B) Wages

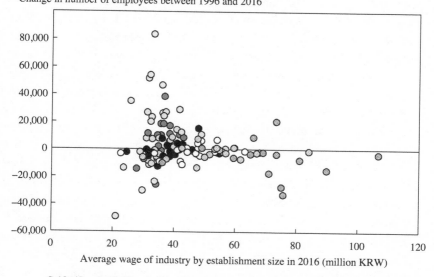

Change in number of employees between 1996 and 2016

Average wage of industry by establishment size in 2016 (million KRW)

○ 10–49　◑ 50–99　○ 100–199　● 200–299　○ 300–499　◔ 500–999　◉ 1000+

Source: Author calculations based on Mining and Manufacturing Survey, Statistics Korea.

Note: KRW=Korean won. Labor productivity and wage measures shown on the horizontal axes are the same as those used in figures 8-6 and 8-7.

Implications for Wage Disparity

What do the above findings imply for wage disparity? First, the widening gap between average wages of small- and large-sized establishments is contributing to an increase in wage disparity.[25] Second, the compositional changes in industries have an ambiguous effect on wage disparity. Wage disparity may either rise or fall depending on the initial distribution of worker wages. The observed changes in wage disparity are the result of both effects combined.

Wage Disparity and Household Income Distribution

Household income is composed of income from different sources. So an important question is the extent to which changes in wage disparity explain changes in household income inequality.

Different Sources of Household Income Inequality

The Gini indices for household income distribution based on market income and disposable income are presented in figure 8-13. There are alternative series of household income Gini indices due to differences in sample and time period coverages.[26] Despite the differences in levels, these indices generally show long-run rising trends from 1990 until the global financial crisis of 2008. For the subsequent period, the market income Ginis have mild downward trends and the disposable income Ginis have significant declining trends. The gap between the market and disposable income Gini indices has increased since 2010 due to stronger income redistribution policies.

Given that increases in firm performance heterogeneity have widened wage disparity, we ask how much the latter has contributed to changes in household income inequality. Individual wage disparity and household income inequality are different in many ways. Wage disparity is solely determined by wage incomes of individual wage workers, whereas household income inequality is determined by all sources of income generated by household members. The latter is especially affected by the number of household members in employment. Furthermore, it is influenced by several different sources of income (wage income, business income, property income, and private income transfers). Changes in individual wage dispar-

FIGURE 8-13. **Household Income Inequality, 1990–2018: Gini Indices**

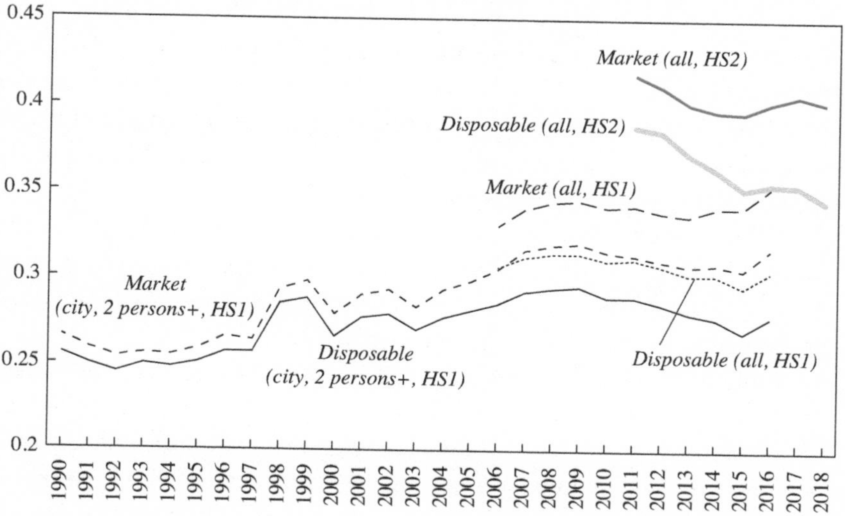

Source: Author calculations based on Household Income and Expenditure Survey (HS1) and Survey of Household Finances and Living Conditions (HS2), Statistics Korea.

ity are only a part of the reason for changes in household income inequality. To address our question, this section presents a decomposition of the household income Gini index by different sources of market income.

One factor to consider is the heterogeneity of incomes from different sources: wage income, business income, property income, and so forth. Assuming that the employment status of household members is not changing, changes in income disparity within each income source affect household income inequality. Conceptually, this effect only reflects changes in income disparity of family members who are already participating in the labor market. We term this effect the *market income disparity effect*.

A second factor is changes in labor market participation of family members. Even when there is no change in market income disparity (wage or nonwage incomes), household income inequality may be affected if an additional family member enters or exits the labor market. We denote this effect the *labor participation effect*. Consider an extreme case where wage and nonwage incomes are constant and uniform for all workers. In that case, the Gini index is solely determined by changes in the number of household members who work. In Korea, most households were single-income-based in the early years of development. As female labor participation gradually rose in the last two decades, the proportion of double-income households rose. The female labor participation rate (ages fifteen to sixty-four) rose from 52.1 percent in 2000 to 58.3 percent in 2016, and the employment rate rose from 50.1 percent to 56.1 percent during the same period.[27] This increased household income inequality as disparity widened between the single-income and double-income households.

A third factor is that an aging population tends to replace high-income households with low-income single-person households. The effect of increases in single-person households on income inequality is ambiguous and depends on the existing income distribution.[28]

Table 8-8 shows the percentages of households with positive income from each type of income source for the years 1996, 2006, and 2016. Column A shows statistics for the sample restricted to city households with two or more family members. We see that the percentage of wage-earning spouses increased dramatically, from 20.7 percent in 1996 to 31.0 percent in 2016, while the proportion of wage-earning heads of household remained stable at about 65 percent. This strongly suggests the presence of a labor participation effect for the period. Column B shows nationwide household statistics, including single-person households, which increased dramatically, from 16.0 percent to 25.5 percent, between 2006 and 2016. For this sample, the proportion of wage-earning spouses did not change much from 2006 to 2016. This can be understood as a result of two offsetting effects: an increase in households with income-earning spouses, and an increase in single-person households (which lowers the proportion of multiple-income households by definition).

Decomposition of Household Gini by Different Income Sources

I now decompose the household Gini index for market income to gauge the contribution of disparity in different income sources to household inequality. We use the decomposition method developed by Lerman and Yitzhaki (1985). Table 8-9 presents the decomposition results for the data sample of city households with two or more persons. Column A shows the inequality contribution of each source of income in absolute terms. The sum of all contributions adds up to the Gini index. Column B shows the relative contribution of each income source. Changes in the contribution of different income sources should be interpreted as the combined effect of the three factors mentioned earlier.

Table 8-8. *Percentages of Households with Positive Income from Each Type of Income Source*

	A. City households with 2 or more persons			B. All households	
	1996	2006	2016	2006	2016
Wage income, head of household	65.7	64.2	65.7	60.9	60.7
Wage income, spouse	20.7	27.8	31.0	23.0	23.8
Business income, head of household	31.8	29.7	23.3	27.2	20.6
Business income, spouse	6.9	7.6	7.1	6.4	5.2
Income of other members	23.4	28.2	30.0	23.7	23.9
Property income	3.2	2.0	2.5	2.1	2.6
Net income transfers	7.5	12.2	11.4	16.0	15.4

Source: Author calculations based on Household Income and Expenditure Survey (HS1), Statistics Korea.

Note: For each income category, income is counted as positive when monthly earnings are greater than 10,000 won.

Table 8-9. *Decomposition of Gini Index by Sources of Income: City Households with Two or More Persons*

	A. Absolute contribution			B. Relative contribution (percent)		
	1996	2006	2016	1996	2006	2016
Wage income, head of household	0.120	0.187	0.177	44.5	60.0	54.9
Wage income, spouse	0.032	0.046	0.065	11.8	14.6	20.3
Business income, head of household	0.070	0.038	0.032	26.0	12.2	10.0
Business income, spouse	0.012	0.016	0.013	4.6	5.1	4.0
Income of other members	0.046	0.040	0.045	17.0	12.7	13.8
Property income	0.004	0.002	0.000	1.6	0.5	0.1
Net income transfers	−0.015	−0.016	−0.010	−5.4	−5.2	−3.1
Gini, overall	0.270	0.312	0.323	100.0	100.0	100.0

Source: Author calculations based on Household Income and Expenditure Survey (HS1), Statistics Korea.

Note: Gini indices are calculated based on market income. The decomposition method developed by Lerman and Yitzhaki (1985) is used.

The relative contribution of different income sources to income inequality has changed dramatically in the last twenty years. In 1996, the main sources of income inequality were wage income (44.5 percent) and business income (26.0 percent) of the head of household. However, in 2016, the main sources have changed to wage income of the head of household (54.9 percent) and wage income of spouse (20.3 percent).

The main reasons for the increase in household income inequality are different for the two decadal periods: 1996–2006 and 2006–2016. Between 1996 and 2006, the Gini index rose appreciably from 0.27 to 0.312. The main income source driving the rise was wage income of the head of household, as its inequality rose from 0.120 to 0.187. Since the percentage of employed heads of household was relatively stable for this period, the rise in wage income inequality for the head of household seems to have been caused by increases in wage disparity. The inequality of spouse wage income also contributed, as it rose from 0.032 to 0.046. Since the percentage of employed spouses rose strongly during this period, the rise in wage income inequality for spouse is likely the result of both the market income disparity effect and the labor participation effect. The inequality of business income for the head of household decreased from 0.070 to 0.038, probably because the proportion of self-employment gradually declined.

The household income Gini index increased more moderately, from 0.312 to 0.323, between 2006 and 2016. The main reason behind the rise was wage income inequality for spouse, as it rose from 0.046 to 0.065.[29] For this period, the increase in wage disparity was smaller, as shown in figure 8-4, while the percentage of spouses with positive wage income continued to rise, as shown in table 8-8. This suggests that the rise in wage income inequality for spouse may be due mainly to the labor participation effect. On the other hand, wage income inequality for the head of household declined slightly from 0.187 to 0.177. This may be due to the combined effects of a stable percentage of employed heads of household, milder increases in wage income disparity, and changes in the head of household demographics.

We observe a similar pattern for nationwide household samples for 2006 and 2016, as shown in table 8-10. The pattern is slightly weakened because single-person households are included. This can result from changes in family demographics that have additional consequences for overall household income inequality.

In sum, the rise in overall household income inequality was substantial in the 1996–2006 period, and it can be explained by both the market in-

Table 8-10. *Decomposition of Gini Index by Sources of Income:
Nationwide Households*

	A. Absolute contribution		B. Relative contribution (percent)	
	2006	2016	2006	2016
Wage income, head of household	0.202	0.199	60.9	56.5
Wage income, spouse	0.047	0.065	14.3	18.6
Business income, head of household	0.044	0.041	13.4	11.5
Business income, spouse	0.016	0.014	4.9	4.0
Income of other members	0.041	0.046	12.4	13.0
Property income	0.001	0.000	0.4	0.1
Net income transfers	−0.021	−0.013	−6.2	−3.7
Gini, overall	0.331	0.352	100.0	100.0

Source: Author calculations based on Household Income and Expenditure Survey (HS1), Statistics Korea.

Note: Gini indices are calculated based on market income. The decomposition method developed by Lerman and Yitzhaki (1985) is used.

come disparity effect and the labor participation effect. Therefore, we observe a positive link between the worsening of household income inequality and the widening wage gap resulting from increased heterogeneity in firm performance discussed in sections 2 and 3. However, the increase in household income inequality was especially strong in this period because of the rise in female labor market participation. In the 2006–2016 period, household income inequality rose less, and the increase can be attributed mainly to the continuing rise in female labor participation. The change in wage disparity was milder and does not seem to have played a conspicuous role for this period.

Concluding Remarks and Policy Implications

This chapter investigates some key questions linking technological change and household income inequality in Korea. It finds that the labor income share does not show a declining long-run trend. Second, wage disparity has increased over time and is driven mainly by a widening wage gap between different-sized firms. Third, larger-sized firms are higher-capacity firms with better human capital, greater capital investment, and higher innovative activity. Fourth, changes in industrial composition have led to greater employment in small-sized establishments, but less employment in large-sized establishments. Fifth, heterogeneous performance between firms of different sizes is contributing to wage disparity. Last, the widening wage gap is only a partial reason for the changes in household income inequality. Rather, a persistent and significant rise in female labor participation was a major factor.

Evidence suggests that technological change may have increased wage disparity and thereby contributed to higher household income inequality, especially during 1996–2006. However, this link is not strong for the 2006–2016 period. While technological change may have changed the composition of industries and widened wage gaps, the proportion of total compensation to human capital—the labor income share—does not seem to have waned during this transition.

Labor Income Share and Policy Implications

Contrary to the belief that technological change favors capital income and reduces the labor income share, our findings suggest that this has yet to happen in Korea. Correctly adjusting for the value added of self-employed businesses with employees, the labor share does not show a long-run declining trend. Since Korea is a leader in digital transformation, this is an intriguing finding.

One possible explanation of the stable labor share is that human capital is complementary to technology. Greater compensation for high-skilled workers may be offsetting the drop in income for less-skilled workers. Labor-saving technology adoption may be in progress, reducing job opportunities for less-skilled workers. But demand for higher-level skills is increasing. Total demand for labor may fall, but technology-complementary labor with inelastic supply may enjoy rising compensation, increasing wage disparity.

Unfortunately, previous studies have put forth biased labor share estimates showing a long-run declining trend in Korea. Policymakers have responded with measures such as sharp increases in the minimum wage (16.4 percent in 2018 and 10.9 percent in 2019) and increases in corporate tax rates for large firms. Empirical studies by Kim (2020) and Kang (2020) show that these policies based on an incorrect diagnosis have led to undesirable consequences for employment.[30] Furthermore, as most minimum-wage earners belong to small-sized firms, the minimum-wage hikes likely hurt in particular the small-sized firms, which have been already battling low productivity. Current policies regarding the labor market and the corporate tax need to be reconsidered.

Accurate measurement of the labor income share, taking into account detailed national accounts data and sectoral distribution, is important. Caution is necessary in interpreting movements in the labor income share and drawing implications for policy.

Widening Wage Disparity and Policy Implications

One important reason for the rise in wage disparity is a widening wage gap between different-sized firms. Workers in large firms may be benefiting more from technological changes as these firms have higher innovative capacity. However, most Korean industries are dominated by minuscule firms. These firms are disadvantaged in adopting new technology and therefore lag behind in productivity and wage growth. The employment share of establishments with fewer than twenty employees was 40.2 percent in manufacturing, and that of those with fewer than ten employees was 43.5 percent in nonmanufacturing, according to the 2015 Economic Census from Statistics Korea. Any effort to mitigate the wage disparity gap will be limited without noticeable changes in firm size distribution.

Not all small firms lack innovative capacity and growth potential. However, in Korea, it is a rare occasion in recent times for a small firm to scale up successfully, as such firms are generally disadvantaged in value creation, new product development, bargaining power, scale economies, and so forth. Moreover, they lack global competitiveness. In 2018, exports accounted for only 10.4 percent of all manufacturing SME sales.[31]

To respond to the widening wage gap, policies should aim to create a business environment attracting innovative productive firms, promote the growth of small firms, and ultimately change the firm size distribution. Firm policies in Korea have not been effective in this respect. Fair trade policies and SME support policies have been introduced, based on the premise that the primary cause limiting small firm growth is unfair business practices between large and small firms. Establishing fair trade practices may be helpful. However, they alone will not be sufficient to revive firm dynamics. The dominance of small firms is prevalent in all industries, regardless of the presence of large firms. Many firms are too small to be transaction counterparts or competitors to large firms. In the manufacturing sector, about half of SMEs do not trade with other firms.

The SME support system that has accumulated over more than thirty years was supposedly designed and targeted to protect SMEs. However, the resulting overprotection seems to have promoted a large population of unproductive, low-capacity small firms that are unsuccessful in scaling up. It is important to revise the system and change the policy approach to achieve competitiveness of SMEs by targeting potential growth and profitability.

The regulatory system discouraging size growth should be reconsidered. SMEs have weak incentives to grow because they face numerous new regulations when they cross the large-firm threshold. A report by the Korea Economic Research Institute (2019) states that 188 new regulations in forty-seven laws are applicable when an SME moves up to large-firm status. According to the OECD Structural and Demographic Business Statistics, Korea ranked first among thirty OECD countries in the employment share of small firms (ten to forty-nine employees) in manufacturing in 2017. Korea also ranked first among twenty-three OECD countries in the employment share of small firms (ten to forty-nine employees) in selected service sectors in 2016.[32]

Overprotection of existing businesses in services is deterring modernization. Innovative services such as IT-based mobility services, long-distance medical services, and large-scale retail services are either blocked or regulated for mostly political reasons. These protective measures hinder potential productivity and wage growth through economies of scale and new high-value-added services. Government should develop a long-run strategy to modernize the services sector, where low-wage jobs are concentrated. Policies should be redirected toward inducing employment to shift to higher-value-added and larger-scale modes of production.

Also, the social safety net should be strengthened to support the necessary transition for scale-up. The emergence of new, growing firms and industries will be associated with substantial firm turnover through entry and exit, resulting in greater frictional unemployment.

Income Inequality and Policy Implications

It is important to understand the nature of the income inequality trend. Our findings indicate that the widening wage gap is only a partial reason for the increase in household income inequality. In recent years, a major driver of rising household income inequality has been the growing number of double-income households, resulting from increasing female labor participation. We need to carefully interpret Korea's data as the economy is still undergoing appreciable demographic transformation, leading to changes in labor market participation that affects income inequality. This transition, as well as technological change, should be taken into account in understanding the rise in income inequality and devising policy responses to it.

Regarding redistribution policy, our findings suggest that even if wage disparity is mitigated through implementation of productivity-enhancement and modernization policies, significant issues about income inequality would remain. Redistributive measures should be carefully designed to incorporate issues regarding demographic transformation, the changing structure of labor participation, an aging population, and increases in low-income single-person households.

NOTES

1. Piketty and Zucman (2014) and Karabarbounis and Neiman (2014). However, Gutiérrez and Piton (2020) document that labor shares may not have declined when corporate sector statistics are correctly measured. Controversies regarding long-run trends of labor income shares for advanced economies are discussed in section 1 of this chapter.

2. Kim (2017) and Park (2019a) both show that performance gaps between large firms and SMEs have widened over the last two decades.

3. The national accounts data are drawn from Bank of Korea (n.d.). For the other surveys mentioned, the author obtained raw data from the Ministry of Employment and Labor and from Statistics Korea. For more information on these surveys, see Ministry of Employment and Labor (n.d.) and Statistics Korea (n.d.).

4. Elsby, Hobijn, and Sahin (2013) and Rognlie (2015) show that imputed wages for the self-employed and the rise in housing value added explain a large portion of the US labor share decline.

5. The harmonized labor shares are recalculated to exclude self-employment and housing services.

6. Lee (2015) and Joo and Cheon (2014).

7. Elsby, Hobijn, and Sahin (2013) estimate that a third of the decline of the US labor income share is influenced by imputed wages for the self-employed.

8. Given that employment in agriculture is counted as self-employed, the decline is strongly related to industrialization, with agricultural labor shifting to formal industrial sectors, a process commonly observed across countries during developmental stages.

9. Gollin (2002) and Elsby, Hobijn, and Sahin (2013) discuss these issues in detail.

10. I use the net-value-added concept of national income for the labor income share calculation. Net value added is equivalent to GDP net of depreciation and indirect taxes. Thus, I do not discuss additional controversies related to estimates of depreciation rates.

11. The decline in the operating surplus of SEs can be understood as mainly the result of the industrialization process, and not of market competition, since a large proportion of SEs in the 1980s were in agriculture (Park 2020).

12. A major problem with approach M2 is that it is difficult to implement correctly, as it requires a detailed breakdown of national income. Unfortunately, most countries' national accounts do not provide the detailed breakdown necessary for an accurate calculation. Korea is no exception, and Park (2020) points out these issues in detail.

13. The business income data for SEs in the Household Income and Expenditure Survey (HS1) from Statistics Korea is not appropriate for our calculation since it is not the operating surplus, but the imputed labor income.

14. This is calculated in Park (2020).

15. Numbers for self-employed persons in SE1 and SE2, obtained from the Economically Active Population Survey from Statistics Korea, are also needed for this calculation. These estimates are based on a strong assumption. However, we do not have any other information to improve the estimates.

16. The number of wage income workers is obtained from the Economically Active Population Survey from Statistics Korea.

17. Oh (2020) and Park (2019b).

18. The dataset is limited to wage workers.

19. Worker age subgroups are twenties, thirties, forties, fifties, and sixties and over. Education subgroups are workers with middle school education or less, high school education, two-year college education, four-year university education, and graduate school degrees. Industry subgroups are formed based on fifteen one-digit industries. Establishment size subgroups are establishments with employees fewer than four, five to nine, ten to twenty-nine, thirty to ninety-nine, 100 to 299, 300 to 499, and 500 and over.

20. Overlapping effect is a cross-term effect derived in the decomposition. It has a vague interpretation and can be understood as a residual.

21. The total employment share of these nine industries in all fifteen industries was 73.3 percent in 2000 and 66.4 percent in 2016.

22. The Mining and Manufacturing Survey (MS) from Statistics Korea is a panel dataset that covers all manufacturing establishments with ten employees or more. The Survey of Business Activities (BS) from Statistics Korea provides panel data at the firm level with fifty employees or more.

23. Declining light and computer manufacturing industries are textiles (17), wearing apparel and furs (18), leather, luggage, and footwear (19), printing and reproduction of recorded media (22), computers (30), and furniture (36). Rising heavy and high-tech industries are chemicals and chemical products (24), rubber and plastic products (25), nonmetallic mineral products (26), basic metals (27), fabricated metal products except machinery and equipment (28), other machinery and equipment (29), electrical and optical equipment (31), medical, precision, and optical instruments (33), motor vehicles and trailers (34), and other transport equipment (35).

24. These industries are chemicals and chemical products (24), other machinery and equipment (29), electronic video and audio, communication equipment (32), and motor vehicles and trailers (34).

25. Although we have provided empirical evidence primarily for manufacturing sectors, this is also true for nonmanufacturing sectors.

26. This is because the existing household income survey (HS1) expanded its sample coverage over time. The samples for household income survey HS1 were limited to city households with two persons or more until 2006. Then the sample was expanded to all household for all regions. A new household income survey (HS2) was introduced in 2011 to correct for underrepresentation of high-income households.

27. The change in male labor participation rate was mild; it changed from 77.2 percent to 78.9 percent during the same period, while the male employment rate changed from 73.2 percent to 75.9 percent.

28. Income distribution in Korea is skewed so that median income is lower than mean income. In this case, it is likely that this replacement lowers income inequality.

29. Choi, Kim, and Park (2018) use Korean Labor and Income Panel Studies data to find that the contribution of household wage income disparity to household income inequality has increased in the period after the global financial crisis. This is consistent with my results. However, my analysis goes further to separate out the wage incomes of heads of household and spouses—in order to distinguish between the market income disparity effect and the labor participation effect.

30. Kim (2020) and Kang (2020) provide evidence that the recent minimum-wage hikes in Korea have led to significant losses in employment.

31. Korea Federation of SMEs (2019).

32. OECD (n.d.). The selected service sectors are wholesale and retail trade, accommodations and food, information and communications, construction, professional, and scientific and technical services.

REFERENCES

Acemoglu, Daron, and Pascual Restrepo. 2018. "The Race between Man and Machine: Implications of Technology for Growth, Factor Shares, and Employment." *American Economic Review* 108, no. 6, pp. 1488–1542.

Autor, David, and Anna Salomons. 2018. "Is Automation Labor-Displacing? Productivity Growth, Employment, and the Labor Share." *Brookings Papers on Economic Activity* 49, no. 1 (Spring), pp.1–87.

Bank of Korea. n.d. National Accounts. https://ecos.bok.or.kr/.

Cette, Gilbert, Lorraine Koehl, and Thomas Philippon. 2019. "The Labor Share in the Long Term: A Decline?" *Economie et Statistique* 510/511, pp. 35–51.

Choi, Jemin, Sunghyun Kim, and Sangyeon Park. 2018. "Income Inequality in Korea in the Post Global Financial Crisis Period." *Korean Journal of Economic Studies* 66, no. 1, pp. 1–28.

Choi, Kyungsoo, and Jungho Kim. 2019. "Decline of Business Growth Dynamics." *Korea Review of Applied Economics* 21, no. 4, pp. 5–44.

Elsby, Michael W., Bart Hobijn, and Aysegül Sahin. 2013. "The Decline of the US Labor Share." *Brookings Papers on Economic Activity* 44, no. 2, pp. 1–63.

Gollin, Douglas. 2002. "Getting Income Shares Right." *Journal of Political Economy* 110, no. 2, pp. 458–74.

Gutiérrez, Germán, and Sophie Piton. 2020. "Revisiting the Global Decline of the (Non-Housing) Labor Share." *American Economic Review: Insights* 2, no. 3, pp. 321–38.

Joo, Sangyoung, and Soomin Cheon. 2014. "Measurement of Labor Income Share: Searching for an Alternative for Korea." *Social and Economic Review* 43, pp. 31–65.

Kang, Changhui. 2020. "Employment Effects of Minimum Wages Increases: Evidence from a Bunching Estimator." *Journal of Korean Economic Analysis* 2, no. 1, pp. 87–136.

Karabarbounis, Loukas, and Brent Neiman. 2014. "The Global Decline of the Labor Share." *Quarterly Journal of Economics* 129, no. 1, pp. 61–103.

Kim, Minho. 2017. "Productivity Growth in Korean Manufacturing Industries: The Role of Young Plants vs. Small Plants." KDI Policy Paper Series 2017–05 (Sejong City: Korea Development Institute).

Kim, Nak Nyeon. 2020. "Korea's Minimum Wage and Employment, 2013–2019." *Journal of Korean Economic Analysis* 26, no. 1, pp. 145–83.

Koh, Youngsun. 2018. "The Wage Inequality in Korea." KDI Policy Study 2018–01 (Sejong City: Korea Development Institute).

Korea Economic Research Institute. 2019. "Differential Regulation Treatment for Large Firms Based on Size Criterion." Press Release, August 29.

Korea Federation of SMEs. 2019. *2018 Survey on Actual State of SMEs: Manufacturing.* Seoul.

Lee, Byung-hee. 2015. "The Issues and Trends in Measuring Labor Income Distribution Rate." *Labor Review*, January, pp. 25–42.

Lee, Yoonsoo. 2020. "Long-Term Shifts in Korean Manufacturing and Plant-Level Productivity Dynamics." World Bank Policy Research Working Paper 9279 (Washington, DC: World Bank).

Lerman, Robert I., and Shlomo Yitzhaki. 1985. "Income Inequality Effects by Income Source: A New Approach and Applications to the United States." *Review of Economics and Statistics* 67, pp. 151–56.

Martinez, Joseba. 2018. "Automation, Growth and Factor Shares." 2018 Meeting Papers, No. 736, Society for Economic Dynamics.

Ministry of Employment and Labor. n.d. Survey on Labor Conditions by Employment Type. https://www.moel.go.kr/english/pas/pasMOEL.jsp#.

OECD. n.d. Structural and Demographic Business Statistics. https://www.oecd.org/sdd/business-stats/structuralanddemographicbusinessstatisticssdbsoecd.htm.

Oh, Jiyoon. 2020. "Change in Labor Income Share: Findings from Firm-Level Data," in *Growth in a Time of Change: Global and Country Perspectives on a New Agenda*, edited by Hyeon-Wook Kim and Zia Qureshi (Brookings Institution Press).

Park, Jungsoo. 2019a. "Growth Slowdown and Low Productivity," in *The Korean Economy Facing Challenges* (Seoul: Hakyeon Publishing).

Park, Jungsoo. 2019b. "Labor Productivity and Wages in the Korean Economy." *Korea Economic Forum* 12, no. 1, pp. 81–112.

Park, Jungsoo. 2020. "Self-Employment Sector and Functional Income Distribution of Korean Economy." *Korea Economic Forum* 12, no. 4, pp. 27–68.

Piketty, Thomas, and Gabriel Zucman. 2014. "Capital Is Back: Wealth-Income Ratios in Rich Countries 1700–2010." *Quarterly Journal of Economics* 129, no. 3, pp. 1255–1310.

Pyatt, Graham. 1976. "On the Interpretation and Disaggregation of Gini Coefficients." *Economic Journal* 86 (June), pp. 243–55.

Rognlie, Matthew. 2015. "Deciphering the Fall and Rise in the Net Capital Share: Accumulation or Scarcity?" *Brookings Papers on Economic Activity* 46, no. 1, pp. 1–69.

Statistics Korea. n.d. Surveys. http://kostat.go.kr/portal/eng/index.action.

Contributors

SANGMIN AUM   is an assistant professor in the Department of Economics at Myongji University. Previously, he was an associate fellow at the Korea Development Institute (KDI). He has also served as an economist at the Bank of Korea. His research and publications cover topics in macroeconomics, technological change and innovation, and labor economics. He received his Ph.D. in economics from Washington University in St. Louis.

FRANÇOIS BOURGUIGNON   is emeritus professor of economics at the Paris School of Economics, and director of studies at Ecole des Hautes Études en Sciences Sociales. He has served as chief economist and senior vice president at the World Bank. He is chair of the Global Development Network Board. He has published extensively on income distribution and economic development, receiving several prestigious awards, including the Dan David Prize. He holds doctorates in economics from the University of Western Ontario and the University of Orléans.

FLAVIO CALVINO   is an economist in the Directorate for Science, Technology, and Innovation at the Organization for Economic Cooperation and Development (OECD). His work focuses on business and employment dynamics, productivity, innovation, and technological change. His research has been published in a number of academic journals and OECD papers and reports. He holds a dual Ph.D. in economics from the Paris School of Economics–Université Paris 1 Panthéon-Sorbonne and Scuola Superiore Sant'Anna (Italy).

SUNGHOON CHUNG is a research fellow in the Department of Economic Policy and Strategy at KDI. His research interests include international trade, environmental economics, and development economics, with a focus on Asian economies. His research has been published in several KDI papers and studies as well as academic journals. He holds a Ph.D. in economics from Southern Methodist University.

CHIARA CRISCUOLO is head of the Productivity, Innovation, and Entrepreneurship Division in the Science, Technology, and Innovation Directorate at the OECD and a research associate of the Centre for Economic Performance (CEP) at the London School of Economics. Prior to joining the OECD, she was a research fellow at the CEP. Her research on productivity, business dynamics, innovation, and international trade has been published widely. She received her Ph.D. in economics from University College, London.

HARRY J. HOLZER is the John LaFarge Jr. SJ Professor of Public Policy at Georgetown University's McCourt School of Public Policy, nonresident senior fellow at Brookings, institute fellow at the American Institute for Research, research fellow at the Institute of Labor Economics, and affiliate at the Stanford Center on Poverty and Inequality. He is a former chief economist of the US Department of Labor. He was a founding faculty director of the Georgetown Center on Poverty and Inequality. He holds a Ph.D. in economics from Harvard University.

MINHO KIM is a fellow and director of the Division of Public Investment Evaluation at KDI. His research interests cover international economics, industrial policy, and firm dynamics. At KDI, he has worked on evaluation of government policies for entrepreneurship, the role of trade in productivity, intangible capital and implications for innovation policy, and application of artificial intelligence in policy targeting. He holds a Ph.D. in economics from Washington University in St. Louis.

JUNGSOO PARK is professor of economics and director of the Nam Duck Woo Economic Research Institute at Sogang University. Previously, he was an assistant professor at the State University of New York at Buffalo. He served as president of the Korea Association of Applied Economics and as a member of the National Economic Advisory Council to the president of Korea. He has published widely on topics in economic growth, technology, productivity, finance, and international economics. He received his Ph.D. in economics from Stanford University.

THOMAS PHILIPPON is the Max L. Heine Professor of Finance at New York University's Stern School of Business. He was named one of the Top 25 Economists under 45 by the IMF in 2014 and received the 2013 Bernácer Prize for Best European Economist under 40. His recent research has focused on financial regulation and the market power of large firms. He has advised the Financial Stability Board, the Federal Reserve Bank of New York, and French monetary and fiscal institutions. He received a Ph.D. in economics from the Massachusetts Institute of Technology.

ZIA QURESHI is a visiting fellow in the Global Economy and Development program at Brookings. His research covers a broad range of global economic issues, including a recent focus on technology's impact on economies and public policy. He previously worked at the World Bank and the IMF, including serving as director, Development Economics, at the Bank, and executive secretary of the IMF-World Bank Joint Ministerial Development Committee. He holds a D.Phil. in economics from Oxford University, where he was a Rhodes Scholar.

CHEONSIK WOO is a senior fellow in the Department of Knowledge Economy at KDI. Previously, he led, as vice president and director, several KDI research departments, including Foresight and National Strategy, Industrial and Corporate Affairs/Competition Policy, and Knowledge Economy. He also served as a senior analyst in the Office of the Secretary-General at the OECD, senior counselor to the deputy prime minister of the Korean Ministry of Finance and Economy, and assistant professor at Clemson University. He holds a Ph.D. in economics from Columbia University.

Index

Figures and tables are indicated by f and t following the page number.

Monopolies: antitrust enforcement
and, 7, 13; copyright and patent
laws, 14; COVID-19 pandemic
and, 11; inequality and, 199;
market concentration and, 6–7, 10
Moore's law, 156
Morelli, S., 184, 187
Mortgage market, 103, 107
M-Pesa, 102–03
Musk, Elon, 128

Nationalist populism, 5, 17, 128
Nedelkoska, Ljubica, 132
Neiman, Brent, 193, 221
Netherlands, automation in, 131
New and young firms: COVID-19
pandemic and, 11; decrease in
United States, 7; disruptions of,
109; employment increases and,
245; Fintech and, 97, 99; market
dynamism declines and, 6, 54;
research and technology transfer
programs for, 15; technology
diffusion support for, 38
Nicoletti, G., 57
Noncompete clauses, 17, 56
Nonlabor income, 192–98, 194f, 203

Occupational Information Network
(O-NET) of US DOL, 131–32
Occupational licensing requirements,
17, 56
Offshoring, 10–11, 245
Oh, Jiyoon, 222
Online learning tools, 137–38, 169
Organizational capacity and technol-
ogy diffusion, 41, 56
Organizational capital. *See* Intan-
gibles, productivity, and digitaliza-
tion; Management practices
Organizational changes for digitali-
zation, 21, 151–76; background,

154–58; data sources, 158–59;
empirical analysis, 161–69, 162t;
organizational fitness and,
154–55; policy implications,
169–71; summary statistics,
161–62, 162t; variable construction, 159–61, 162t
Organization for Economic Cooperation and Development (OECD)
economies: automation and
displacement of workers, 131–32;
Going Digital Project, 74; ICT
Access and Usage by Business
Database, 88; ICT uptake in,
44–45; labor market changes in,
8–9; OECD MultiProd project,
48; productivity database of,
225–26; Programme for the
International Assessment of Adult
Competencies (PIAAC) survey
data, 131; robotics, increase in use
of, 182, 183f; slowing productivity
and increasing inequality, 3, 6,
35–36, 53–54; Structural and
Demographic Business Statistics
on Korea, 258; technology
diffusion and, 44–49
Osborne, Michael, 131, 204

Paid family leave, 140
Palma, Stefania, 111
Park, Jungsoo, 217, 219, 221–24,
226–28
Patent systems, 7–8, 14, 37, 52,
131–32
Patent thickets, 52
Payment apps, 102, 117
Pennacchi, George, 104
Perla, J., 56
Personal loans, 103
Peters, Bettina, 80
Petrin, Amil, 81